DEMOCRACY IN SPITE OF THE DEMOS

Reinventing Critical Theory

Series Editors:
Gabriel Rockhill, associate professor of philosophy, Villanova University
Jennifer Ponce de León, assistant professor of English, University of Pennsylvania

The Reinventing Critical Theory series publishes cutting edge work that seeks to reinvent critical social theory for the 21st century. It serves as a platform for new research in critical philosophy that examines the political, social, historical, anthropological, religious, aesthetic, and/or economic dynamics shaping the contemporary situation. Books in the series provide alternative accounts and points of view regarding the development of critical social theory, put critical theory in dialogue with other intellectual traditions around the world, and/or advance new, radical forms of pluralist critical theory that contest the current hegemonic order.

Titles in the Series

Commercium: Critical Theory from a Cosmopolitan Point of View
    Brian Milstein
Resistance and Decolonization
    Amílcar Cabral, translated by Dan Wood
Critical Theories of Crisis in Europe: From Weimar to the Euro
    Edited by Poul F. Kjaer and Nicklas Olsen
Politics of Divination: Neoliberal Endgame and the Religion of Contingency
    Joshua Ramey
Comparative Metaphysics: Ontology After Anthropology
    Pierre Charbonnier, Gildas Salmon, and Peter Skafish
The Invention of the Visible: The Image in Light of the Arts
    Patrick Vauday, Translated by Jared Bly
Metaphors of Invention and Dissension
    Rajeshwari E. Vallury
Technology, Modernity and Democracy
    Edited by Eduardo Beira and Andrew Feenberg
A Critique of Sovereignty
    Daniel Lock, Translated by Amanda DeMarco
Democracy and Relativism: A Debate
    Cornelius Castoriadis, Translated by John V. Garner
Democracy in Spite of the Demos: From Arendt to the Frankfurt School
    Larry Alan Busk

DEMOCRACY IN SPITE OF THE DEMOS

From Arendt to the Frankfurt School

Larry Alan Busk

ROWMAN &
LITTLEFIELD
───────INTERNATIONAL
London • New York

Published by Rowman & Littlefield International, Ltd.
6 Tinworth Street, London SE11 5AL
www.rowmaninternational.com

Rowman & Littlefield International, Ltd. is an affiliate of
Rowman & Littlefield
4501 Forbes Boulevard, Suite 200, Lanham, Maryland 20706, USA
With additional offices in Boulder, New York, Toronto (Canada), and London (UK)
www.rowman.com

Copyright © 2020 by Larry Alan Busk

All rights reserved. No part of this book may be reproduced in any form or by any electronic or mechanical means, including information storage and retrieval systems, without written permission from the publisher, except by a reviewer who may quote passages in a review.

British Library Cataloguing in Publication Information
A catalogue record for this book is available from the British Library

ISBN: HB 978-1-78661-525-1

Library of Congress Cataloging-in-Publication Data Is Available

ISBN 978-1-78661-525-1 (cloth)
ISBN 978-1-5381-4817-4 (pbk)
ISBN 978-1-78661-526-8 (electronic)

For Eli

in friendship, admiration, and love

If all political tendencies could make use of democracy, then this proved that it had no political content and was only an organizational form; and if one regarded it from the perspective of some political program that one hoped to achieve with the help of democracy, then one had to ask oneself what value democracy itself had merely as a form.

—Carl Schmitt

CONTENTS

Preface *Antonio Y. Vázquez-Arroyo*	xi
Acknowledgments	xv
Introduction	xvii
1 The Categorical Imperative of Democracy	1
2 Arendt's Island of Freedom	23
3 Democracy at Its Limits: Rancière, Mouffe, and Laclau	51
4 From "False Democracy" to False Demos: Adorno, Marcuse, and Climate Skepticism	85
5 What Is Elitism?	107
Notes	129
Bibliography	155
Index	171
About the Author	173

PREFACE

Antonio Y. Vázquez-Arroyo

Democracy in Spite of the Demos is that rare book: important and original but also unsettling and necessary. Necessary because it unsettles. And unsettling because it calls into question many a notion held dear by left-liberal democratic theorists, even defenders of socialist democracy, along with many axioms about emancipatory political life in contemporary political theory and discourse. Armed with a calm but critical disposition, Larry Busk's original philosophical voice is couched in the kind of sharp lucidity one finds among the best philosophical essayists active today (say, from different latitudes, Raymond Geuss and Gabriel Rockhill), who bring an analytical edge to careful engagement with works frequently steeped in so-called continental traditions of thought, occasionally of forbidding difficulty. The book's title adduces the core of the book's concern and critique. Yet unlike many seemingly tepid but decidedly antidemocratic liberal-democratic theorists who, in the wake of the resurgence of "populism" across the globe, sneer at the figure of the demos, Busk calls into question the figure of the demos from a decidedly radical and critical perspective that enables the possibility of a genuinely radical account of democracy. And he does so by meeting head-on some of the questions that right-thinking democratic theory scuffles away from.

Unencumbered by the ways in which democracy has become an unquestioned value at a time in which its spread and dilution of meaning move on a par, Busk critically interrogates "the figure of democracy as a critical category in contemporary political thought" and immediately changes the terms of the discussion: "What is called for in this case is not a theory of 'false democracy' but a theory of false demos. The question, then, would not be 'How do we give the people a voice?' but 'Why do the people speak so wrongly?'" That seems straightforward enough: Still: Why switch the question? Part of Busk's contention in this book is to criticize idealizations of the demos that only zone in on the forms of demotic action that fall within the parameters of right-thinking action and discourse, which is often coextensive with liberal democratic doxa and its attendant platitudes, even by thinkers that purport to operate outside the liberal-democratic galaxy. This is an operation that he convincingly traces back to Hannah Arendt's work and is reproduced by vastly different thinkers, from Ernesto Laclau and Chantal Mouffe to William E. Connolly and Jacques Rancière. Each is carefully read, but Busk's coruscating interpretation of Rancière stands out, as does the brief but level-headed engagement with Connolly; and, most important of all, unlike many accounts of Laclau and Mouffe, he gives Mouffe's own work attention in its own right. And this is accomplished through a critical but scrupulous use of the broad range of scholarly literature, as ideas are probed and distilled.

Busk formulates the formal and theoretical operation at work in these constructions in terms of a constitutive exclusion that runs through all these otherwise distinctive oeuvres. While given a different content by the different thinkers discussed, this exclusion is formally reproduced in their theorizations. Busk calls it "the categorical imperative of democracy" and maps it out by zoning in on "the figure of democracy as a critical category" in contemporary political theory; and figurations of democracy pivot around an idealized figure of the demos that, in turn, relies on a constitutive exclusion of those forms of demotic expression considered to be beyond the pale.

In a telegraphic formulation, he explains this imperative: "The categorical imperative of democracy rejects the notion that there is some definitively correct political result external to its democratic iconography, rightly seeing that this would void the normative specificity of democracy; its theorists likewise distance themselves from majoritarian understandings of democracy, and so the problem of 'bad majorities' is something of a nonstarter. Yet the impulse to disqualify certain political movements as undemocratic on the basis of their content remains intact. . . . But the right-wing demos, unfortunately for the democratic turn, is still the demos."

Not fashionable—let alone palatable—thoughts for many. But these deliver an important truth that a genuinely realist critical theory of democracy has to meet head-on and reframe outside of the typical antidemocratic categories of liberal-democratic practice and discourse. Yet none of the necessary theoretical and political work to go beyond the parameters of liberal democratic orders and practices that paved the way to the current depletions of collective life can be done by relying on the ruses of the categorical imperative the book carefully delineates.

As if the necessary and penetrating identification and critique of the categorical imperative of democracy were not enough, Busk breaks away from idealizations of the demos by formulating an intriguing if a bit clipped account of "social delusion" that draws on early Frankfurt School critical theory, a source not much tapped within contemporary democratic theory. In doing so, he offers a highly suggestive reworking of ideology and an original recasting of the problem of elitism that offers an important corrective to readings of Adorno's legacy vis-à-vis political questions related to democracy. Out of his interpretation of Adorno and Marcuse, Busk gives a fresh meaning and content to the question of a "false demos" and why it seems often to "speak so wrongly" while raising questions of political literacy that current discussions only tacitly assume but never thematize, or that remain altogether disavowed.

Democracy in Spite of the Demos is a work of *Ideologiekritik* in the best sense of this term, as well as genuinely original political theorizing that unsettles predictable patterns and raises hard and difficult questions for those of us committed to a socialist figuration of democracy in which shared power by ordinary people remains paramount. Yet like any ambitious work written with an economy of prose, *Democracy in Spite of the Demos* unavoidably raises a number of questions that fall outside its avowed focus but nevertheless remain within its purview. For instance, what is it about liberal-democratic theory and practice that breeds and sustains a politically illiterate demos? What other resources are there in Marcuse and Adorno to make sense of it or offer a corrective? What about Brecht's own version of plebeian politics and the need to politically educate the dominated as a precondition of undoing their binds? And how would Busk respond to current defenses of plebeian democracy? *Democracy in Spite of the Demos* speaks to all these concerns and should be required reading for any engagement with the fate of popular rule today.

Similarly, Busk's treatment of radical democracy needs to (1) be complemented by a historicization of the antisocialist background of post-Marxism and the ways in which formulations of radical democracy are unthinkable—or at least unintelligible—without it, and to (2) historicize the ideological ruses involved in these theorizations and the sedimentations left by this historical moment—an anti-Marxist and antisocialist moment that encouraged the kind of depoliticization and political illiteracy, concomitant with the ethical turn in the human sciences since the late seventies, that is consistent with his analysis—and pose the question of political literacy, which is central for the project he lays out through his engagement with the Frankfurt School, Marcuse, and Adorno.[1]

Yet there is one figure who would complicate Busk's argument in an enabling way but is treated too cursorily: Sheldon S. Wolin, who sits more uneasily within contemporary political discussions than that the few references accorded to him may suggest. It is Wolin who reminds us that any meaningful emancipatory politics needs genuine democracy, as the latter is nothing less than the attempt by ordinary people "to translate social weakness into political power" and change their lot and the orders and forms that make it legitimate; democracy therein emerges as nothing less than "the means by which the many have sought to access political power in the hope that it could be used to redress their economic and social lot."[2] But Busk's penetrating critique and prognosis holds. It constitutes a necessary corrective of any sanguine view of these prospects: emancipatory action is the task of a politically literate demos at odds with democratic theory's contemporary figurations and the delusions involved.

—Antonio Y. Vázquez-Arroyo,
Rutgers University, Newark, New Jersey

ACKNOWLEDGMENTS

This book grew out of conversations with friends and colleagues, above all Eli Portella, to whom it is dedicated, and Billy Dean Goehring. My intellectual and personal debts to them cannot be overstated. The project likewise benefited from sharing thoughts, ideas, complaints, and grievances with Greg Farough, Coyoté Rooves, Kenny Knowlton, Ricardo Valencia, Joshua Kerr, Sabeen Ahmed, Mark McGinn, and Filipa Melo Lopes. I should also acknowledge members of the Arendt Circle (especially Lucy Benjamin, Matt Wester, and Yasemin Sari) for tolerating my heresies with patience and good humor. Further gratitude is due to Joshua, Sarah, and Mary Kerr, for their hospitality and indispensable friendship; to John Schwartz and Patrick Jones, for their excellent cinephile company; and to my family, especially Larry, John, and Judy, without whom I could not have completed this project.

Because this is my first book, and something of a culmination of an education in philosophy that I began ten years ago, I should thank my first teachers: Don Morse, Britt-Marie Schiller, and David Carl Wilson. Along with the entire Webster University philosophy department, they were instrumental in my decision to take up this subject (special thanks to Don for introducing me to the work of Adorno). I also want to mention a few professors outside of philosophy: Chris Parr, for his unwavering encouragement; Emily Thompson, *parce qu'elle m'a appris une nouvelle langue*; and Alan McNeill, for two life-altering courses.

This education continued at the University of Oregon, and I owe one form of gratitude or another to each professor I worked with there.

Conversations with Bonnie Mann and Colin Koopman were indispensable for the evolution of my work; Anita Chari provided inspiration to think the kind of thoughts that led to this project. I also cannot go without mentioning the supportive graduate student community at Oregon, both inside and outside of philosophy.

During the final stages of this book's composition, I taught at California State University Stanislaus, and I want to thank the incredible philosophy department there, in particular Jason Winfree, for providing a good home. I am likewise indebted to the editorial staff at Rowman and Littlefield International (especially Frankie Mace, Rebecca Anastasi, and Sarah Campbell), the anonymous reviewers, and the editors of the Reinventing Critical Theory series for a smooth and timely production process.

Finally, I thank the two guardian angels of my intellectual and professional development: Gabriel Rockhill, whose enthusiasm for this project rekindled my desire to complete it, and Rocío Zambrana, the best mentor I could have asked for, who supported and encouraged these ideas from beginning to end.

Part of chapter 3 was previously published as "Radical Democracy with What Demos? Mouffe and Laclau after the Rise of the Right," in *Radical Philosophy Review* 21, no. 2 (2018): 225–48.

INTRODUCTION

We are suffering from a democratic deficit, the story goes. Our democracy has been systematically undermined, or perhaps it has not yet been truly realized, or perhaps it can never be *truly* realized. Our emancipation lies in its restoration, or its expansion, or its creation, or in striving toward its impossible ideal. We must escape this false democracy and achieve, or at least try to achieve, a true democracy. These are the key terms for a critique of contemporary society, we are told, and the way forward lies in increasingly refined and sophisticated forms of a qualitative and quantitative demand: *more democracy!*

All but ubiquitous, this story is arguably the dominant narrative of political resistance today, and yet conspicuously absent from its account is a sustained reflection on what is actually, at least from an etymological point of view, the most crucial aspect of democracy: the demos. We know the setting of the play: the democratic form and its iconography (popular sovereignty, equality, speech, debate, difference, *doxa*, plurality, and public space). But who are the characters? This is a most pressing question, not only because the entire relation between democracy and critical resistance hinges there but also because some of the characters we are confronted with today are so unsavory. If we were to take a sober look at the state of things, which would include looking at racist and xenophobic popular movements, mass protofascist demonstrations, and commonplace climate skepticism, then our chant of "more democracy!" might be effectively answered by the proverb about wishing carefully in case the wish comes true.

This book examines the limits of the figure of democracy as a critical category in contemporary political thought. I frame the analysis around a structural tension that pervades the work of several theorists who make use of democratic iconography in an axiomatic way, a tension I term "the elitist-populist ambivalence." This theoretical tendency regards democracy as a categorical imperative—that is, as a foundational normative principle and an end in itself—but selectively focuses its attention on certain elements of the demos and categorically disqualifies others, thereby violating the parameters of a categorical imperative by specifying conditions. In other words, it appeals to formal categories but decides the political content in advance. It advocates democracy on its own terms: democracy in spite of the demos. But if democracy has critical purchase only under certain conditions, then our theoretical intervention must be based on these conditions rather than on the figure of democracy.

There are situations, to take the point a bit further, when what constitutes a problem is not a "democratic deficit" but, in fact, the opposite. In a time of pervasive popular ignorance and delusion, a reliance on democratic iconography obfuscates the potentially questionable character of the demos, rendering us incapable of comprehending or confronting dangerous and pathological political tendencies (e.g., climate skepticism, xenophobia). What is called for in this case is not a theory of "false democracy" but a theory of false demos. The question then would not be "how do we give the people a voice?" but "why do the people speak so wrongly?"

This book focuses on three main bodies of literature: the work of Hannah Arendt, the tradition of radical democracy (exemplified by Jacques Rancière, Chantal Mouffe, and Ernesto Laclau), and early Frankfurt School critical theory (Theodor Adorno and Herbert Marcuse). Though Arendt betrays no particular commitment to the term "democracy," she has been decisively influential for the democratic turn in Continental political theory. Her work is of interest to this project because, in my estimation, it represents the clearest and starkest expression of the democratic categorical imperative and its concomitant elitist-populist ambivalence. The discussion of Rancière, Mouffe, and Laclau highlights the extent to which these figures reproduce not only Arendt's democratic motifs but also her constitutive exclusion (even if it is not the same exclusion). Albeit with divergent political commitments and disparate theoretical concerns, both Arendt and radical democratic theory appeal to democracy in spite of the demos. Finally, Adorno and Marcuse provide an alternative to the categorical imperative of democracy. By critically confronting popular ignorance, irrationality, and delusion, and by understanding these phenomena as inextricably linked to the contradictions of a given social totality, the early Frankfurt School perspective displaces the normative force of the figure of democracy by a critique of the actually existing demos. This critique, I argue, allows us to steer a theoretical course between the perils of elitism and the equivocations of populism.

Contemporary political theory abounds with competing claims to offer the most "robust" account of democracy at both normative and descriptive registers.[1] The only thing taken for granted across the spectrum is that democracy as such is a political-theoretical baseline—"we're all democrats now," as Wendy Brown remarks ironically.[2] As I noted at the outset, theorists with a critical orientation focus their attention on the distance between the realities of prevailing nominal "democracies" and something (a structural change, a better procedure, an impossible ideal) that would constitute a "real" or "true" democratic politics.[3] My concern in this book is not with determining the right theory or model of democracy, nor with envisioning its as yet unrealized true form. Rather, I am interested in whether democracy (however understood) functions coherently as a critical category in our present political moment. The central question is: If we are interested in thinking the conditions for the possibility of a less antagonistic, oppressive, and self-destructive world, can the figure of democracy and its accompanying iconography function as a critical tool of analysis? By answering in the negative, I do not mean to suggest that critical theory become "antidemocratic," which would simply trade one formalism for another. Still less do I mean to proscribe the use of the term in situations where it might be strategically effective. The figure of democracy has historically served an important function in various emancipatory movements that have produced positive results. The same could be said for the figure of nationalism, but this does not establish the critical-theoretical force of nationalist iconography for the present conjuncture.

Defining at the outset what I mean by "democracy" would be counterproductive, as the analysis will be guided in each case by how the philosopher under discussion understands it. The word, as Robert Dahl notes, "is like an ancient kitchen midden packed with assorted leftovers from twenty-five hundred years of nearly continuous usage."[4] I refer to "the figure of democracy" because "figure" captures the rhetorical function and kaleidoscopic connotations of the term while allowing variation in its theoretical content in a way that "idea" or "concept" does not; a figure is less than a concept but more than an empty signifier. My use of "iconography" is likewise meant as a placeholder to track all of the evocative markers or indicators of democracy without reducing it to a set of necessary and sufficient conditions in advance. The suggestive homage to religious reverence is intentional and will, I hope, be justified by the end of the discussion.

This book dwells in a particular domain of democratic theory. Different theoretical models—deliberative, participatory, liberal—make use of somewhat different iconography. Through the examples in chapter 1, we will see an elitist-populist ambivalence present in deliberative theorists, Marxists, liberal humanists, and others. But I focus on radical democratic theory because it represents the most explicit and sustained attempt to suture the figure of democracy to the projects of critique and resistance. It is my hope that, mutatis mutandis, the terms of the analysis will apply to other variations on the democratic theme as well, insofar as they posit a relationship between democracy and the emancipatory aims of critique.[5]

I
THE CATEGORICAL IMPERATIVE OF DEMOCRACY

"It is the task of the left," writes Todd May, "to think and act upon democracy. In many ways, it has always been the task of the left to do so. . . . Conservatism by its nature seeks to resist change, or at best to allow change to happen slowly." If this is true, then the problematic of this project becomes a kind of non sequitur: there is no need to explain why the formal terms of democratic iconography are inevitably instantiated with a particular content, because this content is synonymous with the democratic form. "Democracy is about everyone," May continues, "not simply those in power. Democracy almost always is a challenge to tradition. That is why its creation is a task belonging to the left."[1] Democracy, then, is a critical, emancipatory category by definition.

There are a few peculiarities in May's train of thought, however. Notice that "change" is taken to mean "change for the better" or "change in a Left-progressive direction"; the changes demanded or accomplished by the Right—for example, the dismantling of social welfare programs, restrictions on immigration—apparently do not count. If one takes *these* changes to be good or necessary, then one could easily reverse May's formulation and say that "the Left by its nature seeks to resist change." The notion of "challenging tradition" is equated with Leftism, without further specification about *which* traditions and *what kind* of challenge, as if being oppositional or heterodox as such were enough to determine the content of one's politics. There is a similar problem with his claim that "democracy is about everyone." Is the Right not included in this "everyone"? If it is, then how is democracy both about *everyone* and about the Left? The category May opposes to "everyone" is "those in power." Are we to believe that the Right covers the category of "those in power" while everyone without power is, by default, a member of the Left?

This passage and its peculiarities represent, in microcosmic form, the current of thought that I want to challenge in this book. The idea that there is some immediate relationship between democracy and a particular kind of politics, that more democracy necessarily translates into a less oppressive or regressive social world, has become a largely unquestioned presupposition in numerous quarters of critically oriented political theory. With this democratic turn, the figure of democracy has taken on a self-evidently emancipatory aura. At the same time, this emancipatory currency depends on the careful delimitation of the demos, a qualification of *which* "people" are to be given "power." Implicitly or (in May's case) explicitly, democracy is understood at once as a formal armature and as containing particular content within it.

This ambivalent moment is ubiquitous enough to show up in figures as otherwise distant from one another as Cornel West and Larry Diamond. In *Democracy Matters*, West states that "the basis of democratic leadership is ordinary citizens' desire to take their country back from the hands of corrupted plutocratic and imperial elites."[2] He also, however, explicitly connects "the deterioration of democratic powers" to the rise of "the Christian Right."[3] Members of the latter apparently do not qualify as "ordinary citizens," and *their* "desire to take their country back" is not democratic enough. Diamond's *In Search of Democracy* doubles down on this collapsing of form and content:

> Imagine a world in which all states were democracies. . . . A world of universal democracy would not be a perfect world. Many democracies would no doubt still be illiberal, but the framework of democracy and an open society would generate public pressure to gradually move them in a more liberal direction. . . . It would be a world of dramatically fewer human rights abuses, greater personal and press freedom, less corruption, less violent conflict, and quite conceivably a world that had put an end to interstate war. It would be a world that no longer sponsored or tolerated mass killings like the Rwandan

genocide. . . . It would be a world without famine. . . . It would be a more just world.[4]

If only Rwanda had more of the "qualities of democracy"—according to Diamond: universal suffrage, elections, multiple parties, access to information, public accountability, and "citizen satisfaction"[5]—the mass slaughter of the Tutsis by the Hutus might have been avoided. Setting aside the gross oversimplification involved in this claim, notice that it assumes a direct correlation between democratic "qualities" and particular results; this denies from the outset the possibility that elements of the demos, and even decisive elements, might still condone or participate in genocide, interstate war, and human rights abuses in spite of fair elections, government transparency, and "public pressure"—they might *be* the public, after all.

Theorists with avowedly Marxist commitments have also made the democratic turn, as exemplified by the opening question of Jerry Harris's *Global Capitalism and the Crisis of Democracy*: "Can the power of democracy overcome the power of global capitalism?"[6] Along these lines, Ellen Meiksins Wood's *Democracy against Capitalism* traces the historical lineage of the concept of democracy back to its etymological roots as "rule by the laboring class," while Richard Wolff's *Democracy at Work: A Cure for Capitalism* argues for employee ownership and management of business enterprises. Also worth mentioning in this context (although she is not a Marxist) is Brown's *Undoing the Demos*, which presents neoliberalism as a system bent on the destruction of democratic values and traditions.

Underpinning all of these analyses is the premise—illustrated by the cover of Harris's book—that people are everywhere clamoring for less capitalism, neoliberalism, and the like, and that certain institutions or certain powerful individuals are thwarting this demand.[7] It then becomes a question of "the people" versus a small handful of elites, as if the people are already opposed to these systems and emancipation is just a matter of giving them a power they lack. This prevents us from considering the possibility that the demos is in some way complicit with the systems under critique and is thus part of the problem. Harris attacks the "market fundamentalism" of politicians such as Jeb Bush[8] but does not dwell on the fact that millions of people have voted for Bush (and many others like him). Wolff asserts that "worker self-directed enterprises" would be more environmentally friendly[9] but does not entertain the prospect that the workers directing a given energy firm may not believe in climate change. In diametrically opposing neoliberalism and democracy, Brown obscures the fact that substantial elements of the demos (the Tea Party in the United States, for example) are in favor of and have even struggled for the neoliberal "stealth revolution." And if, to take up Wood's argument, the actually existing laboring class does not understand its oppression as a product of capitalism, then democracy versus capitalism is a false dichotomy insofar as increased power for this class would not, automatically, translate into anticapitalist politics. This is no mere logical point, as it indicates the terms by which capitalism is to be critiqued and the place of democracy in such an undertaking.

This ambivalence is also present in attempts to demarcate a conceptual boundary between democracy and "populism." While some theorists (such as Mouffe and Laclau) regard these terms as essentially synonymous, others have sought to define populism as antagonistic to truly democratic institutions, procedures, or movements; still others, such as Panizza, regard populism as "neither the highest form of democracy nor its enemy, but a mirror in which democracy can contemplate itself, warts and all."[10] In the most common of the proposals for a sharp division, democracy is understood as "open" and "limited," that is, as recognizing that no single movement or form of politics could ever encompass "the people" in a final and definite way, whereas populism represents "closure" insofar as it imposes a fixed and monolithic vision of who the *real* people are. "Populists reject any limits on their claims to embody the will of the people," Ochoa Espejo writes. "Liberal-democratic movements, by contrast . . . frame this appeal [to "the people"] in a way that guarantees pluralism and presents any particular cause as fallible, including their own."[11] In a slightly different register, Mudde and Kaltwasser distinguish between "inclusionary" and "exclusionary" populism; the former wants to include those "people" that have been excluded, while the latter wants to exclude, in the name of the "people," those who have been included too much.[12]

The problem with these distinctions is that they require an *interpretation* of their key categories (openness and closure, inclusion and exclusion), which is itself incompatible with a consistent application of these categories. Suppose a right-wing populist movement claimed that secular, liberal multiculturalism represented a "closure" of democratic embodiment, enforcing coercive recognition of a particular set of universalist values, while *its* intervention represented a pluralistic affirmation of *different* cultures, *different* peoples, *different* races. A response to this claim would require a subsequent distinction between *real* openness and *false* openness, a distinction that would categorically decide which political interventions *really* conform to democratic values and which do not, thus enacting the same "closure" the original distinction was meant to criticize. With regard to Mudde and Kaltwasser's terminology, this movement might likewise claim that *its* people have been "excluded" by the political correctness of globalized liberalism and that it is now only demanding their rightful "inclusion." As we will discuss further in chapter 3, this is the actual rhetoric of many right-wing populist parties, and the distinctions made by Ochoa Espejo and Mudde and Kaltwasser cannot justify any negative appraisal without collapsing under the weight of their own formalism.

Distinctions like these function as ways of maintaining the normative value of democracy while refusing to acknowledge the potentially troubling results of democratic politics. Instead of recognizing the limits of democracy, we simply recategorize movements with offensive content as not *truly* democratic, as "populist" (or "exclusionary populist") instead. Panizza's approach falls in line with this tendency, too, as when he describes populism as "representing the ugly face of the people[13]— "ugly" according to what standard of political beauty? Why is this face "democratic" when it is attractive and "populist" when it is not? By drawing a distinction that relies on the difference between the Ancient Greek word for "people" and the Latin word for the same thing, these theorists surreptitiously reveal what is really at stake: some people and the political movements that coalesce around them are good, others are bad. But the impulse to base a normative political theory on "the rule of the people" is so strong that the latter group must be conjured away into another category altogether, one made up of people who want to rule but that somehow does not express the rule of the people. This is the equivocation involved in the elitist-populist ambivalence. It echoes a comment made by Adolphe Thiers in the middle of the nineteenth century: "It is the masses [*la multitude*], not the people [*le peuple*], that we want to exclude."[14]

All of the figures mentioned so far take for granted that certain Left-progressive content is automatically implied by the term "democracy," be it liberal humanist (Diamond, Ochoa Espejo) or socialist-communist (the Marxists). This project will focus on a more self-conscious justification for the democratic turn, one that not everyone mentioned so far would assent to but one that offers an argument for treating democracy as an end in itself.

AUTONOMY AND INDETERMINACY

It is difficult to give a singular name to this argument, because its advocates employ widely varying vocabularies. It operates according to two basic, closely related hypotheses. First, it states that "the political" is "autonomous" and irreducible with regard to other categories like "the economic"; the former possesses its own structure, its own problems, and its own rewards.[15] Second, it understands the political as the realm of opinion and debate, of *doxai* in confrontation with one another, and not as a matter of truth, guided by reason, struggling to overcome illusions and establish the definitively right kind of society—a characterization that would lend the political the qualities of a science or a metaphysics and thus deprive it of its specificity.

A succinct and oft-cited expression of the first thesis can be found in Paul Ricœur's 1957 essay "The Political Paradox," where he posits "the relative autonomy of the political [le politique] compared to the socio-economic history of societies."[16] If "the political" has a specific and autonomous logic, then there are specifically *political* goods and harms, and it is this specificity that endows the figure of democracy with its normative force. The second thesis is encapsulated in Claude Lefort's frequently quoted phrase from a 1983 essay: "[D]emocracy is instituted and sustained by the *dissolution of the markers of certainty*."[17] The basis of legitimate political power, his argument goes, has been unmasked as an "empty place,"[18] historically contingent and lacking any ultimate foundation that might be uncovered through rational inquiry or analysis. A democratic society is one that organizes itself around this indeterminacy, while totalitarianism attempts to deny the absence of an ultimate ground by appealing to some substantial foundational myth. Both of these moments entail a renunciation of the philosophical ambition to prescribe definitive or authoritative political content (both Ricœur and Lefort articulate this explicitly).[19] Because the political is autonomous and because its markers of certainty have dissolved, Plato's philosopher kings and Rousseau's general will appear at best as hopeless intellectual endeavors and at worst as oppressive totalitarian fantasies. Politics is about *doxa*, not about truth, and it is likewise not a mechanism for bringing about the "right" kind of society. The only political system—or axiological principle—adequate to this understanding of "the political" is democracy.

Through various iterations and formulations, these two theses inform a current of the democratic turn in political theory concerned with suturing the critical project of emancipation to the figure of democracy.[20] Insofar as its appeal to democratic iconography as a critical foundation draws on these two ontological postulates, I will refer to this tendency as *the categorical imperative of democracy*. The reference is, of course, to the Kantian moral system, and specifically to the way Kant characterizes the relationship between the categorical imperative and autonomy:

> If the will seeks the law that is to determine it anywhere but in the fitness of its maxims for its own legislation of universal laws, and if it thus goes outside of itself and seeks this law in the character of any of its objects, then heteronomy always results. The will in that case does not give itself the law, the object does so because of its relation to the will. This relation . . . admits only of hypothetical imperatives: I ought to do something because I will something else. On the other hand, the moral, and hence categorical imperative says that I ought to act in this way or that way, even though I did not will something else.[21]

The categorical imperative is capable of prescribing a moral law because it is not determined by any external demand or circumstance but only by the internal structure of the will itself. The democratic categorical imperative likewise establishes its normative currency on the formal structure of "the political" over against any specific political content. Acknowledging the ontological priority of autonomy and the dissolution of certainty means granting democracy the status of an end in itself, not consigning it to merely instrumental or conditional value (i.e., rendering it a hypothetical imperative); determining the "correct" kind of politics by means of something other than its own nature—reducing it to economic interests or deciding it by appeal to facts—is to introduce something heteronomous into the political and thus distort its status as such.

At the same time, however, this formalism is supposed to coincide with an emancipatory, progressive political orientation, just as Kant's rarefied and abstract moral law, ostensibly cleansed of anything empirical, ends up conforming to the Christian mores of his time.[22] More or less surreptitiously, the heteronomy that was banished reasserts itself. The formal categories are infused with a content that does not essentially belong to them, and this unsanctioned admixture is what really lends the figure of democracy its critical purchase. This is accomplished by delimiting the demos, that is, by selectively focusing theoretical attention on instantiations of formal democratic iconography that coincide with a particular content and relegating other, undesirable content to a status beneath or opposed to the formal categories, or by simply ignoring it. This is what I mean by "democracy in spite of the demos." As we have already seen, this logic is present in the democratic turn at a broad level, but since my project focuses on a particular manifestation of this turn (the categorical imperative), I will concern myself with how it shows up in the context of this manifestation.

Let me cite a few examples of the tendency I have in mind. Over the course of several books, William Connolly has developed an account of "deep pluralism," which he sums up succinctly as a "bicameral orientation to political life." This orientation involves maintaining two sometimes conflicting perspectives: first, a commitment to one's own "faith, doctrine, creed, ideology, or philosophy," be it "Marxism . . . a branch of Christianity . . . orthodox Judaism, Kantianism, Rawlsianism, neoconservatism, or pragmatism," and second, an appreciation of "how [this creed] appears opaque and profoundly contestable to many who do not participate in it," together with a "struggle against the tendency to resent this very state of affairs."[23] Connolly's approach goes beyond advocating for formal legal protection of private beliefs, insisting that deep pluralism requires a "public ethos" and that its understanding of politics must be "multidimensional" (i.e., not limited to representative government).[24] Although he does not articulate it in exactly these terms, his account of bicameral pluralism draws on a conception of the political as autonomous and indeterminate in the ways described above. He also understands this form of pluralism as essential to democracy and vice versa.[25]

Against this backdrop, Connolly occasionally remarks that the contemporary political situation has dimmed the prospects for a realization of this democratic aspiration. "The agenda of deep pluralism," he writes, "is not in the cards 'today' because the right wing holds so many of those cards."[26] Side by side with a leveling of content—Christianity, Marxism, and neoconservatism are all so many "creeds"—there is the suggestion that certain ("right wing") political commitments are fundamentally inappropriate; content is exiled as irrelevant and then returns as decisively important. Ostensibly, the explanation for this is that right-wing politics is inherently antipluralist, and therefore violates the categorical imperative demanded by "bicameralism." But with pluralism defined in such formal terms, there is no a priori reason why the Right should be denied admittance on the basis of its content. Connolly gives no account of how or why certain "creeds" would lend themselves more easily to bicameral political life than others; both liberal humanism and Christian conservatism could be pluralist (cognizant of and comfortable with the contestability of its creed) or antipluralist (dogmatic and closed to discussion). There is consequently no explanation of why one is necessarily more democratic than another. By equating Left-progressive politics with pluralism and excluding the Right, Connolly collapses form and content at the same time as he defends a strictly formal normative political theory.

Connolly might argue that the Right, once in power, tends to be antipluralist by universalizing its particular creed (free market fundamentalism, traditional Christian mores, etc.) in the form of legislation that marginalizes or oppresses other viewpoints. But from the perspective of those who subscribe to this creed, the secular liberal humanism of the other side does the same thing once in power; they could (and do) understand legalized abortion, for example, as an attack on their religious belief system, a coercive universalizing of secular values at the expense of others. If the Left held more cards, the Right would have equal cause to denounce the monochromatic political climate and accuse its opponents of stifling pluralism. By eliding this possibility, not recognizing that the Left seems as antipluralist to the Right as vice versa, Connolly performs the very failure of bicameralism that his theoretical intervention was meant to address.

We find a more detailed example of this ambivalence in Nancy Fraser's *Scales of Justice*. Her central thesis is that a political theory concerned with justice must combine the economic and cultural dimensions of "redistribution and recognition" with an attention to specifically *political* inequities and misrepresentations. Appealing to "the irreducible specificity of the political,"[27] she argues that a unique form of injustice occurs when certain actors are denied access to the process of "frame setting," that is, determining who can be counted as a political subject and what can be counted as a political issue—"the meta-discourses that determine the authoritative division of political space."[28] Disparities in access and representation occur not just at the level of particular policy decisions but also at the level of the "grammar" through which politics is made intelligible, at the level of social ontology. The persistence of the "Westphalian model," in which politics concerns only "citizens" and takes place strictly within and between "states," has led to a "democratic deficit" that is not appropriate to an increasingly globalized and complex world. It thus becomes necessary for a theory of justice to include "struggles for meta-political democracy,"[29] establishing avenues through which politically marginalized actors can express grievances of "misframing" and enact change at this level. The point is not to arrive at the final or "right" frame but to provide mechanisms by which frames can be contested and multiplied.

Both moments of the categorical imperative are present in Fraser's approach: the political has a specific logic, but its content is indeterminate and open to contestation. A normative political theory must therefore root itself in democracy. But notice that Fraser appeals simultaneously to the necessity of democratizing the process of frame setting and to a notion of "misframing." Will those who endorse the outmoded "Westphalian" model of politics be included in the democratic frame-setting process, even though we have decided in advance that their frame is inadequate? The response might be that this model is the dominant one, while democracy at the level of frame setting is meant to give voice to forms of oppression unintelligible within the prevailing system. The consequence of this, however, would be an indiscriminate legitimization of any novel "grammar" insofar as it is understood as novel by its advocates. I have already alluded to the Tea Party; one might well conceive this movement as the struggle for a previously unrecognized hyperlibertarian "frame" in which taxation and social welfare programs are forms of oppression against "entrepreneurs." The objection that such a social ontology is not truly novel does not go very far: for devotees; this "oppression" is sufficient to warrant a new movement and new vocabulary.

Of course, Fraser is not interested in endorsing all novel political grammars as such. "Social movements disclose new dimensions of justice," she writes, "when they succeed in establishing as plausible claims that transgress the established grammar of normal justice, which will appear retrospectively to have obscured the disadvantage their members suffer."[30] A new question forms: What counts as success and plausibility? By any quantifiable metric, the Tea Party movement has had success in shifting public discourse and policy in the United States (and by extension the world).[31] Fraser does not want to say that all political contestations are automatically legitimate, and so she combines the "multi-dimensional social ontology" informing the project with a "normative monism": "As soon as we accept that injustices of misframing can exist in principle, we require some means of deciding when and where they exist in reality. Thus, a theory of justice for abnormal times requires a determinative normative principle for evaluating frames."[32] She finds this monism in "the all-subjected principle," which states that "all those who are subject to a given governance structure have moral standing as subjects of justice in relation to it."[33] With this criterion, we could determine that the feminist movement's appeal to "misframing" is legitimate and that the claims of the "men's rights activists" are not.[34] This is because women *are* subjected to the governance structure of patriarchy, while men *are not* actually oppressed in any way by feminism, "political correctness," and the like.

At this moment the argument becomes circular, as an account of who is subject to what "governance structure" will depend upon a particular "frame"—a given social ontology or "grammar"—and so the criterion for adjudicating between legitimate and illegitimate frames already assumes what it is meant to appraise. In other words, we can only apply the normative principle from within a given frame, and so it cannot function as a means of evaluating when a social movement has "established a plausible claim." If one's political grammar includes "the war on Christmas,"[35] to take another example, then this frame passes the test of "the all-subjected principle" insofar as, in this imaginary, devout Christians are subjected to a form of governance by secularism, academic elites, or whatever. Normative monism cannot determine if this contestation represents a genuine injustice of misframing without reinstating the same "democratic deficit" that it sought to remedy. While the entire project hinges on a democratic multiplication of frames that rejects "appeals to authority,"[36] a particular frame is taken as a fait accompli. Again, the gulf between form and content cannot be bridged without sacrificing one or the other.

A final example: Oliver Marchart's *Post-Foundational Political Thought* offers a self-conscious reflection on the problem I have been articulating, drawing explicitly on Ricœur and Lefort. He insists on the ontological (as opposed to merely ontic) consequences of the autonomy and indeterminacy of the political; the "post-foundational turn" does not only mean that the "ground" for any particular politics is undermined, but also and more significantly that the notion of a "final ground" itself has become untenable.[37] Political movements can and should still attempt to provide grounds for themselves, but always against the backdrop of this constitutive limit (what he calls a "quasi-transcendental"[38]), the impossibility of arriving at an uncontestable and exhaustive foundation. Drawing on Mouffe and Bonnie Honig, Marchart argues that traditional political philosophy is an attempt to "displace" politics itself by appealing to a fixed and final foundation.[39] The interesting moment for our purposes comes when he considers the implications of this ontological thesis for our ontic concerns:

> If we take seriously the notion of a politico-ontological difference, then we should recognize that we will never be able to secure an ontological ground that would found or determine a particular ontic politics (emancipatory or not)—such a move would clearly be self-contradictory. And . . . we can easily imagine a conservative post-foundational skepticism which is not necessarily democratic or emancipatory. [*Notice the distancing of conservatism and democracy.*] So, if to derive a particular politics from a post-foundational stance would be a clear *non sequitur*, then it seems that the only political argument which can be made starting from the political difference is a *non sequitur* argument.[40]

To a certain extent, his line of thought here seems to mirror my own: a recognition of the autonomy and uncertainty of the political does not entail or correspond to any political content. He goes so far as to say—

pace Ricœur and Lefort, Connolly and Fraser—that it does not even entail democracy. He explicitly criticizes the equation of "postfoundationalism" and Leftist/progressive political aims, referring to this false equivalence as "emancipatory apriorism."[41]

Marchart then retreats from this conclusion, first by reattaching the postfoundational turn to the figure of democracy and then by bringing emancipation back into the fold:

> [D]emocracy is to be defined as a regime that seeks, precisely, to *come to terms* with the ultimate failure of grounding rather than simply repressing or foreclosing it. . . . Claude Lefort's argument as to the dissolution of the markers of certainty and as to the emptying of the place of power in democracy implies that democracy is the regime which comes closest to *accepting* the absence of an ultimate ground.
>
> [T]he displacement of politics is an act that tries to conceal its own political nature, and thus its own contingency, historicity, conflictuality and ungroundable status. If, on the other hand, democracy and emancipation must be conceived of in a post-foundational way . . . then it is of vital importance for an emancipatory project to defend a post-foundational approach.[42]

Through this gesture, he sutures the categorical imperative of democracy and emancipatory politics from the other direction—claiming that emancipation necessarily entails "the specificity of the political" and "the dissolution of the markers of certainty," rather than vice versa. Though the categorical imperative of democracy is no longer a sufficient condition for Left politics, it is still a necessary condition. In this case, content is not surreptitiously introduced into form, but form into content. Our critical question can likewise be reversed: Would it not be of equally vital importance for a conservative right-wing project that regarded itself as democratic to defend a postfoundational approach? If, as Marchart argues above, there is no necessary connection between a postfoundational understanding of the political and emancipatory politics, then there is also no necessary connection between the latter and democracy—which is defined by the extent to which it "comes to terms" with its indeterminate situation. To say that an emancipatory project demands a postfoundational approach is another non sequitur, as this approach is demanded by *any* project that does not "conceal its own political nature," regardless of its content. In foregrounding the relationship between postfoundationalism and Left-progressive political content, minimizing the potential relationship between the former and any other project, Marchart rehearses the categorical imperative of democracy in spite of his critique of "emancipatory apriorism."

These examples are only sketches. The next two chapters of this book attempt to trace in detail the ambivalent structure of the democratic categorical imperative, first in Arendt and then in the "radical democracy" of Rancière, Mouffe, and Laclau. Beginning with Arendt may seem counterintuitive, as she does not advocate a Left-progressive political project in any unambiguous way. Her work is of central importance for this discussion not only because of its strong influence on the Left's democratic turn but also because it lays bare the elitist-populist ambivalence at work in the categorical imperative. She develops a political ontology anchored in democratic iconography—conforming to the two theses articulated by Ricœur and Lefort above—but at the same time excludes much of the demos from the status of "the political." My argument in the third chapter is that Rancière, Mouffe, and Laclau repeat this basic Arendtian maneuver, albeit with a different object of exclusion. In their hands, this democratically oriented political ontology is meant to coincide with a critical, emancipatory political project—but this coincidence is accomplished by, as it were, staying faithful to Arendt and disqualifying parts of the demos from consideration.

In pointing to an elitist-populist ambivalence, I do not have in mind the "paradox in the theory of democracy" as described by Richard Wollheim and others. In this account, there is a potential contradiction between one's desire for a certain outcome and the desire that this outcome be decided democratically.[43] If I support democracy and also support policy x, and if policy x is decided against by the democratic process, then I both support and do not support policy x. Theorists in the critical milieu, however, do not typically understand democracy as proclaiming, "Whatever policy the majority supports should be enacted," nor are they content to combine this principle with liberal-constitutional safeguards to protect against "the tyranny of the majority" or with "proceduralist" caveats that insist on a fair and open deliberation process. If democracy is to be critical, the argument goes, it must have a more fundamental, deeper, or (as we will explore in chapter 3) more "radical" meaning than just "majority rule." The ambivalence comes when this democratic depth is taken, without justification, to coincide with particular political projects and to exclude others a priori. The problem does resemble Wollheim's inasmuch as it relates to the tension between form and content. Here, however, it is not a matter of two potentially conflicting commitments (a commitment to democracy and a commitment to certain outcomes) but the supposition that these commitments are actually identical.[44]

DOXA OR DELUSION?

The categorical imperative of democracy and its elitist-populist ambivalence would be an innocuous theoretical oversight if the object of its exclusion were only a negligible extremity. If the examples we consider (France's *Front national*, men's rights activism, climate denial) were only liminal or speculative cases, my critique would likewise remain at an abstract, ahistorical level, content to point out the surreptitious and ambivalent introduction of content into the nominally formal iconography of democracy. The Left democratic turn carries a more serious danger, however, when its "other"—the part of the demos that it refuses to esteem as democratic—attains a dominant or decisive position in actually existing politics. When ignorance, right-wing extremism, and delusion solidify into active and successful political movements, the theory that maintains the figure of democracy as a critical foundation is forced to make one of two choices: either grant these phenomena an emancipatory or progressive status or ignore them altogether. Except in occasional and cautionary moments, typically accompanied by an unjustified disqualification (as we have already seen and will see again throughout chapter 3), the democratic turn has opted for the second option. At best, it characterizes pernicious political tendencies as the responsibility of a small handful of elite powers exerting their will over and against the will of the people (e.g., Harris, as discussed above). The possibility that "the people" also will these pernicious tendencies is thus denied from the outset. By its very structure, the categorical imperative of democracy prevents us from acknowledging the *popularity* of regressive or pathological political positions, thereby also preventing us from critically analyzing or confronting them. West, for example, writes:

> As I've traveled across this country giving speeches and attending gatherings for the past thirty years, I've always been impressed by the intelligence, imagination, creativity, and humor of the American people, then found myself wondering how we end up with such mediocre and milquetoast leaders in public office. It's as if the best and brightest citizens boycott elected public office.[45]

This becomes less mysterious if we admit the unpleasant reality that drastically more people in this country attend sermons by evangelical preachers than lectures by public intellectuals. The real danger of the democratic turn does not lie in any logical incoherence but in its failure to come to terms with this disturbing fact about the present political conjuncture.

The "other" of the democratic turn, in other words, is not a thought experiment. Around 50 percent of the US population remains skeptical of the scientific consensus on anthropogenic climate change, and many do not believe that the climate is changing at all.[46] Elected officials like Senator James Inhofe—who brought a snowball to the floor of the Senate to discredit climate science, authored a book on the subject called *The Greatest Hoax*, and served as chair of the Committee on Environment and Public Works—continue to command decisive constituent support.[47] Around a third of this population also disbelieves that human beings have evolved to their present state, and 29 percent think that former president Obama is a Muslim.[48] In several states, school textbooks are rewritten to expunge the history of American racism—one actually referring to slaves as "workers."[49] On the public stage of political discourse, we can hear major politicians claim that the United States has never supported dictatorships.[50] During one of the 2016 primary debates, former Senator Rick Santorum opined that "Islam is not just a religion. Islam is Sharia Law. It is also a civil government. It is also a form of government. The idea that that is protected under the First Amendment is wrong. There will have to be a line drawn." The large audience then applauded.[51] These widespread and egregious misrepresentations—by no means limited to the United States and by no means exhausted by this list—are not mere harmless mistaken beliefs; at our present historical moment, they are assuming a position of momentous political significance. Shortly after the US presidential election, Oxford English Dictionaries named "post-Truth" the word of 2016,[52] and a top advisor in the new administration made headlines when she referred to "alternative facts."[53] Facing all of this, one is tempted to invoke Tocqueville's *Democracy in America* and declare that "a new political science is needed for a totally new world."[54] At the same time, the increasing visibility of this phenomenon should not lead us to think that it is new. What we are experiencing now is only a particularly stark expression of a politics of delusion that long predates the 2016 election and that made this historic moment possible.

When the democratic turn appeals to "the people" (which it does in various sophisticated ways), it does not mean the people who applauded Senator Santorum's "Islam is Sharia Law" comment. When it valorizes "new social movements," it does not mean the Tea Party or "men's rights activism."[55] When it ontologizes *doxa* as the essence of the political, it does not have in mind the *doxa* that anthropogenic climate change is the greatest hoax. But are these people not also people, these movements not also movements, these *doxai* not also *doxai*?

This line of thought may invite an objection from democratic theorists of a deliberative persuasion. They might argue that democracy can only fully function, and thus maintain its normative force, if the democratic citizenry is "informed." What democracy holds in esteem is not "raw public opinion," to use James Fishkin's terminology, but the voice of the people "after it has been tested by the consideration of competing arguments and information conscientiously offered by others who hold contrasting views."[56] Or, following Joshua Cohen's formulation, we might say that a commitment to democracy requires a recognition of "reasonable pluralism" rather than an indiscriminate legitimation of all values that any element of the demos might hold. A value is "reasonable," according to Cohen, "just in case its adherents are stably disposed to affirm it as they acquire new information and subject it to critical reflection."[57] Ostensibly, then, climate skeptics and xenophobic nationalists would be excluded from the normative winners' circle because their positions, according to the intellectually demanding conceptions of democracy established here, are not "informed" or "reasonable" and thus not yet fully democratic.[58]

If we take this objection at its word, we arrive at the bizarre conclusion that the demos may be thoroughly undemocratic, and that democratic values may bear absolutely no relation to "the people" as they are presently constituted—an oxymoronic result expressed by the title of Yascha Mounk's *The People vs. Democracy*. We should ask, in this case, why the term "democracy" is maintained even if its form is entirely divorced from the empirical demos. This question is especially pertinent insofar as the "informed opinion"/"reasonable value" stipulations posit a divide between the current "voice of the people" and something that would constitute its *true* voice, raising the further question of how this divide could be bridged while respecting democratic principles.[59] Unless the criterion for establishing what counts as an "informed opinion" or a "reasonable value" is also arrived at through the democratic process, in which case the proviso becomes meaningless, the stipulation that the demos be of a certain rational caliber shifts the normative force away from democracy and toward rationality or reasonableness, but still identifies the former with the latter. The peculiarity of this Rousseauian conclusion—that the people must be *shown* how to properly exercise their own will—is expressed succinctly by Carl Schmitt: "The consequence of this educational theory is a dictatorship that suspends democracy in the name of a true democracy that is still to be created. . . . [O]nly political power, which should come from the people's will, can form the people's will in the first place."[60]

The ominous implications of Schmitt's argument aside, the reasonable/informed caveat has devastating consequences for a theory that regards democracy as an end in itself. If we are confident that proper deliberation will yield results that point away from positions like climate skepticism and xenophobia, then we have decided the correct political result in advance of the democratic process. We are, in effect, identifying democracy with the right politics and then dismissing the wrong politics on the grounds that it is undemocratic, no matter how much popular support it commands. If a commitment to democracy means that we want the people to have power *provided that* the people hold certain values and believe certain things—which may not coincide with what they actually believe and value—then everyone is a democrat, and our differences come down to differences of content. Christian absolutists could profess a faith in democracy provided that everyone is a Christian. Commitments to democracy with provisos about "informed" or "reasonable" views—where "informed" is taken to mean "believes in climate change" and "reasonable" to mean "has a critical perspective on the history of racial oppression"—accomplish the same thing. Liberal constitutionalism fares no better in maintaining the normative specificity of democracy, as the power of the people can always be checked by an appeal to the protection of rights, the understanding of which is not itself established democratically. Even a monarchist could support democracy, provided that the demos always defers to the monarch, and this is why Schmitt claims that "dictatorship is not antithetical to democracy."[61] These are so many forms of democracy in spite of the demos. As soon as we assume that certain results will follow from democratization, and justify democracy on that basis, the critical weight is placed on the results rather than the democratization. If, on the other hand, we are *not* confident that deliberation will point away from climate skepticism and xenophobia, and regard the success or failure of democracy strictly on the basis of its procedure,[62] then we must ask ourselves if a commitment to democracy is worth these potentially troubling outcomes.

The categorical imperative of democracy rejects the notion that there is some definitively correct political result external to its democratic iconography, rightly seeing that this would void the normative specificity of democracy; its theorists likewise distance themselves from majoritarian understandings of democracy, and so the problem of "bad majorities" is something of a nonstarter. Yet the impulse to disqualify certain political movements as undemocratic on the basis of their content remains intact, as we have already seen and will see again in chapter 3. But the right-wing demos, unfortunately for the democratic turn, is still the demos. Climate skepticism and xenophobia are still parts of its voice, its potential *kratos*. I am not suggesting that critical political theory should begin taking these positions seriously in that sense that one takes well-given advice seriously; rather, my claim is that we should take these phenomena seriously in the sense that one takes an eminent danger seriously. The categorical imperative of democracy prevents us from doing the latter and, if it were consistently maintained—which it rarely if ever is—would demand that we do the former. It wants it both ways: to avoid conferring legitimacy on these pathological and far-Right views and to avoid a critical analysis of them that might drift into "antidemocratic" territory. Given the increasingly evident dangers harbored by the politics of delusion, we can no longer remain in abeyance here; we are forced to make a choice.

The last two chapters of this book explore what form this choice might take. Chapter 4 engages with Adorno and Marcuse, focusing on the former's "Opinion Delusion Society" and the latter's "Repressive

Tolerance." In these pieces and elsewhere, they develop an account of pathological political "opinion" as an expression of antagonistic, contradictory social relations. This culminates in what I will call a theory of "socially necessarily delusion," otherwise called "ideology." I argue that our present political conjuncture is better theoretically understood and critically confronted by a theory of social delusion than by the logic of democracy as a categorical imperative. The democratic ethos of the Left, as I hope to have indicated already and to explore more deeply in chapter 3, is fraught with a tension between its political content (whereby it excludes certain perspectives as inadmissible in some way) and its formal normative categories (which preclude the possibility of such exclusion). The theory of ideology developed by Adorno and Marcuse allows us to go beyond this elitist-populist ambivalence by confronting the normative force of the figure of democracy with a critical appraisal of the actually existing demos. Rather than providing and defending a formal concept of "the political" while surreptitiously or unjustifiably determining its content, they orient their analysis at the level of the latter.

The final chapter responds to one of the criticisms of ideology critique that has led to its perceived obsolescence in recent years: the charge of "elitism." Ideology critique, its opponents suggest, presupposes a fundamentally antidemocratic division between intellectual knowledge and mass culture, a division that preserves the power of an elite intelligentsia by making it the guardian of a truth inaccessible to the multitude. To address this concern, I will provide a brief history of the argument for elitism—which I call "the incompetence principle"—that has been part of Western political philosophy since Plato. I will then distinguish this argument from the approach of the early Frankfurt School. For the incompetence principle, the prevailing ignorance and irrationality of the demos reveals an essential characteristic of its nature; for Adorno and Marcuse, however, the phenomenon of "socially necessary delusion" reflects a contingent, historically specific situation that can and must be transformed through critical education and practice.

This distinction will allow me to respond to the charge of elitism. The democratic turn criticizes ideology critique as elitist, but this judgment depends on an equivocation between an essentialist claim about the abilities or prerogatives of a given class or group of people (the incompetence principle) and a diagnosis of the momentous political problem of mass delusion, which is not necessary and eternal but reflects a historically specific reality (Adorno and Marcuse). The latter, I argue, should not properly be called elitism. In fact, insofar as it insists on withholding altogether the title of "the political" from certain (right-wing) political movements, the elitist label belongs more appropriately to the categorical imperative of democracy than to ideology critique. Returning to the early Frankfurt School, we are in a position to avoid both the classist implications of the incompetence principle and the equivocations of the democratic turn, both elitism and populism.

2

ARENDT'S ISLAND OF FREEDOM

There is a tension in Arendt's thought between her valorization of democratic iconography and her restrictive demarcation of political space. Her identification of politics with the public sphere—a space where a plurality of persons can appear, speak to one another, give their opinions, and undertake collective or individual action—is undermined by her categorical relegation of necessity (the reproduction of material life) to the private, nonpolitical realm. This bifurcation has the effect of excluding a priori from politics all those who have not secured the "liberty" (independence from material necessity) to exercise "freedom" (the ability to act on the public stage). For her, the collapse of this strict dichotomy—that is, increasing democratization, the rise of "the masses"—has engendered the most disastrous political events of our time, including the rise of totalitarianism. Arendt's political ontology is thus torn between a consecration of plurality and a restless insistence on exclusivity. In other words, she has faith in democracy but no faith in the demos. Her work is therefore a stark expression of the elitist-populist ambivalence that concerns this book and will indicate the terms by which it can be understood and analyzed. The aim of this chapter is to elaborate the origins, consequences, and meaning of this ambivalence in Arendt's work.

A POLITICAL ONTOLOGY

Arendt makes a fundamental distinction between "the public sphere"—the place of appearance, plurality, and speech, and therefore the political—and "the private sphere"—the place of the maintenance of material necessities. She frequently associates the public sphere with the polis and the private sphere with the household. This distinction, which runs like a fault line throughout her work, lays the foundation for her ambivalent political ontology.

Taking cues from (her reading of) Aristotle, Arendt argues that human beings are political by condition owing to two closely related phenomena: the fact of plurality and the faculty of speech. This condition is what gives meaning to the notion of "world"—the shared space between the plurality of individuals in which they all have a stake and in which they "appear" to one other:

> While all aspects of the human condition are somehow related to politics, this plurality is specifically *the* condition—not only the *condition sine qua non*, but the *condition per quam*—of all political life. (*The Human Condition*, 7)

> Wherever the relevance of speech is at stake, matters become political by definition, for speech is what makes man a political being. (*The Human Condition*, 3)

> To live together in the world means essentially that a world of things is between those who have it in common, as a table is located between those who sit around it; the world, like every in-between, relates and separates men at the same time. (*The Human Condition*, 52)

The polis represents the space in which human beings (I will replace Arendt's sexist language for now—more on this later) come together in their equality and distinction, to appear to one another and to speak. It is the public sphere in its purest form, the political itself. Her choice of the term "polis" is not accidental, as she understands the ancient Athenian model as the clearest possible expression of the public/political. The public sphere is also the place of "freedom," which will become clearer when we discuss "action" below, but which we can begin to flesh out by discussing the opposite of the public.

The private sphere is where human beings are when they are not exposed to the plurality of their fellows seated around the common table of the "world," when they are not "appearing" in public. The private is what belongs to the individual as opposed to what is shared in common, and it therefore includes private property. Importantly, the private is also the realm of "necessity," "in the original sense of being necessitated by having a body" (*The Human Condition*, 73). For Arendt, it is not only that private concerns like property and the reproduction of life are properly outside of the public sphere but that a *prerequisite* for participation in the public sphere is a mastery of these "necessities" such that one is no longer beholden to them. Furthermore, since appearance in public represents what is properly political (plurality and speech), and what is properly human is the political (note the overtones of Aristotelian teleology), to be fully beholden to necessity is to be not fully human. She again takes her cue from ancient Athens:

> What all Greek philosophers . . . took for granted is that freedom is exclusively located in the political realm, that necessity is primarily a prepolitical phenomenon, characteristic of the private household organization, and that force and violence are justified in this sphere because they are the only means to master necessity—for instance, by ruling over slaves—and to become free. (*The Human Condition*, 31)

> It is . . . not really accurate to say that private property, prior to the modern age, was thought to be a self-evident condition for admission to the public realm; it is much more than that. Privacy was like the other, the dark and hidden side of the public realm, and while to be political meant to attain the highest possibility of human existence, to have no private place of one's own (like a slave) meant to be no longer human. (*The Human Condition*, 64)

> Private wealth, therefore, became a condition for admission to public life not because its owner was engaged in accumulating it but, on the contrary, because it assured with reasonable certainty that its owner would not have to engage in providing for himself the means of use and consumption and was free for public activity. . . . If the property-

owner chose to enlarge his property instead of using it up in leading a political life, it was as though he willingly sacrificed his freedom and became voluntarily what the slave was against his own will, a servant of necessity. (*The Human Condition*, 64–65; cf. *The Promise of Politics*, 116–19)

When the aristocratic master enters the public realm, he must leave behind his concern for his private property and his economic privilege; this concern is dealt with in private by domination over others. While we still need to discuss "action" to get a full account of Arendt's notion of "freedom," we can say that, for her, freedom at least includes freedom *from*—freedom from the necessity of having to maintain one's own necessities. Since freedom from necessity is the condition for access to the public sphere, and mutatis mutandis the condition for political life, it follows that those who are "servants of necessity" are unable to participate in politics. With this argument, Arendt establishes a negative correlation between economic precarity and political participation. Those whose lives are defined by the maintenance of bare necessities are not properly political beings, and properly political beings have their necessities provided for such that, when they enter the public realm, they can focus on properly political things.

The categories of the public and the private are correlated to the concepts of labor, work, and action. Labor is the reproduction of the basic necessities of life; the human being conceived in terms of labor is referred to as the *animal laborans*. Work is the construction of lasting and stable structures (e.g., buildings, monuments, works of art). Unlike labor, the objects of work have a sense of permanence and therefore immortality; they are not constructed merely for the sake of "bare life." The human being defined by work is called *homo faber*. Action is the unique, ephemeral capacity of human beings "to begin something new," which Arendt here and elsewhere describes as a kind of "miracle." Action depends upon the existence of a public realm and is associated with great deeds or "glory." It is also characterized by its unpredictability, in contradistinction to labor and work.[1]

Furthermore, action depends upon plurality and relates to speech in ways that labor and work do not. Accordingly, it is the only one of these three domains that is uniquely political, the only one that relates to positive freedom (the freedom *to* begin something new), and therefore the category most expressive of the human condition: "[H]uman plurality is the paradoxical plurality of unique beings. Speech and action reveal this unique distinctness. Through them, men distinguish themselves instead of being merely distinct; they are the modes in which human beings appear to each other, not indeed as physical objects, but *qua* men" (*The Human Condition*, 176). In later works, Arendt will go so far as to identify action and freedom (*Between Past and Future*, 151). Finally, action is also, even more than work, the promise of "earthly immortality": "Without this transcendence into a potential earthly immortality, no politics, strictly speaking, no common world and no public realm, is possible" (*The Human Condition*, 55).[2]

We can see already the ambivalent structure of Arendt's thought: an exaltation of human plurality as the meaning of politics, and a simultaneous acknowledgment that significant portions of the population are excluded from the political realm and are therefore not part of this human plurality. Politics is what takes place between free human beings, but the condition for the possibility of this freedom is not itself a political issue. So far, however, Arendt is only discussing ancient Athens, and her account may only be a description of Athenian political life and not a prescriptive account of how we should understand politics today. Domination over slaves was necessary for the Athenian polis, but this does not amount to an apology for any contemporary economic inequalities. Let us turn, then, to her motivations for developing a political ontology, using ancient Athens as a model.

Arendt puts the public/private/labor/work/action schemata to work in diagnosing what she takes to be an affliction of "the modern era": the rise of "the social." She argues that, owing to a complex constellation of causes, the necessities formerly consigned to the private sphere have been made objects of public concern. "The social" or "society" is the name she gives to this "curiously hybrid realm where private interests assume public significance" (*The Human Condition*, 35). In other words,

> The distinction between a private and a public sphere of life corresponds to the household and the political realms, which have existed as distinct, separate entities at least since the rise of the ancient city-state; but the emergence of the social realm, which is neither private nor public . . . is a relatively new phenomenon whose origin coincided with the emergence of the modern age and which found its political form in the nation-state. (*The Human Condition*, 28)

> [T]he dividing line is blurred, because we see the body of peoples and political communities in the image of a family whose everyday affairs have to be taken care of by a gigantic, nation-wide administration of housekeeping . . . "collective housekeeping"; the collective of families economically organized into the facsimile of one super-human family is what we call "society," and its political form of organization is called "nation." (*The Human Condition*, 28–29)

> Society is the form in which the fact of mutual dependence for the sake of life and nothing else assumes public significance and where the activities connected with sheer survival are permitted to appear in public. (*The Human Condition*, 46)

This development amounts to the destruction of what is proper to both the public and the private (*The Human Condition*, 59, 69). In society, the accumulation of wealth, the maintenance of necessities, and the reproduction of life as such—to paraphrase, economic concerns—displace the properly political activities of action and speech that characterized the polis. The *animal laborans*, previously defined precisely by its nonpolitical (economic) mode of being, has now attained dominance in public sphere at the expense of human "action," that is, at the expense of the truly political.

Arendt finds theoretical expression of this development in the work of Marx (and to a lesser extent Nietzsche), who (she claims) simply inverts the ancient hierarchy according to which labor was inferior to work and action (*The Human Condition*, 17).[3] Arendt develops an understanding of Marx's work as the apex of "socialization," where the formerly despised status of the reproduction of the life process is glorified and transfigured into the content of politics. To make this clearer, see how Arendt characterizes the status of labor in the Athenian context:

> To labor meant to be enslaved by necessity, and this enslavement was inherent in the condition of human life. Because men were dominated by the necessities of life, they could win their freedom only through the domination of those whom they subjected to necessity by force. The slave's degradation was a blow of fate and a fate worse than death, because it carried with it a metamorphosis of man into something akin to a tame animal. A change in a slave's status,

therefore, such as manumission by his master or a change in general political circumstance that elevated certain occupations to public relevance, automatically entailed a change in the slave's "nature." . . . It is in this sense that Euripides calls all slaves "bad": they see everything from the viewpoint of the stomach. (*The Human Condition*, 83–84, 84n)

In Marx, as in the rise of the social, this "viewpoint of the stomach" becomes "good," the "tame animal" who labors due to being enslaved by necessity becomes politically meaningful (something unthinkable to the Athenians). According to Arendt, this amounts to the dissolution of political experience as such. In society, as in Marx, "the *animal laborans* was permitted to occupy the public realm; and yet, as long as the *animal laborans* remains in possession of it, there can be no true public realm, but only private activities displayed in the open" (*The Human Condition*, 134). Marx's political utopia, then, is actually more of an antipolitical dystopia, the final instantiation of what, since Plato, had been the philosophers' dream: to be finished with politics altogether (*The Human Condition*, 222; cf. this point with Rancière). Arendt, once very sympathetic to Marx,[4] developed this damning criticism while laboring over a book that was never completed, tentatively titled *Totalitarian Elements in Marxism* (designed as a kind of sequel to *The Origins of Totalitarianism*, it was eventually abandoned, and elements of it found their way into *The Human Condition* and various other later writings). This will become significant later, when we consider the extent to which the categorical schema of *The Human Condition* was motivated by a reaction to the calamity of totalitarianism.[5]

The rise of the social, Arendt argues, effects an inversion of the political means/ends relationship that prevailed in ancient Athens. In classical antiquity, the mastery of necessity was a means to the end of political life, of distinguishing oneself in the realm of appearances. In the modern era, the reproduction of life is an end in itself, and politics is understood as a means to that end. This phenomenon, along with the epistemological crisis initiated by the rise of modern science, is the meaning of modern "world alienation" as Arendt understands it:

> [W]e have almost succeeded in leveling all human activities to the common denominator of securing the necessities of life and providing for their abundance. Whatever we do, we are supposed to do for

the sake of "making a living"; such is the verdict of society, and the number of people, especially in the professions who might challenge it, has decreased rapidly. (*The Human Condition*, 126–27)

This development is so problematic because it diminishes the capacity and motivation for action, and thus results in the hypostatization and mechanization of a given way of life. At precisely the time when a reflection on means and ends is most warranted—the era of totalitarianism and the atomic bomb—we are predisposed against this task by the nature of "society." This is why Arendt, from this work through the *Eichmann* book and her last, unfinished text, *The Life of the Mind*, is concerned with the faculty of thinking. Thinking is by no means the same as action, but at the moment of action's fall from grace, it is incumbent upon us "to think what we are doing" (*The Human Condition*, 5).

This means/end inversion is closely related to another modern phenomenon that Arendt finds dangerous: the emergence of a relatively liberated *animal laborans* as a being with (quasi-)political power. Technological advances have lessened the burden of the reproduction of life, leaving the *animal laborans* with relatively more free time to pursue other ends, including "political" activity. The problem is that a laborer understands only labor and consumption (i.e., the reproduction of life) and "sees everything from the viewpoint of the stomach," as Arendt put it above. Even when the burden of necessity is lifted, then, the *animal laborans* cannot make productive use of the newly won freedom but can only approach the political in terms of the social. This terminates in a "society of laborers without labor," making, in effect, the entire society into a nonpolitical laboring/consuming society:

> The modern age has carried with it a theoretical glorification of labor and has resulted in a factual transformation of the whole of society into a labouring society. The fulfillment of the wish . . . comes at a moment when it can only be self-defeating. It is a society of laborers which is about to liberated from the fetters of labor, and this society does no longer know of those other higher and more meaningful activities for the sake of which this freedom would deserve to be won. (*The Human Condition*, 4–5)

> [T]he spare time of the *animal laborans* is never spent in anything but consumption, and the more time left to him, the greedier and more craving his appetites. That these appetites become more sophisticated, so that consumption is no longer restricted to the necessities but, on the contrary, mainly concentrates on the superfluities of life, does not change the character of this society, but harbors the grave danger that eventually no object of the world will be safe from consumption and annihilation through consumption. (*The Human Condition*, 133)

At this moment the complexion of the argument begins to change, and a critical question presents itself: Assuming that the economically impoverished represent a contemporary manifestation of the classical *animal laborans* (the "servant of necessity" corresponding to the ancient slave), does this mean that the poor cannot participate in politics without destroying the purity of the public realm? These passages seem to suggest not only this but also that those who were once materially dispossessed will continue to act out of "greedy and craving appetites" even when they attain a higher standard of living: once poor in body, always poor in spirit. Notice how closely this line of thought matches up with a classically aristocratic disdain for bourgeois society and the crass materialism of the nouveaux riches.

Arendt carries the argument further by suggesting that the expansion of this society of laborers without labor, this "mass culture" (*The Human Condition*, 134), has at least an elective affinity with the rise of totalitarianism. In such a society, "action as such is entirely eliminated and has become the mere 'execution of orders'" (*The Human Condition*, 223)—notice that she is already looking ahead to the encounter with Eichmann. The elitist tendency in this argument comes to the fore when the figure of the "masses" takes on a momentous and frightening significance for Arendt. See her characterization of the potential "ochlocracy" of this laboring society:

> If tyranny can be described as the always abortive attempt to substitute violence for power, ochlocracy, or mob rule, which is its exact counterpart, can be characterized by the much more promising attempt to substitute power for strength . . . [and] there is always the danger that, through a perverted form of "acting together"—by pull and pressure and the tricks of cliques—*those are brought to the fore*

who know nothing and can do nothing. (*The Human Condition*, 203–4, my italics)

There is, indeed, much evidence to suggest that Arendt's study of totalitarianism motivates the disjunctive categorical schemata of *The Human Condition*.[6] Looking back to *The Origins of Totalitarianism*, we see an explicit connection between imperialism (the principle progenitor of totalitarianism, according to Arendt) and the displacement of the political by the social, as well as an explanation of the category of "the mob" as a symptom of the modern capitalist (i.e., "social") world (*The Origins of Totalitarianism*, 123–57). There is even an explicit association between the dislocation of *homo faber* by *animal laborans* (using these terms) and totalitarian ideology (*The Origins of Totalitarianism*, 475). While Arendt insists that the existence of masses is not a sufficient condition for totalitarianism (*The Origins of Totalitarianism*, 313), she does claim that it is a necessary one: "Without the masses the leader is a nonentity" (*The Origins of Totalitarianism*, 325). Consider also this rhetoric, from the essay "Truth and Politics": "[Deliberate falsehood in politics] is clearly an attempt to change the record, and as such, it is a form of *action*. . . . This is frequently done by subversive groups, and *in a politically immature public*, the resulting confusion can be considerable" (*Between Past and Future*, 245, my italics). Compare this with the passages cited above about the masses' propensity for totalitarian manipulation and about the connection between this propensity and the status of the *animal laborans*. A theme emerges: a lack of faith in the populous to be politically responsible, the suggestion that the "impotence" of "mass democracies" (*The Promise of Politics*, 98) gives rise to a "politically immature public" prone to calamitous political mistakes. A certain "ochlophobia," or fear of "the masses," pervades Arendt's work, and her disdainful remarks about "the realm of necessity" suggest something about the socioeconomic status of these masses.[7] For all her glorification of human plurality, she is nervous about extending this plurality too far. If totalitarianism is the destruction of plurality, it is also, paradoxically enough, the result of too much plurality of the wrong kind.

On one reading, then, Arendt's diagnosis of the modern age and its afflictions represents elitism in a stark, unequivocal way. If the *animal laborans*—the "servant of necessity" who "sees everything from the viewpoint of the stomach"—is the cause of our modern political perils, then responsibility for "world alienation" is placed squarely on the shoulders of the poor. In Athens, politics was possible because subordinate classes took care of the necessities, leaving others the freedom to be free in the public realm. But now the interest of the subordinate classes (economics) has infiltrated the public realm, destroying it and our common world with it. In this interpretation, it is the politicization of material inequality that is the root cause of modern society's ills. Would the solution, then, be to force economic concerns back into the private realm, to once again restrict public access to those whose material needs are satisfied, thus perpetuating already established economic inequalities? In this case, Arendt's thought would seem to participate in one of political philosophy's oldest motifs: the notion that the economically underprivileged cannot and should not participate in politics.

This is one of the most perplexing tensions in Arendt's work: a celebration of "freedom" as the authentic space of politics, and a recognition of the fact that this freedom is predicated on domination. As Gines puts it, "[Arendt] acknowledges that in order to participate in public/political space, one must be liberated from the burdens of life in the private realm and also that this liberation is most often achieved by forcing life's burdens onto other people."[8] Even more unsettling is the suggestion, easily inferred from the schemata discussed above, that these "private" forms of domination are not of public concern and are therefore not politically significant.[9] Arendt's consistent use of the Athenian polis as an exemplar does not do her any favors on this account, as the women and slaves (and therefore the majority of people) of ancient Athens were consigned to the "private sphere," destined to live as the *animal laborans*, not fully human. Multiple feminist critics have taken Arendt to task on this point.[10]

If we wanted to avoid conclusions that would paint Arendt in elitist tones, we might point out that the reading developed so far relies on an equivocation between "the *animal laborans*" and "the poor." But the *animal laborans*, we might say instead, is not a person or a class of people. The rise of the social is the ascendancy of a certain disposition or mentality, not of certain individuals. When Arendt assigns qualities to the *animal laborans*, she is not evoking classist stereotypes about the poor; rather, she is pointing out the mode of behavior common to everyone in this "society of laborers without labor." Likewise, her use of Athens as a model is not meant to suggest that slavery was justified, or that we should return to it, but rather to illustrate the specificity of the "freedom" that has been covered over in the modern age. The animating impulse of Arendt's work, then, is the recovery of the cherished public sphere without the relations of domination that accompanied it in the Athenian context.[11]

There is some plausibility to this more generous interpretation. Peppered in between these passages reflecting a pronounced fear of the demos are moments of apparently genuine democratic thinking. In an interview titled "Thoughts on Politics and Revolution," Arendt says this: "Not everyone wants to or has to concern himself with public affairs. In this fashion a self-selective process is possible that would draw together a true political elite in a country. Anyone who is not interested in public affairs will simply have to be satisfied with their being decided without him. But each person must be given the opportunity" (*Crises of the Republic*, 233). From what has been said above, it would seem as though the expansion of opportunity to the impoverished constitutes a catastrophe in Arendt's eyes. But here she extends access to public affairs to "each person." This rhetoric leads some critics to conclude that there really is no elitist/populist tension in Arendt's thought.[12] But we must tread carefully here: if we accept the claim that Arendt's "public sphere" is available to anyone regardless of economic status—which she suggests in the quote just given, but which seems to be in conflict with her descriptions elsewhere—this still would not mean that "private" economic concerns are subject to public debate. So political space may be accessible to the poor but only on the condition that they not speak about their poverty. In the passage above (*The Human Condition*, 133), however, we are led to believe that the dispossessed cannot approach politics except in terms of possession (and therefore not at all).

The categorical schemata of *The Human Condition* have been subject to numerous criticisms on various grounds. Several scholars have taken note of the antinomy that I am describing as an elitist-populist ambivalence.[13] At the same time, as I have just mentioned, many readers deny that Arendt is as contradictory as she seems, and they take up the task of exonerating what *appears* as elitism in her work.[14] A consistent and initially compelling way of salvaging Arendt's thought from some of its troubling implications is to read her conception of the political together with her populist impulses as articulating the necessity for a radical (though nonviolent) reorganization of society or redistribution of resources. The train of thought runs like this: Arendt insists that liberation from necessity is a prerequisite for political participation *and* sometimes says that "each person" should be allowed political participation. So her conception of politics impresses on us the task of making sure that everyone is liberated from necessity enough to engage in public affairs.[15] Perhaps in spite of herself, Arendt offers a radical, emancipatory politics with her claim that political freedom requires freedom from toil; it expresses the task of working toward the increasing democratization of freedom from toil so as to make political space more available for all.

There are some passages that lend credence to this interpretation. In the same interview I quoted a few paragraphs above, Arendt says, "Our problem today is not how to expropriate the expropriators, but, rather, how to arrange matters so that the masses, dispossessed by industrial society in capitalist and socialist systems, can regain property" (*Crises of the Republic*, 214). Or consider Arendt's reply to Michael Gerstein's question about the status of class and property in her thinking: "To make a decent amount of property available to every human being—not to expropriate, but to spread property—then you will have some possibilities for freedom even under the rather inhuman conditions of modern production" (*Hannah Arendt*, 320). Better still, see the following from the essay "Public Rights and Private Interests":

> [I]ndeed, freedom, political life, the life of the citizen—this "public happiness" I've been speaking of—*is* a luxury; it is an *additional* happiness that one is made capable of only after the requirements of the life process have been fulfilled. . . . So if we talk about equality, the question always is: how much have we to change the private lives of the poor? . . . Before we ask the poor for idealism, we must first make them citizens: and this involves so changing the circumstances of their private lives that they become capable of enjoying the "public." (107)

As attractive a possible appropriation of Arendt's political ontology this reading may be, and as much as these (relatively obscure) passages lend it support, it is difficult to reconcile with her work as a whole, especially *On Revolution*.

ISLANDS OF FREEDOM AND SEAS OF NECESSITY

Arendt's primary objective in contrasting the French and American Revolutions is to form a hypothesis as to why the former "ended in disaster" while the latter was "so triumphantly successful" (*On Revolution*, 46). Her conclusion is that the American experiment was based on "freedom" and was therefore a truly political revolution able to found an enduring republic, while the French attempt was based on "the social question" and was as a result a spectacular failure. By "the social question," Arendt means "the existence of poverty" (*On Revolution*, 50), and she refers to this struggle as "liberation" in contradistinction to "freedom" (*On Revolution*, 20–24). This is consonant with the way she characterizes "the rise of the social" in *The Human Condition*, that is, when economic concerns (like the miserable poverty that defined the lives of the lower classes in the *ancien régime*) take on political significance (she once again describes "society" as "that curious and somewhat hybrid realm which the modern age interjected between the older and more genuine realms of the public or political on one side and the private on the other" [*On Revolution*, 113]). In other words, the French Revolution's critical error was that it tried to abolish poverty politically, to achieve a private end with public means:

> The social question began to play a revolutionary role only when . . . men began to doubt that poverty is inherent in the human condition, to doubt that the distinction between the few, who through circumstances or strength or fraud had succeeded in liberating themselves from the shackles of poverty and the labouring poverty-stricken multitude was inevitable and eternal. (*On Revolution*, 12–13)

> All rulership has its original and its most legitimate source in man's wish to emancipate himself from life's necessity, and men achieved such liberation by means of violence, by forcing others to bear the burden of life for them. This was the core of slavery, and it is only the rise of technology, and not the rise of modern political ideas as such, which has refuted the old and terrible truth that only violence and

> rule over others could make some men free. Nothing, we might say today, could be more obsolete than to attempt to liberate mankind from poverty by political means; nothing could be more futile and more dangerous. (*On Revolution*, 104)

The notion that only "the rise of technology" could relieve the necessity of "private" economic domination troubles the potentially emancipatory interpretation alluded to above, and renders all the more confusing Arendt's talk of "changing the circumstances of [the poor's] private lives that they become capable of enjoying the 'public.'" Was this not the fatal mistake of the French Revolution, according to her description? Perhaps the attempt to abolish poverty with politics is permissible only now, since technology has made this possible. But at the same time, she insists that "today . . . nothing could be more futile and more dangerous" than the attempt to alleviate poverty by political means.

The argumentative structure of *The Human Condition* shows up in *On Revolution* in other ways as well. Just as the former did, the latter explicitly associates the disastrous "rise of the social" with Marx and Marxism, suggesting that prioritizing economic restructuring and redistribution amounts to a perversion of the political means/ends relationship and to the dissolution of "freedom" in the name of "the life process":

> If Marx helped in liberating the poor, then it was not by telling them that they were the living embodiments of some historical or other necessity, but by persuading them that poverty itself is a political, not a natural phenomenon, the result of violence and violation rather than scarcity. [Marx] finally strengthened more than anybody else the politically most pernicious doctrine of the modern age, namely that life is the highest good, and that the life process of society is the very centre of human endeavour. . . . Not freedom but abundance became now the aim of revolution. (*On Revolution*, 52–54)[16]

On Revolution drives home this point again and again: the French Revolution was a disaster because it was not a truly political revolution, and it was not a truly political revolution because it was concerned with "the life process of society," with poverty and hunger, "the invasion of the public realm by society" (*On Revolution*, 213). It was a revolution "from the point of view of the stomach," doomed as an uprising "whose end is impotence, whose principle is rage, and whose conscious aim is not freedom but life and happiness" (*On Revolution*, 103). The fact that Arendt uses the same conceptual apparatus to discuss the downfall of the French Revolution should cast doubt on some of the more generous readings of *The Human Condition*, for example, that the rigid class structure of ancient Athens bears no relation to her larger point.

This brings me to another theme from *The Human Condition* that carries over to *On Revolution*: Arendt's low estimation of the political maturity of the materially dispossessed and her fear of the dangerous power of the masses, which she brings up in both the French and American contexts:

> [T]his multitude, appearing for the first time in broad daylight, was actually the multitude of the poor and the downtrodden, who every century before had hidden in darkness and shame. What from then on has been irrevocable, and what the agents and spectators of revolution immediately recognized as such, was that the public realm—reserved, as far as memory could reach, to those who *were* free, namely carefree of all the worries that are connected with life's necessity, with bodily needs—should offer its space and its light to this immense majority who are not free because they are driven by daily needs. (*On Revolution*, 38)

> [T]he trouble was that the struggle to abolish poverty, under the impact of a continual mass immigration from Europe, fell more and more under the sway of the poor themselves, and hence came under the guidance of the ideals born out of poverty, as distinguished from those principles which had inspired the foundation of freedom. For abundance and endless consumption are the ideals of the poor: they are the mirage in the desert of misery. . . . And while it is true that freedom can only come to those whose needs have been fulfilled, it is equally true that it will escape those who are bent upon living for their desires. (*On Revolution*, 130; cf. *Thinking without a Bannister*, 373–81)

These passages should be read against interpretations that construe Arendt's apprehension about the *animal laborans* and the "rise of the social" as a strictly analytical concern, as a question of mentality or disposition. It *is* a certain mentality that Arendt finds troubling—the conception of politics as instrumental, as a means of the end of material life—but she is also convinced that the poor, when they are given power, act out of this mentality ("the ideals born of poverty") and will continue to do so even when they cease to be poor. This unmistakably antipopulist rhetoric—which should be familiar from *The Human Condition*—contravenes her democratizing gestures elsewhere, the sentiment that "each person . . . must be given the opportunity" to participate in public affairs. If this democratizing gesture means that political space must be accessible to the poor (who are *not* free), then Arendt seems to be recommending her own worst nightmare ("the rise of the social," etc.). If the gesture means instead that collective life should be reorganized and resources redistributed such that the poor are "liberated" (as she sometimes hints), then she is recommending what she diagnoses as the crucial misstep of an ill-fated revolution.

Before continuing the discussion of *On Revolution*, we should to pause to note the curious ambivalence that emerges from this argument. Arendt knows that political freedom is impossible without "freedom from toil" (liberation) and yet insists that "everyone must be given the opportunity" to participate in politics. But here she says that increasing economic liberation has only been made possible with "modern technology" and cannot be attempted by "political means." Her thought on this point articulates a necessity and then systematically blocks the realization of this necessity. Freedom (from toil) is the condition for the possibility of access to political life in the public realm, and yet the political is categorically not allowed to act on the conditions of this freedom from toil (lest it lose its status as political). So increasingly democratized access to politics *should* happen (if everyone is to be given the opportunity to participate), but it is not clear how this *could* happen without political action. What Arendt grants with one hand she takes away with the other.[17] The only possibility for including "each person," then, is the liberation brought by technology. But there is a problem here as well: in *The Human Condition*, Arendt warns against the "society of laborers without labor" that results when the *animal laborans* is granted more spare time by technological advances. So the "labouring poverty-stricken multitude" is dangerous if it tries to liberate itself actively, and also dangerous if it is liberated passively by "the rise of technology."

The primary difference in the situations preceding the respective revolutions, according to Arendt, was that "poverty was absent from the

American scene." She immediately amends this claim to read "what were absent from the American scene were misery and want rather than poverty" (*On Revolution*, 58). This enabled the American founders to orient their revolutionary project around the "rights of the citizen" as opposed to "the rights of Man," as the French would (*On Revolution*, 140). Arendt once again looks to antiquity to augment her distinction, this time to Rome:

> The distinction between a private individual in Rome and a Roman citizen was that the latter had a *persona*, a legal personality. . . . Without his *persona*, there would be an individual without rights and duties, perhaps a "natural man"—that is, a human being or *homo* in the original meaning of the word, indicating someone outside the range of the law and the body politic of the citizens, as for instance a slave—but certainly a politically irrelevant being. . . . [T]he men of the French Revolution had no conception of the *persona*, and no respect for the legal personality which is given and guaranteed by the body politic. (*On Revolution*, 96–98)

This gives more detail to her claim that the American Revolution succeeded where the French failed because it was a truly *political* revolution. It was concerned with the foundation of a body politic where "legal personalities" capable of speech could appear, their "natural" necessities a non sequitur.

There are two other, closely related factors that make the American Revolution so successful in Arendt's estimation. One is its status—sometimes in spite of its founders' self-understanding—as a foundation and a beginning. The other was its predilection for public debate, discussion, and deliberation in town halls, councils, and wards. The local town halls, like the Athenian polis, were places where personae could appear to one another and speak, that is, the properly "public sphere" described in *The Human Condition*. Arendt is clear that these councils, in which the "public happiness" (*On Revolution*, 110) she cherishes is embodied and secured, have an explicitly *political* (not social/economic) function (*On Revolution*, 266). As we have seen, "the social question" played no role in (Arendt's account of) the American Revolution. "Political freedom," she says in this context, "means the right 'to be a participator in government,' or it means nothing" (*On Revolution*, 210). But the high recommendation of the council system returns us to our familiar question: *Who* is granted access to this public sphere? Who can, should, or must attend the town hall meeting? Who has this right of political freedom? Her brief comment on this score is important for our problem:

> The phenomenon I am concerned with here is usually called the "elite," and my quarrel with this term is not that I doubt that the political way of life has never been and will never be the way of life of the many, even though political business, by definition, concerns more than the many, namely strictly speaking, the sum total of all citizens. . . . My quarrel with the "elite" is that the term implies an oligarchic form of government, the domination of the many by the rule of a few. From this, one can only conclude . . . that the essence of politics is rulership and that the dominant political passion is the passion to rule or to govern. This . . . is profoundly untrue. The fact that political "elites" have always determined the political destinies of the many and have, in most instances, exerted a domination over them, indicates . . . the bitter need of the few to protect themselves against the many, or rather to protect the island of freedom they have come to inhabit against the surrounding sea of necessity. (*On Revolution*, 267–68; cf. *Thinking without a Bannister*, 382)

Although she is skeptical of the term "elite" insofar as it associates politics with ruling, the disjunctive political ontology of *The Human Condition* shines through clearly: islands of "freedom" and seas of "necessity." The exclusionary nature of the polis remains in full force, as those whose lives are characterized by the maintenance of bodily needs are not, and cannot be, properly political subjects. Refraining from the temptation to expand this island by political means, to democratize the public sphere—that is, to secure everyone's necessities such that they can participate in public life—is precisely the virtue of the American Revolution over and against the French Revolution.

Arendt's admiration for America is qualified, however. She claims that the authentically political aspect of the founding of the United States has been lost in its subsequent history—in fact, the glorious moment was lost almost immediately. The heritage of "freedom" represented by the revolutionary movement was mitigated by the emergence of the representative form of government as opposed to Jefferson's "ward" system (*On Revolution*, 209ff). While the early stages of the Revolution had been characterized by active popular participation, "action," and the singular experience of foundation, the developing nation stabilized and relaxed into a complacent "social" state, its popular power transferred to elected officials entrusted solely with the task of protecting "private" interests. Paradoxically, then, the very achievement of the American Revolution (founding a stable state) led to the decline of the ethos of its achievement. "Representative government," she writes, "has in fact become oligarchic government" (*On Revolution*, 261). To recover the lost treasure of true politics, she suggests, as we have already guessed, replacing elected officials with voluntary participation in councils, and she refers to this—in scare quotes—as "an 'aristocratic' form of government" (*On Revolution*, 271). Interestingly, Arendt also describes the development of the representational system in the following way: "The 'élite sprung from the people' has replaced the pre-modern élites of birth and wealth" (*On Revolution*, 269). Now, one could read this comment with a positive connotation according to the democratic impulses in Arendt's work (political power has shifted from the wealthy to the larger populous). One could also read it with a negative connotation according to the elitist aspects of her work (the politically immature "people" have been given political power they are not worthy of). Given her judgment about representative government, coupled with her remarks about what kind of "elite" would characterize her ideal council system, the latter reading seems more plausible.

The historical accuracy of *On Revolution* has been called into question numerous times, especially Arendt's "Disneyland version"[18] of the American Revolution. Scholars have also debated the consequences of these inaccuracies for her theoretical argument.[19] While we should not pretend that Arendt is only offering an instructive fable in her account of the Revolutions, we should also not suppose that its factual inaccuracies determine the value of her work or constitute its most serious problems. More will be gained by looking at what the factual inaccuracies *reveal* about her political ontology. Her valorization of the Athenian polis and her lionizing of the American Revolution should be considered together, not only because they perform the same function in the structure of her argument but also because they reveal the same antinomy of her thought, namely, that the "space of freedom" is constituted by domination. It is no secret that the American "founding fathers," whom Arendt admires for their commitment to "freedom," conceived their "Republic" as belonging to land-owning white men only.[20] The

American Revolution was, in fact, so characterized by "freedom" that it emerged and sustained itself on the shoulders of a massive slave trade and the genocide of an indigenous population. But what is decisive here is the fact that Arendt is perfectly aware of these historical realities: "The absence of the social question from the American scene was, after all, quite deceptive . . . that abject and degrading misery was present everywhere in the form of slavery and Negro labour. . . . [Slavery is] the primordial crime upon which the fabric of American society rested" (*On Revolution*, 60–61).[21] Whatever the status of the hideous violence concomitant with the "foundation" Arendt admires, it was apparently not enough to provoke her to rethink her account of the virtues of the American Revolution. And yet there is little here that explicitly contradicts the political ontology laid out in *The Human Condition*. Slavery, the subjugation of women, and the condition of the laboring landless are, after all, "private" matters.[22] The Americans succeeded where the French failed, according to Arendt, because they accorded a privileged status to the political persona. This is true, and all of our qualms about *On Revolution* disappear, if we assume that only landowning white men count as personae. The American Revolution was a "success" and the French a "failure" only from the perspective of the safety and prosperity of this elite group.

The preceding enables us to articulate the relationship between Arendt's elitism and her democratic iconography in another way, in terms of its *isonomic* character. The term "isonomy" is usually understood as something like "abstract equality in law," that is, as the formal legal equality of all citizens regardless of social or economic position. Arendt, in her customary fashion, resignifies the term according to her understanding of its Greek roots: "*Isonomia* does not mean that all men are equal before the law, or that the law is the same for all, but merely that all have the same claim to political activity, and in the polis this activity primarily took the form of speaking with one another. *Isonomia* is . . . essentially the equal right to speak" (*The Promise of Politics*, 118). But this "equality" of "all" takes on a peculiar form in Arendt's hands, as she says on the same page: "Freedom does not require an egalitarian democracy in the modern sense, but rather a quite narrowly limited oligarchy or aristocracy, an arena in which at least a few or the best can interact with one another as equals among other equals. This equality has . . . nothing to do with justice." So the public sphere is isonomic but exclusionary. The isonomic equality of speaking beings is predicated on and inseparable from the material and social inequality that renders such isonomy possible. Social, material differences are at once politically irrelevant *and* determinant of the extent to which one is a political being. Arendt's elitism does not merely run alongside her democratic iconography but is inscribed within it.[23]

Both sides of this ambiguity—that social differences both do and do not have political significance—are expressed by Arendt in different ad hoc pieces. One side of this tension is notoriously expressed in the "Reflections on Little Rock" essay, in which Arendt protests against the enforced desegregation of Southern public schools in the 1950s. I will refrain from summarizing or critiquing her argument as a whole, but I will cite one passage that expresses the curious status of isonomy in her work:

> Segregation is discrimination enforced by law, and desegregation can do no more than abolish the laws enforcing discrimination; it cannot abolish discrimination and force equality upon society, but it can, and indeed must, enforce equality within the body politic. For equality not only has its origin in the body politic; its validity is clearly restricted to the political realm. Only there are we all equals. Under modern conditions, this equality has its most important embodiment in the right to vote, according to which the judgment and opinion of the most exalted citizen are on a par with the judgment and opinion of the hardly literate. . . . What equality is to the body politic—its innermost principle—discrimination is to society. (*Responsibility and Judgment*, 204–5)

Notice that here we "are all equals" in the political realm, and that she is content in this instance to associate this with voting, which includes "the hardly literate." This is not the idea of "the political" we have been given to understand from her other work. But in any case, what is developed in this passage is a dissociation of relevance between political equality and social inequality. The latter is not the concern of the former, and attempts by the former to act upon the latter are a transgression of its inherent limits (note the same theme from *On Revolution*). If we take her seriously in her more elitist moments—as opposed to this passage in which illiterates get to participate in politics by voting—then it would seem that, as we have suggested before, the economically underprivileged have no political recourse to address their situation.[24]

At the same time, we must point out the disconcerting character of her racism when considered alongside her sophisticated reflections on the "social" conditions of European-American Jewish experience.[25] "When one is attacked as a Jew, one must defend oneself as a Jew" (*Essays in Understanding*, 12), but African Americans have to defend themselves as "citizens." Drawing on Arendt's reflections on the figure of the "pariah"—in the first third of *Origins*, her book on Rahel Varnhagen, and various other "Jewish writings"—is a common strategy of rescuing her from the more problematic implications we have mentioned, and of mending the damage done by "Reflections on Little Rock."[26] Also worth mentioning in this context is "On the Emancipation of Women," a review of a book by Alice Rühle-Gerstel that Arendt wrote while still in Germany. Here she is sharply critical of the movement for formal, legal equality for women that neglects what she will later call "social" equality (*Essays in Understanding*, 66–68).

CONCLUSION

Though she has no particular attachment to the term, Arendt's political ontology is defined by the iconography we have come to associate with democracy—public space, plurality, speech, debate, and the freedom to begin something new.[27] It is also clear, however, that she has a devastatingly low opinion of the demos in the original sense of this term: the poor, the laboring, and the dispossessed.[28] Not only does she categorically disqualify "the maintenance of bodily needs" from political concern but she also goes so far as to suggest that the rising status and centrality of the *animal laborans* constitute the abolition of politics and therefore the catastrophe of modern life. For her, the political itself is effaced when "the multitude of the poor and the downtrodden"—those "politically immature" masses "who know nothing and can do nothing" and who "see everything from the viewpoint of the stomach"—try to alter their conditions of life by political action, for they can only act with "the ideals born out of poverty." This is therefore not an elitism that merely ignores the dispossessed but an elitism that keeps them in their place—a place in which they must be kept if politics is to be possible for others. It is a denial of the *capacity* of the economically underprivileged to act politically, an ontological dispossession of the already materially dispossessed. Scholars consistently refer to Arendt's idea of "plurality" to allay the problem of her elitism,[29] but a plurality of elites is still a plurality. The other features of the political ontology cannot help those not included: democratic iconography is cold comfort to a disqualified demos; an island of freedom means nothing to one adrift in the sea of necessity. Despite her endless admonition of the philosophers' retreat into the worldless realm of "Man" (as opposed to the world of "men"), Arendt returns there with a vengeance. In her disdainful exclusion of material necessity from the political realm, she betrays her own cardinal rule, forgetting that the majority of "men" who inhabit the world are hungry, needy, and precarious.

Indicting Arendt for her elitism is not my primary concern here. I am interested, rather, in the relationship between this elitism and her conception of the political, particularly the notion—celebrated by many of her admirers—that politics is an end in itself. As we have seen, the "rise of the social" transfigures politics into a means to the end of the reproduction of life, consumption, and private happiness, destroying the uniquely political "public happiness" once known by the ancient Athenians and the American founding fathers. This happiness consists in making oneself seen and heard in the public sphere, expressing one's opinion, engaging in debates and deliberations with others, persuading them and being persuaded, being one of a "plurality," acting to bring forth something new, and determining the conditions of one's own life. The figure of the political as an end in itself, sometimes referred to as "the autonomy of the political," is taken up by many as Arendt's most compelling contribution to political theory.[30]

As I have struggled to show throughout this chapter, however, the "autonomy" that Arendt grants to the political is purchased at the price of ontologically disqualifying the maintenance of material necessity from the status of politics (even if it is the condition for the possibility of politics) and by extension those whose lives are defined by (or were defined by) this maintenance. Democratic iconography has foundational status *only insofar* as economic concerns are not subject to discussion and *only insofar* as the economically underprivileged are excluded. The essence of politics is discussion but only a discussion of *certain things*. It is defined by appearance but only the appearance of *certain people*.

This is a formalism that narrowly circumscribes its content in advance. Arendt disqualifies the dispossessed because she abhors the political content that results from their inclusion—so much so that she refuses to call it politics. Political action is an end in itself only once we have delimited what counts as a political subject. Its autonomy is heteronomous.

This raises the question of what we might call the "content lacuna" of Arendt's conception of political action.[31] It is never entirely clear what is to be *done* in the public sphere, what taking action is supposed to accomplish if it is not allowed to infringe upon the private. At a symposium devoted to the latter's work, Mary McCarthy posed this question to Arendt directly: "If all questions of economics, human welfare, busing, anything that touches the social sphere, are to be excluded from the political scene, then I am mystified. I am left with war and speeches. But speeches can't be just speeches. They have to be speeches about something" (*The Recovery of the Public World*, 316). Arendt's response—which, as attendee Richard Bernstein notes,[32] satisfied no one present—is revealing. She first says that the content of political action will be determined by the political problems of a particular time and place. When pressed on what makes a problem political, she responds, "There are things where the right measures can be figured out. These things can really be administered and are not then subject to public debate. Public debate can only deal with things which—it we want to put it negatively—we cannot figure out with certainty." Politics is concerned with things that are "somehow *really* debatable" as opposed to "everything which can really be figured out, in the sphere Engels called the administration of things—these are social things in general. That they should then be subject to debate seems to me phony and a plague." As an example of these "things where the right measures can be figured out," Arendt offers the issue of public housing: "There shouldn't be any debate about the question that everybody should have decent housing" (*The Recovery of the Public World*, 316–18).

So politics, in this conception, is the space of debate and opinion—but only about those issues that are "somehow *really* debatable," those that "we cannot figure out with certainty." Ostensibly, the material/economic concerns that Arendt excludes (like the existence of poverty) fall outside of this category; the mistake of the sansculottes was to put "the administration of things" (like the distribution of resources) into question. One problem with this response—as I will explore in later chapters—is the usefulness of such a conception of the political at a time in which the most momentous subjects of debate are often issues "which can really be figured out" in an even more obvious way (e.g., the reality of climate change). In this respect, Arendt's thought repeats the deliberative tradition's *"informed* opinion" stipulation that we discussed in chapter 1: the essence of politics is the exchange of a plurality of *doxai*, but such *doxai* as are not deemed properly informed (or in Arendt's terms, debates about subjects that are not truly debatable) are excluded. This is how the elitist-populist ambivalence gets to have its cake and eat it too: there are no right answers in politics unless you have the wrong answer. This association of political life with the epistemically uncertain disqualifies those who are ignorant of or incredulous toward those things that *are* certain, and it is only through this exclusion of vast swaths of contemporary "political" actors that we can justify theorizing politics as an open-ended end in itself.[33] Again, we confront this curious ambivalence: Arendt's identification of politics with *doxa* directly contravenes the Platonic motif of the philosopher king, but her work is also seized by an aversion to the demos that would not be out of place in Plato.[34]

Central to Arendt's thought, as we said, is the thesis that the political—understood as the activity or performance of speech, plurality, debate, and dissensus—is an end in itself. We must now add a caveat: the political is an end in itself inasmuch as it concerns *doxa* rather than certainty or truth. This addendum is not incidental, for if the answers to political questions "could really be figured out," then politics would not be an end in itself, and there would be no need to posit democratic iconography as its essence.

In this thesis and its crucial caveat, Arendt's work has a broad affinity with the democratic ethos prevailing in critical political theory (and often directly informs it). Her conception of "public happiness" and her association of politics with *doxa* resonate with the turn (discussed in the introduction and the next chapter) toward democracy as a normative foundation for the Left, what I have called the categorical imperative of democracy. This chapter has argued, however, that in Arendt's hands this categorical imperative comes with certain conditions: not everyone can be counted as a political subject; the demos must be carefully circumscribed. The democratic turn, I claim, reproduces this exclusionary moment as well (even if the object of exclusion is different).

It is important to note that the categorical imperative of democracy, like its namesake in the Kantian moral system, has both normative and ontological moments (never neatly separable). A set of formal characteristics is posited as belonging essentially to "the political," and then these characteristics are exalted as "good" in themselves. Because the political *is* autonomous, one *ought* to treat it as such. Because "true" politics admits of no "certain answers," to pretend otherwise is both an intellectual and an ethical failure ("phony and a plague," as Arendt says). The most grievous error—in both senses, again—would be to understand the iconography of the political as being *for* something else (such as "the reproduction of life" or "a good society"), or as a good *only if* certain other conditions are met first (i.e., if the content of speech and debate is determined in advance). This would reduce political action to a means to some external end, that is, to a *hypothetical* imperative, thereby annulling the "good in itself" that politics truly *is* and mistaking the "management of the social" for the properly political. So when Arendt introduces conditions into her framework, she betrays not only her own normative injunction but her ontological commitments as well. As we have seen and will see again in chapter 3, the Left democratic ethos follows suit.

Despite the intrusion of content into her formal categories, it is difficult to count Arendt as a partisan for any particular political position or project. She has been described as a liberal humanist, a "classical Republican" opposed to "liberal democracy," a "radical conservative," a Whig, a theorist of political *virtù*, an agonist, and a "reluctant modernist."[35] She considered herself neither a liberal nor a conservative nor a socialist: "So you ask me where I am. I am nowhere" (*The Recovery of the Public World*, 336). When pressed for her stance on capitalism, she replied, "I do not share Marx's great enthusiasm about capitalism" (*The Recovery of the Public World*, 334). The democratic theorists of the next chapter, however, are in various ways and to varying degrees committed to a progressive and/or leftist project of social transformation, that is, a structural change in the social, political, economic order that will address the inequalities, antagonisms, and oppressions wrought by racism, sexism, heterosexism, and the capitalist world system. Chapter 3 will consider how the categorical imperative of democracy plays out in the work of these figures.

3

DEMOCRACY AT ITS LIMITS

Rancière, Mouffe, and Laclau

"**R**adical democratic theory," while not a consistently applied term, refers to a current of critical political thought that emerged at the end of the twentieth century, situated geographically in and around the French intellectual context and historically near the decline of the Soviet Union. It is usually framed as a reaction against (1) the "consensus" model proffered by the tradition of deliberative democracy and (2) the "reductionist" tendency of Marxism to subsume "the political" to "the economic." While getting more specific would require a treatment of individual figures, we can comfortably say with Breaugh et al. that "what distinguishes this tradition is a particular preoccupation with indeterminacy, difference, or division."[1] They are also right to point out that this milieu is heavily indebted to Arendt's political ontology.[2] Who counts as a "radical democrat" will depend on how one carves up the philosophical subdivisions,[3] but Laclau, Mouffe, and Rancière are perhaps the three figures most frequently cited as exemplars of this theoretical current (the former two having originated or at least popularized the term), and so it is with their work that I engage here. The aim of this chapter is to show that as radical democracy reproduces Arendt's democratic iconography (the populist element of her work, democracy as a categorical imperative), it also reproduces her exclusionary political "island" (the elitist tendency, democracy in spite of the demos). The point is not to criticize this exclusionary moment as such, to argue that

Rancière, Mouffe, and Laclau *should* include those whom they exclude, or to expose a contradiction in service of a "refutation." Rather, my purpose is to reveal the limits of democracy as a critical category by narrating the tension produced when the radical democratic approach selectively imports particular content into its formal theoretical landscape.

RANCIÈRE: DEMOCRACY AGAINST PHILOSOPHY

Rancière begins *On the Shores of Politics* with a striking metaphor: for fear of the unstable, unpredictable "democratic assembly" (the sea), philosophy attempts to ground politics on a firm theoretical foundation (the shore). Beginning with Plato, philosophy has sought to subsume politics under its own domain, to have rid of the messy political world that upsets its secure and durable categories: "The sea smells of sailors, it smells of democracy. The task of philosophy is to found a different politics, a politics of conversion which turns its back on the sea" (*On the Shores of Politics*, 1–2). Our first radical democratic theorist understands himself to be challenging this tradition, attempting to think the sea on its own murky terms.

Like Arendt, Rancière takes ancient Athenian political philosophy as his point of departure. In his reading, the tradition's foundational texts present a vision of the political as "geometrical equality" (as opposed to "arithmetical equality"), that is, the appropriate distribution of "parts" in a community. "Wealth" is the part owed to "the smallest number," while "excellence" belongs to "the best"; the "part" owed to "the people" (demos) is "freedom," and this part, paradoxically, also belongs to the whole, and so it is in a sense *no part* (*Disagreement*, 6–9). This distribution and its justifications are, however, contingent rather than necessary. The "counting" of the parts is therefore always "a false count, a double count, or a miscount" (*Disagreement*, 6). So while Plato (and the subsequent tradition of political philosophy) conceives politics as the correct distribution of parts, Rancière claims that it is the *contestation* of this precarious counting—by those who are miscounted—that gives politics [*la politique*] its meaning: "There is politics—and not just domination—because there is a wrong count of the parts of the whole.... Politics exists when the natural order of domination is interrupted by the institution of a part of those who have no part" (*Disagreement*, 10–11). This intervention consists in the juxtaposition of the basic fact of "equality"—"the absence of *arkhe*, the sheer contingency of any social order" (*Disagreement*, 15)—and an inegalitarian order of domination.

The uncounted can interrupt this order because they are capable of speech, which is the condition for the possibility of political action.[4] Equality is always already presupposed in domination, Rancière argues, because "in order to obey an order at least two things are required: you must understand the order and you must understand that you must obey it. And to do that, you must already be the equal of the person who is ordering you. It is this equality that gnaws away at any natural order" (*Disagreement*, 16). Politics, then, is the ephemeral appearance of the contradiction between equality and inequality, identity and nonidentity, "the introduction of an incommensurable at the heart of the distribution of speaking bodies" (*Disagreement*, 18–19). What we usually call "politics"—the maintenance of a given order, "the simple management of the social" (*On the Shores of Politics*, 11)—Rancière nonpejoratively terms "the police" (*Disagreement*, 28–30).[5] A given police order breaks down when its schema of distribution, its count of who counts as a speaking being, is disrupted by a new, incompatible "partition of the perceptible" (*Disagreement*, 24: *le partage du sensible*, also translated as "the distribution of the sensible"). Rancière gives several examples of this phenomenon, including Jeanne Deroin presenting herself as a candidate in an 1849 election, even though women were barred from holding office (*Disagreement*, 41), and Auguste Blanqui responding "proletarian" when asked to state his profession during trial (*Disagreement*, 37).

In Rancière's understanding of ancient Athenian political ontology, the demos referred to those who had no part, "the great beast of the populace" (*On the Shores of Politics*, 2) counted as not counting by the police order. Rancière likewise equates his account of politics with democracy: "Wherever the part of those who have no part is inscribed, however fragile and fleeting these inscriptions may be, a sphere of appearance of the demos is created, an element of the *kratos*, the power of the people, exists. The problem is to extend the sphere of this materialization, to maximize this power" (*Disagreement*, 88). He defines the term similarly in *Shores* as "first and foremost the space of all those locations the facticity of which tallies with the contingency and resolve of the egalitarian inscription in the making" (*On the Shores of Politics*, 90). In fact, he distinguishes "democracy" from "politics" only to say that the former is the latter's "mode of subjectification" (*Disagreement*, 99); a few pages later, he writes that "democracy . . . is the institution of politics itself. . . . Every politics is democratic in this precise sense . . . in the sense of forms of expression that confront the logic of equality with the logic of the police order" (*Disagreement*, 101). The meaning of "democracy," then, is the articulation of division and dissensus as opposed to the "unified mass" that troubled Plato's imagination, which is better termed "ochlocracy" (*On the Shores of Politics*, 32). Against various forms of antidemocratic rhetoric (which he catalogs in *Hatred of Democracy* and associates with Arendt on 23) and against an "epistemocracy" (*Hatred of Democracy*, 45) of experts who would decide on the right form of politics (a task that belongs to the police order and to the history of political philosophy), Rancière advocates a faith in "the intelligence of the people" (*Disagreement*, 23–25), the "wisdom of the many" (*On the Shores of Politics*, 35), or the "equality of intelligences" (*On the Shores of Politics*, 51–52) and understands this faith as a precondition of the political. "The denunciation of 'democratic individualism,'" he writes, "is simply the hatred of equality by which a dominant intelligentsia lets it be known that it is the elite entitled to rule over the blind herd" (*Hatred of Democracy*, 68).

While his use of the term "democracy" is idiosyncratic, Rancière's theory resonates with much of Arendt's democratic iconography (he refers to her work frequently, almost always neutrally or positively; the passage I pointed to in the preceding paragraph is an exception).[6] They share a certain privileging of speech, appearance,[7] and debate,[8] as well as a mistrust of philosophy's ambition to prescribe the right content of politics. Rancière's approach, however, could be utilized to critique Arendt's elitist dimension. Instead of a public space free from the needs of the *animal laborans*, the political would be instantiated precisely when the *animal laborans* contests this exclusion and demands a place at the table as a speaking being. Rancière could count Arendt, in spite of her anti-Platonic protestations, as part of the philosophical project of abolishing politics, because, as the last chapter argued, she still turns her back on the "sea" of the demos (using, remarkably, the same metaphor).

Rancière does not identify democracy/politics with economics or with class struggle, however. Hesitant to specify or determine in advance what content it will or should take, he speaks instead of "emerging" subjects "who take . . . wrong [*tort*] in hand, who expose the substance of the irreconcilable grievance while simultaneously beginning the process of addressing it by means of disputation. Politics exists by virtue of the democratic mobilization of this apparatus of appearance, imparity and grievance" (*On the Shores of Politics*, 97).[9] Politics is therefore "autonomous" in the sense discussed at the end of the last chapter, and democracy a process that makes sporadic historical appearances but never terminates in a final "end" that is external to itself. The figure of democracy also shows up in a normative register when Rancière criticizes contemporary state governments for working against the resurgence of democracy in a vain attempt to achieve "the end of politics."[10] He thus falls into the camp of theorists who criticize the prevailing nominal "democracies" in the name of an unrealized *real* (or radical) democracy; in his case, however, this real democracy is never "realizable" as such.[11]

For all this, Rancière is not without an "antidemocratic" tendency of his own. He advances a formal theory of democratic contestation but selectively determines the content of this contestation in advance, proscribing certain "partitions of the sensible" in spite of his own interdiction against this.[12] In both *Disagreement* and *Shores* he characterizes the rising tide of racism and xenophobia in Europe as a *negative example* of his democratic model of dissensus: "The trouble is that racism is not the symptom [of "consensus" thinking] but the disease—the disease, in fact, of consensus itself" (*On the Shores of Politics*, 104). His use of the term "disease" here is not strictly metaphorical, as he goes on to pathologize these racially charged nationalist views:

> The subject of the [racist] opinion says what he thinks of Blacks and Arabs in the same real/simulated mode in which he is elsewhere invited to tell about his fantasies [*fantasmes*] and to completely satisfy these just by dialing four figures and as many letters. The subject who opines accordingly is the subject of this new mode of the visible where everything is on display, up for grabs, a subject called on to live out all his fantasies in a world of total exhibition. (*Disagreement*, 119–20; and see the whole discussion from 117–21)

But it is not clear, at a formal level, why xenophobic populism would represent "consensus" against the backdrop of liberal multiculturalism, or why this "contestation" would not count(!) as "the introduction of an incommensurable at the heart of the distribution of speaking bodies."[13] Ostensibly, those participating understand themselves to be doing something like this, rather than enacting a confused pathology—living out their "fantasies" and the like. So why is this interruption, this "subjectification" not an example of democracy but of its polar opposite? What about the "equality of intelligence" of *these* people? Rancière selectively chooses his positive examples from historical cases of leftist or progressive politics.[14] But given his formalistic categories, the rise of neoliberalism could just as well be a disruption of the Keynesian police order that produces "emerging subjects" appearing in public to demand that corporations be "counted" as speaking beings.[15] For better or worse, right-wing extremism also represents "a tear in the common fabric, a new possibility that makes itself visible and that challenges the obviousness of a given world" (*Moments Politiques*, viii–ix). Rancière, however, takes for granted that all such "tears" will be progressive or leftist.

It might be objected here that, contrary to what I have just suggested, right-wing extremism represents the police rather than politics. In what sense could xenophobic and racist nationalism be said to operate on the presupposition of "equality"? This points to a certain ambiguity in Rancière's thought. As we have seen, he sometime speaks of the political as the juxtaposition of "the basic fact of equality" with the contingent inequality of a given police order. At other times, as we have also seen, he characterizes politics as the *creation* of specific political identities that juxtapose one partition of the sensible with another, or "an operator performing an opening" (*Recognition or Disagreement*, 93). In one case, a given distribution of parts is challenged by the impossibility of a "right" distribution of parts; in the other, a given count is disrupted by the articulation of a *different* count.[16] Rancière's examples confirm both interpretations. When Jeanne Deroin presents herself as a candidate for office, this exemplifies the former conception: the police order that decrees that men can hold office while women cannot is disrupted by the assertion of the equal capacity of women. But when Auguste Blanqui states his profession as "proletarian," he seems to be doing something else: giving voice to a new partition of the sensible that includes "proletarian" as a part, contesting a police order that does not count it. Here we have the emergence of a new "operator" and therefore an example of the latter conception of politics—a declaration of inequality against the presupposition of equality, rather than the opposite. This ambiguity comes down to what Rancière means by "a false count, a double count, or a miscount" of parts. On one hand, *any* count of parts is always false insofar as there is no "right" count; on the other, a count can be false to the extent that it renders invisible a given part by identifying this position with the whole of society ("no part"). The second understanding, however, requires a condition made impossible by the first: that there are better and worse counts of parts.[17]

This difficulty could be resolved if we make use of a distinction between necessity and contingency, as Rancière frequently does. There is no "right" distribution of parts in the sense that one is valid necessarily and eternally, but in the present inegalitarian order, there are true and false articulations of how this order distributes its parts. Right-wing xenophobia, then, would be a false "contestation" insofar as it based on a false partition of the sensible ("white nationals are being oppressed by a dangerous foreign force and need to defend themselves") *and* insofar as it is based on the false presupposition of necessary inequality (white supremacy, nationalism). In this case, we could make a distinction between those contestations that are legitimate (LGBTQ activists demanding to be "counted" without violence) and those that are not (men's rights activists claiming that feminism is oppressive to men).

Rancière, however, denies us the theoretical tools to make either of these distinctions. Adjudicating between partitions of the sensible, deciding which "contestations" are right and which wrong, would place us back in the position of an antidemocratic philosophy that eliminates politics. If political theory determines the correct count of what is owed to whom (LGBTQ activists are owed recognition and solidarity in struggle; men's rights activists are not), then we return to the "epistemocracy" of those who claim expertise over and against those who are ignorant of how things really are.[18] As we have seen, this is a position that Rancière associates with the police and (what amounts to the same thing) the Platonic project, the *end* of politics and likewise of democracy. Rancière does say that there are better and worse police orders (*Disagreement*, 30–31); for him, however, they are not better or worse on the basis of their particular distributions of parts (their content), but only by the extent to which they allow for the interruption of politics/ democracy. So a police order that counts LGBTQ activism but not MRA is not better as such, and one that systematically blocks the emergence of MRA would be *worse* as such. One might object, again: LGBTQ activism is based on the presupposition of equality, while MRA is based on the conceit of natural hierarchy. In this case, we are back where we started: certain movements are based on truth (the contingency of any social hierarchy) and others are based on illusion (the necessity of a certain distribution of parts). But Rancière's criticism of elitism, pivotal to his argument, dissolves the possibility of even *this* distinction, which is also pivotal to his argument.[19] To make this clearer, we should look at the former in more detail, tracing its lineage back from *Disagreement* and *Shores* to his earliest work.

Rancière's conception of "the equality of intelligences,"[20] inextricable from his theory of democracy,[21] is rooted in the critique of philosophical elitism initiated by his first book, *Althusser's Lesson*. There, he criticizes his former teacher's categorical division between "the science of intellectuals" (*Althusser's Lesson*, 61) and the illusions of "the agents of production" (workers), which reproduces a "partition of the sensible" according to which common people cannot speak for themselves: "[Althusser] gives to philosophers the power to be the word-keepers" (*Althusser's Lesson*, 96). If the realities of workers' lives do not match up to the intellectuals' theory, then so much the worse for those realities. Such a theoretical maneuver, Rancière argues, functions to guarantee the legitimacy of the intellectual's place in a given police order and consequently poses no meaningful challenge to that order. He continues this line of thought in *The Philosopher and His Poor*, where he draws an analogy between Plato's "philosopher kings" and Marx's distinction between "materialist science" and the false consciousness engendered by the capitalist production process. Marxism is only "Platonism sociologized," as it presumes "the permanence of optical illusions, the necessary non-concordance between what the scientist knows and what the peasant sees" (*The Philosopher and His Poor*, 131).[22] The innovation of unorthodox teacher Joseph Jacotot, the subject of Rancière's *The Ignorant Schoolmaster*, was to abandon this presupposition of the inequality of intelligences, to replace the pedagogical logic of "explication" (which assumes and therefore solidifies an intellectual division in the social fabric) with that of "emancipation" (which assumes the equality of intelligences and can therefore unsettle that fabric). The figure of the intellectual/educator as one who fosters correct consciousness by way of expertise, Rancière claims, hopelessly resembles the old Platonic project: "The intelligent caste's management of the stupid multitude" (*The Ignorant Schoolmaster*, 131).[23] He even equates the notion of "progress" with this elitist, paternalist perspective: "Progress is the new way of saying inequality. . . . The century of Progress is that of the triumphant explicators, of humanity pedagogicized" (*The Ignorant Schoolmaster*, 119–20).[24]

This line of criticism continues to play a role in Rancière's current work. In one of the contributions to his debate with Honneth, he returns to this theme: "[In explicative logic], the role of the schoolmaster is posited in the act of suppressing the distance between his knowledge and the ignorance of the ignorant. Unfortunately, in order to reduce the gap, he has to reinstate it ceaselessly" (*Recognition or Disagreement*, 138). He goes on to claim that since democracy consists in the contestation of a certain partition of the sensible, the conceit of a *right* form of politics that the learned might illuminate to the ignorant is fundamentally antidemocratic. "The distribution of the sensible is not a matter of illusion or knowledge," he writes. "It is a matter of consensus or dissensus" (*Recognition or Disagreement*, 136).[25] From *Althusser's Lesson* to this recently published piece, we see the repetition of a basic opposition: on one hand, the contestation of those who claim they are miscounted, the voice of the people capable of speech, *democracy*, and on the other hand, the pedagogical disposition, "Platonism sociologized," the distance between "the intelligent caste" and "the stupid multitude." The latter side of this opposition reduces politics to "explication," a matter of knowledge as opposed to ignorance, and therefore abolishes democracy. If we are to leave the all-too-comfortable "shores of politics" and think the sea, we must abandon the elitist logic that posits some truth that might be explained to those outside the know.[26] He expresses this opposition in many places:

> I always try to think in terms of horizontal distributions, combinations between systems of possibilities, not in terms of surface and substratum. Where one searches for the hidden beneath the apparent, a position of mastery is established. I have tried to conceive of a topography that does not presuppose this position of mastery. . . . I constructed, little by little, an egalitarianism or anarchist theoretical

position that does not presuppose this vertical relationship of top to bottom. (*The Politics of Aesthetics*, 49–50)

Rancière always constructs his argumentation as a re-staging of a limited number of . . . scenes or events of discourse. It is also important to remark that he introduces no hierarchy in the selection of its scenes. The Marxist tradition and all the tradition of social science distinguishes two kinds of words: there are the words in which people express a situation as they feel it, and there are the words by which science accounts for a situation and for the ways in which those who are part of it can feel it and express their feeling. But, for Rancière, words are still words, arguments are still arguments, narratives are still narratives. The main point is not what they explain or express, it is the way in which they stage a scene or they create a commonsense. ("A Few Remarks on the Method of Jacques Rancière," 117)

Key to Rancière's work is a decisive movement away from the paternalistic truth/illusion/knowledge/ignorance disjuncts that characterized the history of political philosophy from Plato to Althusser (and beyond) and toward a figure of thought that allows a "people"—who are not a given datum but are created through their enunciation as such—to speak for themselves.

How, then, are we to situate the rise of extreme right-wing populist movements? This question is all the more pressing when we read passages like this: "For me the point is not pathology and how to heal this pathology; the point is that we have conflicting ways of describing or constructing a common world" (*Recognition or Disagreement*, 119–20). As we have seen, however, Rancière does not describe the rising tide of racism and xenophobia as just another way of "constructing a common world"; he describes it as pathology in need of a critical diagnosis. He does write, immediately after the passage just cited, that "of course, we can prefer one of those constructions to the other." But if we are content to offer pathologizing accounts of certain constructions, then in what sense are we still dealing with "preferences"? Consider again the example of men's rights activism. Those involved understand themselves to be giving voice to a form of domination made invisible by the prevailing "police order," articulating a partition of the sensible in which feminism is oppressive to men.[27] We might be inclined to say (I certainly am) that this "contestation" does not name a real "wrong" but is only a pathetic and desperate attempt to reassert a privilege that has been threatened or that its basic conceit assumes a completely illusory natural hierarchy, or that feminism represents "progress" while MRA represents "regression." But notice what we have done in this case: reinstantiated a gap between knowledge and ignorance, between "surface" and "substratum," as though we could "explicate" certain truths (feminism is not actually a form of oppression against men, patriarchy is actually a contingent historical violence and is not rooted in a metaphysical hierarchy of the sexes, etc.) to those who think otherwise. Is diagnosing this movement and others like it as ignorance or pathology still "Platonism sociologized" and therefore fundamentally antidemocratic? Are words still words, arguments still arguments, narratives still narratives? Or do we find ourselves on the "shores" of politics yet again?

Rancière has a solution to this problem. In "The Populism That Is Not to Be Found" (his contribution to the *What is a People?* volume), he denies that right-wing extremism has any democratic support:

> Whatever the grievances expressed daily regarding those called immigrants . . . they are not expressed in popular mass demonstrations. . . . Some good souls on the left like to see [racist, xenophobic] measures as an unfortunate concession made by those in power to the extreme "populist" right for "electioneering" reasons. But none of them were taken under pressure from mass movements. . . . The so-called populist extreme right does not express a specific xenophobic passion emanating from the depths of the body popular; it is a satellite that profits from the strategies of the state and distinguished intellectual campaigns. (103–4)[28]

The "populist right," he claims, is only a convenient fiction devised by academic and governmental elites intent on maintaining their power against true forms of democratic contestation. So insofar as right-wing extremism exists, it is a pathology (as we saw above), but it has little to no popular support and so cannot be called a popular movement. Beyond being patently false, this claim is also manifestly irresponsible. The recent histories of Europe and the United States make it overwhelmingly clear that xenophobic right-wing populism *is to be found* and that it constitutes a serious political problem. It cannot be counted, however, by Rancière's model without legitimating it as an example of democratic dissensus; diagnosing xenophobia, racism, and the like as ignorance or pathology means abandoning democracy for the elitist pedagogical disposition of political theory. The solution is to pretend as though the rise of extreme right-wing populism has not occurred.

With this claim, Rancière's thought reaches its logical conclusion—and its antithesis. He abandoned "the science of intellectuals" as pursued by Plato and "the Marxist horizon" (*The Philosopher and His Poor*, 127–35) because it assumed the right to speak *for* the people whose positions, conditions, and interests it was meant to represent. It claimed to be the arbiter of the divisions between truth and illusion, knowledge and ignorance. What would the people say, Rancière asks, if we let them speak for themselves? "Who were these people, what did they do, think, want, say?" ("Jacques Rancière," 240). Sometimes, as his book *Proletarian Nights* and his numerous examples corroborate, the result is inspiring, instructive, and enriching. Sometimes, however, "the people" do, think, want, and say xenophobic, racist, misogynist right-wing extremism. Sometimes what they do and say reflects ignorance and illusion. In this case, we must either pathologize these positions (in direct contradiction with our firm stance against "explication") or simply pretend, in spite of all evidence, that they do not exist, ignoring "the people" for the sake of theoretical consistency—precisely the sin of the old master Althusser. In the last instance, then, Rancière's thought reverts to exactly what it began as a reaction against.[29] He advocates a commitment to "the wisdom of the many," but not *this* many. He takes himself to be departing from what Arendt characterized as an "island of freedom" (the place of political purity insulated from all that which is not true politics); for him, although politics is still rare, anyone can be a political subject and anything can become an object of political contestation. Ultimately, however, he only manages to *expand* this island.[30] Despite his intentions, he still protects himself from the sea; it still smells of sailors he finds distasteful. The philosopher who devoted a body of work to criticizing the distance between philosophy and democracy, who laments that elitist political theory that does not listen to the people and presumes to speak for them, closes his ears to their voice at this crucial moment.

MOUFFE: AGONISM WITHOUT AGONY

Mouffe begins with the premise that the political is inherently antagonistic (always involving an inside and an outside, an "us" and a "them") and argues that the attempt to evade this reality—through the prevailing "consensus model" (*The Democratic Paradox*, 7)—threatens the preservation and advancement of democracy. This antipolitical "illusion of consensus and unanimity" (*The Return of the Political*, 5) is represented in politics by the heralded "end of history" following the triumph of global capitalism; it is represented in theory by the various avatars of "rationalist," "deliberative" democracy (among whom she counts Rawls and Habermas) *and* by the Marxist or communitarian critics of this perspective.[31] Against this development, she advocates both a politics and a theory of *agonistic, pluralistic, liberal, radical democracy* that recognizes the nature of the political.

Some terminological clarifications. Mouffe distinguishes between "the political" and "politics," the former being "the dimension of antagonism that is inherent in human relations" and the latter being "the ensemble of practices, discourses and institutions which seek to establish a certain order and organize human coexistence in conditions that are always potentially conflictual" (*The Democratic Paradox*, 101). The former is "ontological" while the latter is merely "ontic" (*On the Political*, 8). Her "political" is thus not quite the same as Rancière's *la politique*, though what she terms "politics" is close to his "police."[32] Both, however, are concerned with the loss of an ontological, definite-article *political* rather than particular forms of politics/police; in this respect, they are both in close proximity to Arendt.[33]

Mouffe also differentiates "antagonism" and "agonism"; the former is characterized by relations between "enemies" who do not accept each other's legitimacy, while the latter involves relations between "adversaries" who are in opposition but nevertheless "tolerate" one another (*The Return of the Political*, 4; *The Democratic Paradox*, 13–14, 102–3). Mouffe's theoretical goal is to establish a politics of agonism in order to acknowledge the indeclinably antagonistic "political" while "sublimating" (*Agonistics*, 8), though never entirely exterminating, some of its dangerous tendencies (*The Democratic Paradox*, 103). "The task of democracy," she writes, "is to transform antagonism into agonism" (*On the Political*, 20).

By "democracy" she does not have in mind the parliamentary procedures of state governments but rather a "symbolic ordering of social relations" organized around the icon of "popular sovereignty" (*The Democratic Paradox*, 18). As for "liberalism," she is perhaps more comfortable with the term than any other radical democratic theorist is, and understands its commitments as "constituted by the rule of law, the defense of human rights and the respect of individual liberty" (*The Democratic Paradox*, 2–3). She is aware that liberal values are sometimes in direct contradiction with democratic ones, but argues that this "paradox" (of *The Democratic Paradox*) is constitutive, rather than prohibitive, for her project: "Democratic politics consists in pragmatic, precarious and necessarily unstable forms of negotiating its constitutive paradox" (*The Democratic Paradox*, 11). In contemporary parliamentary states, there is a tendency to overvalue the liberal side of liberal democracy, creating a "democratic deficit" (*The Democratic Paradox*, 3–4); the adjective "radical" is necessary to make clear that "popular sovereignty" is not achieved by periodic elections and a government limited to the protection of individual rights; rather, it also involves "a profound transformation of the existing power relations" (*On the Political*, 52). It is important to note, however, that to Mouffe's mind, liberal democracy is "a political form of society that is defined exclusively at the level of the political, leaving aside its possible articulation with an economic system" (*The Democratic Paradox*, 18). So her vision is neither necessarily capitalist nor necessarily socialist, not wedded to a particular set of policies, "not . . . the search for an inaccessible consensus to be reached through whatever procedure—but . . . an 'agonistic confrontation' between conflicting interpretations of the constitutive liberal-democratic values" (*The Democratic Paradox*, 9). This is closely tied to her idea of pluralism, or "the end of a substantive idea of the good life . . . the legitimation of conflict and division, the emergence of individual liberty and the assertion of equal liberty for all." She claims that pluralism is not merely a description of an existing fact but also an "axiological principle" (*The Democratic Paradox*, 18–19).

Mouffe's insistence that agonistic pluralism is essential to liberal democracy is informed by her ardent "anti-essentialism," which she develops from readings of philosophers like Derrida and Rorty. She rejects the attempt (again, she names Rawls and Habermas as culprits) to provide a "foundation" for any form of politics, claiming that there is "no longer a role to be played in this [liberal democratic] project by the epistemological perspective of the Enlightenment" (*The Return of the Political*, 10). Such a perspective errs, she thinks, in presupposing a rational, disinterested subject and in assuming that there is some "truth" from which the "right" form of political life would be derived. "Our societies today demand to be approached from a nonessentialist perspective" (*The Return of the Political*, 11), and it is necessary for radical democracy "to renounce any claim to universality" (*The Return of the Political*, 13) along with "the rationalist belief in the availability of a universal consensus based on reason" (*On the Political*, 11). This does not mean that rationality as such will be jettisoned entirely, but that "we need to broaden the concept of rationality . . . to recognize the existence of multiple forms of rationality" (*The Return of the Political*, 14). As she understands it, the normative currency of her approach does not follow from its universality, rationality, or truth, but is part of a project of hegemony.[34] One more passage is important for us: "Hannah Arendt was absolutely right to insist that in the political sphere one finds oneself in the realm of opinion, or 'doxa', and not in that of truth, and that each sphere has its own criteria of validity and legitimacy" (*The Return of the Political*, 14).[35]

At the same time, however, some forms of rationality and some opinions should *not* be recognized. In several places, Mouffe correlates the neglect of "the political" with the rise of extreme right-wing populist movements (*The Return of the Political*, 5–6; *The Democratic Paradox*, 7, 96; *On the Political*, 66–72; "The 'End of Politics' and the Challenge of Right-Wing Populism"; "For an Agonistic Public Sphere," 129), arguing that this troubling and dangerous development is a symptom of the "consensus" approach of contemporary mainstream political parties. Because individuals are given no real alternatives in the prevailing liberal "democracies," the antagonism constitutive of the political is forced to express itself in harmful, destructive (i.e., right-wing) ways: "The tendency to privilege exclusively [the liberal component of liberal democracy] and to treat the democratic element as obsolete has serious political consequences. It is the source of the growing success of right-wing populist parties, which pretend to re-establish popular sovereignty against elites" ("For an Agonistic Public Sphere," 129). Her argument here is similar to Rancière's insofar as both invoke the figure of right-wing extremism as a self-evidently undesirable consequence of ignoring their theoretical interventions. For Mouffe, however, these populist movements *do* represent a return of the political (as opposed to the antipolitical consensus model), but an unwelcome or inadmissible return: "The solutions [Jean-Marie Le Pen] proposes are of course unacceptable but one cannot deny the political character of his discourse" (*On the Political*, 68). She also recognizes, unlike Rancière, that such movements have commanded broad popular support.

Several questions arise here. Why, in this account, did the triumph of the consensus model precipitate the rise of *right-wing* populism rather than a Left return of the political? More importantly for our immediate concern: Why is this eruption of antagonism "of course unacceptable"? Reading Mouffe, one might think that it should be celebrated as a resurgence of democracy over and against the antipolitical "illusion of consensus and unanimity" as well as a contestation of the universalist pretensions of "rationalism." Despite its formal similarities to her normative categories, Mouffe does not take right-wing populism seriously as a democratic demand, even as she recognizes that it represents a return of the political. Why? We have already seen that, for her, these movements only "pretend" to restore popular sovereignty. There are more problems:

> We should realize that, to a great extent, the success of right-wing populist parties comes from the fact that they provide people with some form of hope, with the belief that things could be different. Of course this is an illusionary hope, founded on false premises and on unacceptable mechanisms of exclusion, where xenophobia usually plays a central role. But when they are the only ones to offer an outlet for political passions, their pretence of offering an alternative is seductive, and their appeal is likely to grow. ("The 'End of Politics' and the Challenge of Right-Wing Populism," 56; cf. *On the Political*, 71)

Right-wing nationalism, however "political" it may be, is based on illusions, false premises, and unacceptable exclusions. But Mouffe has already denied us the use of these discriminating categories when it comes to politics. If the political is the realm of *doxa*, how can we dismiss the political aspirations of the Right as illusory? Once we have "renounced any claim to universality," abandoned our "rationalist" perspective and affirmed "multiple forms of rationality," we have no grounds to criticize the *foundations* of such movements as "false" or their intentions as "pretend."[36] Mouffe states again and again that political divisions are not (and should not be understood as) a matter of rationality or truth: "How are we going to enact a 'politics of truth' in the terrain of real politics? Such an injunction is clearly incompatible not only with . . . liberal democratic pluralism . . . but also with any project of radical democracy. Thus, it leads us into a political dead end" (*Agonistics*, 17). Even supposing the inherent superiority of liberal democracy belongs to the obsolete "rationalist" approach (*On the Political*, 88). When it comes to right-wing populism, however, the truth is somehow on our side, and those identifying with these movements are under the sway of an illusion.

Perhaps, then, the theoretical right to dismiss these political movements as "unacceptable" comes from elsewhere, from the "unacceptable mechanisms of exclusion" (like xenophobia) on which such movements are based. An immediate problem with this approach is the fact that few people self-identify as "xenophobic"—they may identify as patriotic, nationalistic, and the like, but "xenophobia" is a term that belongs to Left critics of right-wing rhetoric. Marine Le Pen does not say, "*Je suis xénophobe*." In fact, she says the opposite—and often sounds not unlike Mouffe in appealing to a "multi-polar world" and accusing her opponents of "stifling democracy."[37] So we are still assuming a divide between the professed self-understanding of a certain demos and the "real" conditions and effects of their actions, declining to engage them on their own terms, like the old-fashioned rationalists of an outdated epistemological project.

Even bracketing this concern, it is unclear how such an account of "pluralism" could adjudicate between exclusions that are unacceptable (like the exclusion of immigrants) and those that are acceptable (like the exclusion of the populist Right). This leads Mouffe to qualify the parameters of the pluralist approach: it must avoid the pitfall of "total pluralism," the supposition that *any* democratic demand is as legitimate as any other. "It is important to recognize," she writes, "the limits to pluralism which are required by a democratic politics that aims at challenging a wide range of relations of subordination" (*The Democratic Paradox*, 20). Put otherwise:

> The pluralism that I advocate requires discriminating between demands which are to be accepted as part of the agonistic debate and those which are to be excluded. . . . But exclusions are envisaged in political and not in moral terms. Some demands are excluded, not because they are declared to be "evil," but because they challenge the institutions constitutive of the democratic political association. (*On the Political*, 120–21)

Our rejection of right-wing populism and its xenophobia is thus not to be cast in moral terms. It is to be excluded from consideration and participation on *political* grounds because it challenges the basic institutions of democratic politics. The interventions of Jean-Marie and Marine Le Pen are therefore both a return of the political *and* a violation of the values of democratic political association. This is consonant with the way she describes the difference between an "adversary" (in her preferred agonism) and an "enemy" (in dangerous but ineradicable antagonism):

> [W]ithin the context of the political community, the opponent should be considered not as an enemy to be destroyed, but as an adversary whose existence is legitimate and must be tolerated. . . . The category of the "enemy" does not disappear but is displaced; it remains pertinent with respect to those who do not accept the democratic "rules of the game" and who thereby exclude themselves from the political community. (*The Return of the Political*, 4)[38]

Movements informed by xenophobia, then, are excluded on the basis of their "unacceptable exclusions"; they become "enemies" because they refuse to recognize certain others (immigrants) as "adversaries" and insist on regarding them as "enemies." In fact, on this account, any politics that does *not* aim to "challenge a wide range of relations of subordination" would automatically lose its right to participate in the agonistic political sphere insofar as it does not accept "the democratic rules of the game," that is, insofar as it is based on "unacceptable exclusions."[39]

We are left with the following conclusion: exclusion is acceptable when we are excluding those with unacceptable exclusions. Petito *principii*. Which exclusions are unacceptable will, of course, depend upon one's "interpretation of the constitutive liberal-democratic values," that is, one's politics. For anyone reading Mouffe (or anyone reading this), the suggestion that France should permanently close its borders to all immigration from the Middle East is unacceptable because it is xenophobic. For Le Pen, however, the suggestion that anti-immigration and anti-multicultural sentiments should be silenced is unacceptable because they are "elitist" or "technocratic."[40] Each side could accuse the other of not following "the rules of the game," of defying "the institutions constitutive of the democratic political association." Each side also understands itself as "challenging a wide range of relations of subordination"; for the *Front national*, patriotic French nationals are subordinated by globalization and multiculturalism.[41] In order to decide between these two interpretations, in order to know when democratic pluralist agonism passes into inadmissible exclusion, we need to have in advance a set of political beliefs and commitments with certain content. Once we have these beliefs and commitments, we can disqualify any opposition as disobeying "the rules of the game" on that basis.[42] Mouffe writes that "modern democracy's specificity lies in the recognition and legitimation of conflict and the refusal to suppress it by imposing an authoritarian order" (*The Democratic Paradox*, 103). But if we can refuse to recognize or legitimate a certain "conflict" because we deem its content unacceptable on the basis of our political commitments, then this "specificity" becomes a tautology: we should accept the political demands we accept, and not accept those we do not. It is difficult to see the agony involved in this kind of agonism.

Mouffe's theory hinges on the relinquishing of "foundations," the end of a "substantive idea of the good life," the ontologization of agonistic confrontation, and a pluralistic political space where conflict, division, and *doxa* are taken as ends in themselves and different interpretations of liberal-democratic values are tolerated and recognized. But the Le Pens and the politics they represent are not to be taken seriously because they have an unacceptable interpretation, a *doxa* we decline to recognize. Like both Arendt and Rancière, Mouffe appeals simultaneously to democratic iconography and to a demos with specifically demarcated content. All political commitments are to be counted as legitimate and given recognition in the agonistic sphere, *except* those that do not share our political commitments. On the same page where she claims that "there is only a multiplicity of identities without any common denominator, and it is impossible to distinguish between differences that exist but should not exist and differences that do not exist but should exist," she reiterates that her position is *not* the same as "valorization of all differences" (*The Democratic Paradox*, 20). So "the people" are to be sovereign, everyone is to be equal, different "forms of rationality" are to be tolerated, there is to be no pretension to universality or authoritarian suppression of conflict, and dissensus is to be maintained as the essence of the political—*as long as everyone plays by "the rules of the game."* We should pursue a radical democratic agonistic pluralism where "the political" is made up of adversaries and none denies the others' right to exist, but only if these others do not challenge "the institutions constitutive of the democratic political association" as we have determined them, and only insofar as all of the adversaries are committed to "challenging a wide range of relations of subordination" as we understand them. There are no common denominators except these common denominators.

LACLAU, LACLAU AND MOUFFE, AND THE UNDEMOCRATIC DEMOS

Many of the theoretical tools Mouffe utilizes were first articulated with Laclau in *Hegemony and Socialist Strategy*, the text that inaugurated the term "radical democracy."[43] Here, Laclau and Mouffe respond to an epistemological "crisis" in Marxist theory and socialist politics, heralded by an increasing recognition of "the opacity of the social" and the "fragmentation of the different positions of social agents" (*Hegemony and Socialist Strategy*, 12). Arguing against what they characterize as the "essentialist" class reductionism of Marxism, they advance a theory of "articulation" in which diverse and dispersed actors (or "elements") construct a precarious and contingent identity around rhetorical "nodal points," constituting themselves as parts (or "moments") of a discursive totality. The unity of this totality (or "formation") is not given—in logic or in experience—prior to its articulation, and so the identities of and relations between the various moments are never fixed and stable. "If we accept . . . that a discursive totality never exists in the form of a simply *given and delimited* positivity," they write, "the relational logic will be incomplete and pierced by contingency" (*Hegemony and Socialist Strategy*, 97). While Foucault's notion of "regularity in dispersion" informs this argument, they draw on Derridean diacritics to develop an account of "antagonism" as the discursive manifestation of "the 'experience' of the limit of all objectivity" (*Hegemony and Socialist Strategy*, 91, 108). Because of the instability and constitutive heterogeneity of all positive signifying terms, the "ambition" of "the social" to "constitute a full presence" (*Hegemony and Socialist Strategy*, 113) always fails. The confrontation of this ambition and its inevitable failure constitutes an antagonism: "It is because a peasant *cannot* be a peasant that an antagonism exists with the landowner expelling him from his land" (*Hegemony and Socialist Strategy*, 111).

Laclau and Mouffe develop their analyses of "articulation" and "antagonism" into a concept of "hegemony." There is a "hegemonic articulation" when discursive formations operate in a field of antagonism, when "phenomena of equivalence" (the constitution of moments, or "subject positions") and "frontier effects" (the recognition of the impossibility of a full constitution) develop alongside one another in a shifting and ambiguous process that never terminates (*Hegemony and Socialist Strategy*, 122). They take this term and its basic theoretical structure from Gramsci but understand themselves as departing from his account insofar as it still held privileged places for the category of class and the ideal of revolution.[44] Laclau and Mouffe look away from the articulation of some determinate, necessary content (like "class struggle" or "communism") and toward "a plurality of political spaces." For them, "pluralism" becomes "radical" when "this plurality of identities finds within itself the principle of its own validity, without this having to be sought in a transcendent or underlying positive ground" (*Hegemony and Socialist Strategy*, 151). Radical pluralism likewise becomes "democratic" when "the autoconstitutivity of each [identity] is the result of displacements of the egalitarian imaginary" (ibid.). They also distinguish pluralistic "democratic struggles" from "popular struggles," which construe a Manichean political space, but still consider the latter to be a variant of the former (*Hegemony and Socialist Strategy*, 118, 124).

A radical and plural democratic politics, then, embraces and works to augment an indeterminate proliferation of "egalitarian" hegemonic articulations, in which the identities of the agents in question are understood as a result of the articulation and not as a datum given beforehand. "Radical unfixity," Laclau and Mouffe write, "makes it impossible to consider the political struggle as a game in which the identity of the opposing forces is constituted from the start" (*Hegemony and Socialist*

Strategy, 154). They understand this as a principle that could revitalize a Left disoriented by the collapse of its Jacobin imaginary; rather than staking its claim on the a priori reality of class struggle, emancipatory politics should orient itself around a "proliferation of antagonisms and calling into question of relations of subordination," thus "deepening . . . the democratic revolution" (*Hegemony and Socialist Strategy*, 147). Radical democracy is presented as a theoretically and strategically viable alternative to the "vanguardism" (a bugbear throughout the work) that would "represent" the "interests" of a preexisting and selfsame "people."[45]

Laclau elaborates and refines the terminology of *Hegemony and Socialist Strategy* throughout his subsequent work. In *New Reflections on the Revolution of Our Time*, he further clarifies the concept of "antagonism" as "the limit of all objectivity . . . that which prevents the constitution of objectivity itself" (17). For him, this does not mean that objectivity is abandoned entirely in a "nihilistic" embrace of unintelligible chaos but that the indispensable task of articulating objectivity will always be restricted by its own impossibility. "What we always find is a limited and given situation in which objectivity is *partially* constituted and also *partially* threatened; and in which the boundaries between the contingent and the necessary are constantly displaced" (*New Reflections on the Revolution of Our Time*, 27). The notion of "displacement" developed here clarifies his understanding of hegemonic articulation as the constant but constantly unsuccessful attempt to stabilize constitutively unstable identity categories and to render clear a necessarily opaque social totality; the boundaries are "displaced" because there is a perpetual renegotiation of the line between what is included (in a given identity or in the social totality) and what is excluded. Likewise in *Emancipation(s)*, Laclau frames the relationship between universality and particularity as one of "permanent asymmetry" (35); particular struggles always express themselves in terms of a universality with which they can never fully coincide. This insoluble paradox—that the articulation of identity/objectivity/fixity/universality is both necessary and impossible—is the condition for the possibility of radical democratic politics. "If democracy is possible," he writes, "it is because the universal has no necessary body and no necessary content; different groups, instead, compete between themselves to temporarily give to their particularisms a function of universal representation" (*Emancipation(s)*, 35).

These "different groups," as we recall from *Hegemony*, are not pre-given and self-identical subjects either. Laclau takes up this theme again in *On Populist Reason*, where he argues that "a people" is constituted by the articulation of "demands" rather than by any unity existing prior to this articulation. This contingent and fragile collective construction, which involves a form of "representation" that is both equivalential and differential (a people is always both the same as and different from the sum of its parts), is "the primary terrain of the constitution of social objectivity" (*On Populist Reason*, 163). Such a "social logic," he claims, is "inscribed in the actual working of *any* communitarian space" (*On Populist Reason*, x). He goes on to argue that the question of "popular identity" is "practically indistinguishable" from the issue of "democratic identity," and that his and Mouffe's "hegemony" model is "profoundly democratic, because it involves launching new collective subjects into the historical arena" (*On Populist Reason*, 168–69). He stops short of directly identifying populism and democracy, however, writing that "the very possibility of democracy depends on the constitution of a democratic 'people'" (*On Populist Reason*, 171). This would suggest that though all democratic subjects are populist, not all peoples are democratic. We will return to this point.

Laclau joins Rancière and Mouffe in understanding "the political" as an *ontological* condition over and against the merely ontic "sedimented forms of 'objectivity'" reminiscent of the "police" and its "distribution of parts" in Rancière or "politics" in Mouffe. Laclau's definite-article "political" is "the moment of antagonism where the undecidable nature of the alternatives and their resolution through power relations becomes fully visible" (*New Reflections on the Revolution of Our Time*, 35).[46] The "alternatives" here are competing and incompatible hegemonic articulations within groups and/or between groups, a plurality of struggles that attempt, through various "demands" and always ultimately in vain, to fill the impossible spaces of group identity and social totality. Because we cannot appeal to the "true" nature of things "behind" the hegemonic articulations, we have no recourse to choose between them on any basis that transcends their strictly *political* confrontation, that is, their conflict and struggle over power and the ineradicable moment of "decision"—without ground—that such a struggle demands; the "undecidability" inherent in the political means that "if two different groups have taken different decisions, the relationship between them will be one of antagonism and power, since no ultimate rational grounds exist for their opting either way" (*New Reflections on the Revolution of Our Time*, 31). He does not flinch from the potential implications of this claim: "From an ultimate ontological and epistemological point of view, religious fundamentalism and the most 'refined' of Western socialisms are on equal footing" (*New Reflections on the Revolution of Our Time*, 242–43).

According to Laclau, the project of "democracy" begins with an affirmation of this undecidability, "the recognition of the constitutive nature of [the absence of ground] and its political institutionalization" (*Emancipation(s)*, 46). Democracy, he writes, "is the very placing in question of the notion of *ground*" (*New Reflections on the Revolution of Our Time*, 78). The "vanguardism" that Laclau and Mouffe criticized in *Hegemony* thus comes to include all forms of "rationalism,"[47] any pretension that political problems could be adjudicated by reason or truth rather than hegemonic confrontation. The figure of the political rationalist takes on an increasingly villainous role in Laclau's work, identified with the "dictatorship of the Enlightenment" (*New Reflections on the Revolution of Our Time*, 4) and the philosopher-king; he goes so far as to suggest a kind of elective affinity between rationalism and totalitarianism.[48] Like Rancière, Laclau repeatedly draws an analogy between Platonic elitism and the Marxist vision of a universal class—eventually extending the second term of the analogy to include rationalist politics as such: "In so far as there is true knowledge, only one particular form of social organization realizes the universal. And if ruling is a matter of knowledge and not of prudence, only the bearer of that knowledge, the philosopher, has the right to rule. *Ergo*: a philosopher-king" (*Emancipation(s)*, 61–62). In *On Populist Reason*, he argues that the denigration of "populism" by political theory (which he again associates with Plato) is "the dismissal of politics *tout court*, and the assertion that the management of community is the concern of an administrative power who source of legitimacy is a proper knowledge of what a 'good' community is" (*On Populist Reason*, x). This "elitist" rejection of populism involves the "discursive construction of a certain normality, of an ascetic political universe from which [populism's] dangerous logics had to be excluded"; he considers such elitism part of "the history of the constitution and dissolution of a social frontier separating the normal from the pathological" (*On Populist Reason*, 19). In abandoning rationalism, radical democracy also leaves behind the elitism that has characterized the history of political philosophy (as well as the political projects informed by this history):

> What we are criticizing is an attitude laying down what people should do in certain circumstances or what they should prefer on the basis of general, abstract reasoning; the kind of attitude that constructs an "interest" and then concludes that it is a case of "non-rational" behavior or "false conscience" when people do not fall into line. (*New Reflections on the Revolution of Our Time*, 217)

Again in tandem with Rancière, Laclau establishes an opposition between democracy, on one hand, and philosophically elaborated "reason," "truth," "knowledge," or "foundation," on the other. The category of "misrecognition" is maintained, however, for the lingering belief in the "identity and homogeneity of social agents." It is still possible, in other words, to misrepresent reality: with the claim that one can represent reality (*The Rhetorical Foundations of Society*, 11–36).

Paradoxically, then, radical democracy is supposed to remind us that socialism is ultimately on "equal footing" with religious fundamentalism *and* to offer a compelling "socialist strategy." We find in Laclau the same equivocal maneuver we encountered in Rancière and Mouffe: determining in advance the proper course of the political belongs to antidemocratic elitism, but democracy belongs to the Left. As was the case for our previous two theorists, all of Laclau's positive examples are taken from progressive or left-wing "articulations"—"feminism, antiracism, the gay movement, etc." (*Hegemony and Socialist Strategy*, 118).[49] Laclau and Mouffe even write that "every project for radical democracy implies a socialist dimension, as it is necessary to put an end to capitalist relations of production, which are at the root of numerous relations of subordination" (*Hegemony and Socialist Strategy*, 162).[50] But *Hegemony and Socialist Strategy* gives no justification as to why radical democratic projects would correspond to any particular content, that is, why certain hegemonic articulations are radically democratic while others are not, except that the former are "the result of displacements of the egalitarian imaginary." We are not told, however, *which* displacements of the "egalitarian imaginary" constitute radical democracy, or why.

The problem is once again one of form and content. Laclau's argument is predicated on an account of "subject positions" as constituted in and by their articulations over and against an understanding of "peoples" and their struggles as "representations" of previously existing "actual" social relations. Inserting a gap between real conditions and their various representations, besides leading inevitably to elitist-rationalist vanguardism, also presupposes an epistemologically untenable division between reality and its articulation that radical democracy rejects: "The main consequence of a break with the discursive/extra-discursive dichotomy is the abandonment of the thought/reality opposition, and hence a major enlargement of the field of those categories which can account for social relations" (*Hegemony and Socialist Strategy*, 96). If we take this line of thought seriously, it would seem to collapse a meaningful divide between true or false representations; there would be only *different* articulations of the social totality locked in hegemonic struggle, sometimes forming "chains of equivalence" and sometimes breaking them. As we have seen, this perspective is consonant with the way Laclau describes political confrontation in *New Reflections*; it is maintained in some of his last writings:

> [W]hile the assertion of the primary ontological character of antagonism . . . gives way to a plurality of contingent investments not predetermining the nature of the social agents resulting from them . . . the aprioristic assertion that those agents are, necessarily, "social classes" can only be made from a teleological-objectivist perspective. (*The Rhetorical Foundations of Society*, 124)

Radical democracy, then, would involve an affirmation of this undetermined plurality of investments and their permanent and unpredictable struggle as the essence of the political. Once we have affirmed this, leaving behind the "teleological-objectivist perspective," on what grounds can we assume that emancipation(s) will have any particular content?

Consider our previous examples: men's rights activism and the *Front national*. They too involve "discursive formations" in a "field of antagonism" and thus constitute hegemonic articulations. As we have seen, they also "call into question" *what they take to be* "relations of subordination"; thus, on a formal level, they should count for Laclau and Mouffe as a "deepening of the democratic revolution."[51] If this is not the case, if democracy is bound to be progressive or leftist in character, then radical democratic theory must tell us why, *without violating the other strictures of the theoretical landscape*. How will we describe these "articulations" once we have abandoned "the thought/reality opposition"? "There is no radical and plural democracy," we are told, "without renouncing the discourse of the universal and its implicit assumption of a privileged point of access to 'the truth'" (*Hegemony and Socialist Strategy*, 175). In this case, must the feminist movement renounce its "assumption of a privileged point of access to 'the truth'" when it confronts the MRA movement?[52] If we want to avoid the "purely pedagogical" attitude of vanguardism (*Hegemony and Socialist Strategy*, 49), are we to refrain from appealing to a "reality" the *Front national* (or for that matter, the climate skeptic movement) might be misrepresenting?

Laclau and Mouffe admit at one point that "the conservative reaction . . . has a hegemonic character," but they never explain why this "reaction" is not on that basis a democratic struggle, why left-progressive hegemonic articulations are democratic while right-wing "displacements of the egalitarian imaginary" are consigned to "the antidemocratic offensive" (*Hegemony and Socialist Strategy*, 155–59). In *New Reflections*, Laclau again acknowledges that his formal theoretical tools might fall into the wrong hands:

> The indeterminacy of the relations between the different demands of the social actors certainly does open the possibility for their articulation by the right; but insofar as such articulations are not *necessary*, the field of possibilities for historical action is also widened, as counter-hegemonic struggles become possible in many areas traditionally associated with the sedimented forms of the status quo. (*New Reflections on the Revolution of Our Time*, 82–83)

If the field of possibility for struggle is widened, it is also widened indiscriminately. Again, we are left wondering why the radical democratic model would lend itself to the Left as opposed to the Right with any greater justification or plausibility. If it does not, then there is a sleight of hand in Laclau and Mouffe's identification of radical democracy with progressive movements and in the suggestion, which frames the entire analysis, that this model represents an orientation for a revitalized Left. Why not simply say that radical democracy is a political-ontological disposition that could be utilized by the Left, the Right, or anything in between as it sees fit? The only possible answer is that Laclau and Mouffe happen to be leftists. This is indeed the answer Laclau gives, after naming the problem we have articulated:

> In our perspective it is a question of historically constituting the subject to be emancipated—indeed, emancipation and constitution are part of the same process. But in that case, why prefer one future over another? Why choose between different types of society? There can be no reply if the question is asking for a kind of Cartesian certainty that pre-exists any belief. But if the agent who must choose is someone who *already* had certain beliefs and values, then criteria for choice—with all the intrinsic ambiguities that a choice involves—can be formulated. (*New Reflections on the Revolution of Our Time*, 83; cf. *Contingency, Hegemony, and Universality*, 85)

At this juncture, we return to the same tautological formulation offered by Mouffe: radical democracy means the affirmation of "the proliferation of new identities and antagonisms" (*New Reflections on the Revolution of Our Time*, xv), *but* we can adjudicate between legitimate and illegitimate "antagonisms" according to our already established beliefs and values.[53] So we formulate our choice for feminism and against MRA not on the grounds of the former's "truth" and the latter's "illusion"—that would be a category mistake and place us back in Platonic elitism/rationalist vanguardism—but on the basis of our (entirely contingent) existing sympathies for the former's project. But if the "plurality" of "democratic struggles," the "proliferation of antagonisms and calling into question of relations of subordination," can be limited and arbitrated according to whatever beliefs we happen to have already, then radical democracy demands very little of us. It asks only that we cease assuming "a privileged point of access to 'the truth'" for our beliefs and corresponding political projects, not that we alter them. The men's rights activist also chooses his commitments on the basis of his already existing beliefs and values.

This conclusion, however troubling it may be on its own, is not consistently maintained. Laclau elsewhere suggests that certain political commitments *will* follow from the abandonment of the rationalist "dictatorship of the Enlightenment," that is, that a certain content *is* inscribed within the formal terms of radical democracy:

> Difference and particularisms are the necessary starting point, but out of it, it is possible to open the way to a relative universalization of values which can be the basis for a popular hegemony. This universalization and its open character certainly condemns all identity to an unavoidable hybridization, but hybridization does not necessarily mean decline through the loss of identity: it can also mean empowering existing identities through the opening of new possibilities. *Only a conservative identity, closed on itself, could experience hybridization as a loss.* (*Emancipation(s)*, 65; my italics)

Once we have affirmed the constitutive "dislocation" of all identity categories and the resulting impossibility of a completely integrated social totality, any hegemonic articulation predicated on a preestablished fixity, fullness, or completion—that is, any hegemonic articulation that does not understand itself as such—is proscribed. "There is democracy," Laclau writes, "only if there is the recognition of the positive value of a dislocated identity" (*Emancipation(s)*, 100). The "conservative identity" denies this positive value and is thus undemocratic. In concert with Rancière and Mouffe, Laclau invokes the *loup-garou* of right-wing nationalist movements to make this point:

> A democratic society is not one in which the "best" content dominates unchallenged but, rather, one in which nothing is definitely acquired and there is always the possibility of challenge. If we think, for instance, of the resurgence of nationalism and all kinds of ethnic identities in present-day Eastern Europe, then we can easily see that the danger for democracy lies in the closure of these groups around fully-fledged identities that can only reinforce their most reactionary tendencies and create the conditions for a permanent confrontation with other groups. (*Emancipation(s)*, 100)

Democracy requires maintaining the openness, fluidity, and hybridization of identities and resting the Manichean tendency to organize social space around a closed circuit of stable subject positions. Hegemonic articulations that fail to meet this condition, no matter how "populist" they may be, are not democratic.[54] This would account for the nondemocratic populisms alluded to in *On Populist Reason* and, in a different register, for the distinction between "popular" and "democratic" struggles mentioned in *Hegemony*.

There are several issues with this attempt to disqualify certain popular movements from the domain of democracy. Notice, first of all, that Laclau has surreptitiously imported certain normative content even as he distinguishes his vision of a "democratic society" from a society with "the best content": the "reactionary" tendencies of these nationalist groups are only reactionary if we assume in advance that certain tendencies are "better" than others. Another problem is one we have encountered already in our discussion of Mouffe: it presumes that all right-wing nationalist movements articulate their demands in terms of permanent closure and the refusal to recognize the value of a "dislocated identity." As we saw when we looked at Marine Le Pen's *Front national*, this is not the case (nor is it the case for Poland's Law and Justice party, to take another example[55]). For Le Pen, it is "multiculturalism" and "globalization" that represent "closure" and French nationalism that opens up "a multi-polar world." We might be able to choose which articulation to endorse (based only on our existing political commitments), but we cannot determine which "closures" are democratic and which are not while maintaining our other stated conditions, because this determination will depend upon the "articulation" we have chosen. If we claim, on the other hand, that *despite* their professed intentions, these right-wing movements are nevertheless operating within a closed discursive space and a denial of the pluralistic and incomplete nature of the social, then we have reintroduced the thought/reality opposition so antithetical to radical democracy.

Finally, this requisite "openness" would also disqualify many progressive/leftist movements from the democratic society. As Laclau admits,[56] political projects such as feminism and racial justice require the total exclusion of certain other identities (the identities of the patriarch and the racialist, for example), the refusal to "hybridize" with them. For that matter, any variation of progressive/Left politics that does not understand itself as a "hegemonic articulation," that is, that understands itself as *representing* a *preexisting social totality* instead of "constituting it" would also be immediately disqualified on that basis.[57] A movement that claimed that society was *really* organized along gender and racial hierarchies, even prior to its articulation as such, would be profoundly undemocratic. In sum: if Laclau and Mouffe are entitled to the distinction between "democratic struggles" and "popular struggles," and if Laclau is entitled to posit the possibility of an undemocratic "people," it cannot be on the basis of where such struggles or people fall on the spectrum of Left/Right or progressive/conservative.[58] According to the strictures they have imposed, *we do not know democracy by its content but only by the extent to which it meets certain formal criteria.* Nevertheless, they feel at liberty to give examples that lean only in one direction and to assert that "every project for radical democracy implies a socialist dimension."

Before concluding, we should make one more note with regard to Laclau. There is a curious passage at the end of *On Populist Reason* when he takes a moment to differentiate his position from that of Rancière (after noting their decisive similarities). Interestingly, he advances much the same criticism as we did:

> [In Rancière] there is no a priori guarantee that the "people" as a historical actor will be constituted around a progressive identity (from the point of view of the Left). . . . Rancière identifies the possibility of politics too much, I believe, with the possibility of an emancipatory politics, without taking into account other alternatives—for example, that the uncounted might construct their uncountability in ways that are ideologically incompatible with what either Rancière or I would advocate politically. . . . To explore the system of alternatives, we need a further step that Rancière has not taken so far: namely, an examination of the forms of representation to which uncountability can give rise. (*On Populist Reason*, 246–47)

If it constitutes a problem that Rancière's model of "the part of those who have no part" does not provide or guarantee any specific political content, we must ask if Laclau's own "articulation of demands" theory fares any better. Does Laclau himself take this further step that he chides Rancière for avoiding, or is this an example of the pot calling the kettle black? According to what criteria are we to "examine the different forms of representation" to which "the articulation of demands" can give rise, once we have left behind our "elitist" presumption to "proper knowledge of what a 'good' community is," without constructing "a certain normality" from which "dangerous logics" have to be excluded?

Like Rancière, both Laclau and Mouffe categorically reject the "vanguardist" division between the "real" interests of "the people" and their prevailing "false consciousness." What is necessary is not the pretension of intellectuals, who claim to know the truth when it comes to politics, but democracy: an open and shifting terrain of demands and articulations in which the demos is not determined in advance but constituted in and through its discursive struggle. When confronted with a demos articulating demands they find unacceptable, however, Laclau and Mouffe's answer is the same as Rancière's: that's not *true* democracy. The gap between prevailing articulations of the demos and what would constitute its "real" articulations, a division resolutely denied by the radical democratic imaginary, is thus reinscribed. However "radical," this is nevertheless a democracy in spite of the demos.

CONCLUSION

Radical democratic theory rehearses the categorical imperative we discussed in chapter 2 with regard to Arendt: the "political"—understood through the democratic iconography of speech, plurality, appearance, debate, dissensus, and *doxa*—is an end in itself.[59] It also rehearses, however, the a priori exclusion of certain content from its formal categories, thus *conditioning* the categorical imperative and nullifying its status as such. The radical democrats do not share Arendt's conviction that the private/economic should not enter the public/political realm, and they have a decidedly more expansive notion of *doxa*; the realm of "what can really be figured out" is far narrower than it was for Arendt, if not eliminated entirely. Nevertheless the elitist-populist ambivalence that characterized her work shows up in another way. The object of exclusion is different: for Arendt it is the *animal laborans* and the material concerns associated with it, while for radical democracy it is the Right and its "distributions of the sensible," "interpretations of liberal-democratic values," or "hegemonic articulations." In both cases the ontological and normative priority accorded to democratic iconography is undermined by a determination of what does and does not count as an acceptable instantiation of this iconography, a determination justified by nothing but an *ex cathedra* decree inconsistent with the theoretical commitments grounding this democratic priority. If certain speech should not be heard, if the "plurality" can be limited as deemed necessary, if some *doxai* are fundamentally inadmissible, then speech, plurality, and *doxa* are not ends in themselves. Instead, the critical currency of the figure of democracy depends upon something else, something outside of democracy.

The nature of this "something else" is a different question, but we find a clue waiting for us in those moments when the radical democrats deign to comment on the rise of right-wing extremism. Consider again Mouffe's formulation: "The success of right-wing populist parties comes from the fact that they provide people with some form of hope. . . . Of course this is an illusionary hope, founded on false premises." Perhaps, in that case, critically diagnosing and confronting the rise of the Right should mean giving an account of these "false premises" and "illusory hopes" rather than an affirmation of dissensus and contestation as the ontological and normative essence of the political, which if consistently maintained would only vindicate the Right and its "illusions."

4

FROM "FALSE DEMOCRACY" TO FALSE DEMOS

Adorno, Marcuse, and Climate Skepticism

> I consider the survival of National Socialism *within* democracy to be potentially more menacing than the survival of fascist tendencies *against* democracy.
> —Theodor W. Adorno, *Critical Models: Interventions and Catchwords*

> It is interesting to think back, and not too long back, when among the American Left the slogan was "Power to the People." The slogan is now used to far less a degree because the question "Who are the people?" cannot for any length of time be postponed.
> —Herbert Marcuse, *Paris Lectures at Vincennes University, 1974: Global Capitalism and Radical Opposition*

In spite of its formal constraints, the categorical imperative of democracy inevitably disqualifies certain elements of the demos from the status of the political. For Arendt, the object of exclusion is the laboring class and its material concerns. For radical democracy (and much of the broader democratic turn), it is right-wing populism, especially in its patently ignorant or pathologically prejudicial forms. How might an account of "the political" and the place of democratic iconography within it be transformed once the radical Right can no longer be dismissed as inconsequential? Once circumstances have necessitated a confrontation with these phenomena, how does the figure of democracy change in its function and its critical force, if it retains any? Can the notion of "false democracy"—an understanding of the contemporary political conjuncture as too little democratic—remain the pivot point for critique? If not, then how could we begin to theorize an alternative *informed by* the social phenomena rendered invisible by the democratic turn?

This chapter will sketch such an alternative by engaging the work of Herbert Marcuse and Theodor W. Adorno, specifically, two key essays in which these figures reflect on what I will call "false demos."[1] Provisionally, this is an account of false and pathological political beliefs and movements as generated and sustained by the contradictory necessities of an antagonistic society, or "socially necessary delusion." This demos is thus not "false" in the sense that it is not the "real" demos but in the sense that its character reflects a false social totality. An account of socially necessary delusion allows critical theory to understand and confront mass ignorance and irrationality without lapsing into a crude paternalism that would posit an essential or ahistorical incongruity between true and false consciousness.

The phenomenon of climate denial provides a timely and illustrative model for elaborating the concepts of false demos and socially necessary delusion. Skepticism about anthropogenic climate change is erroneous to the point of absurdity, yet necessary if society is to function in its current form. I follow Adorno in conceiving a "model" as an analysis of a particular phenomenon that represents the whole in and through its particularity rather than as an "example" that instantiates a general concept that is indifferent to its instantiations.[2] In other words, climate denial is not an incidental case of "social delusion as such," an abstract or eternal category. Rather, we form a concept of social delusion through an analysis of the phenomenon of climate skepticism as it appears in the present political conjuncture. This is only one possible model among many; a critical analysis of other forms of social delusion (e.g., Holocaust denial or biological racism) would require attention to the specifics of each model. This is likewise not a theory of political belief as such or a hypothesis as to how it is formed.

I foreground climate denial for three principal reasons. First, it represents a stark and unambiguous disparity between prevailing "public opinion" and reality. Second, it is illustrative as a belief that is systematically and heteronomously produced, completely unintelligible as a spontaneous eruption of the "will of the people." Finally, it is a useful model because it is so overwhelmingly dangerous; in this "difference of opinion" lies the possibility of a sustainable and inhabitable world.[3]

SOCIALLY NECESSARY DELUSION AND THE LOGIC OF OPINION

In criticizing the function and effect of "tolerance" as a political and philosophical value, Marcuse does not mean to repudiate "the elimination of violence" and "the reduction of suppression" as an ideal; to this extent, tolerance remains an "end in itself" ("Repressive Tolerance," 82). His key observation, rather, is that under prevailing conditions, the exaltation of tolerance comes to contravene this ideal and to sustain its opposite. For Marcuse, contemporary capitalist society is organized according to an antagonistic class structure, stratified by deeply entrenched hierarchies and relations of subordination, and maintained by organized campaigns of indoctrination and misinformation. In this situation of "total administration," the value of tolerance serves to safeguard the prerogatives of the privileged elite and to legitimate the distortions produced to justify these prerogatives. By leveling all political interventions to the common denominator of "opinion" according to a standard of neutral "impartiality," tolerance "actually protects the already established machinery of discrimination" ("Repressive Tolerance," 85).

At this point, we could mistake Marcuse's theoretical agenda for a critique based on "subject positions," that has some currency today. The argument goes like this: we cannot evaluate the "opinions" of the oppressor and the oppressed according to the same criterion, because the opinion of the oppressor will always be informed by privilege and/or because the oppressed have access to an experience unknown by the oppressor and therefore a certain epistemic authority.[4] We could also mistake "Repressive Tolerance" for articulating the "paradox" most famously expressed by Karl Popper, namely, that it is necessary to be intolerant of intolerance to protect tolerance.[5] While these lines of thought are consonant with Marcuse's approach up to a point, he has something decidedly different in mind. By taking aim at the normative institution of tolerance, he is attacking the presumed separation of truth and political dispute, a separation made in the name of democracy. "In endlessly dragging debates over the media," he writes,

> The stupid opinion is treated with the same respect as the intelligent one, the misinformed may talk as long as the informed, and propaganda rides along with education, truth with falsehood. This pure toleration of sense and nonsense is justified by the democratic argument that nobody, neither group nor individual, is in possession of the truth and capable of defining what is right and wrong, good and bad. Therefore, all contesting opinions must be submitted to "the people" for its deliberation and choice. ("Repressive Tolerance," 94)

Political differences, the logic of tolerance tells us, cannot be adjudicated according to some "right answer" that everyone would be made to accept, and everyone is entitled to their opinion. To think otherwise is antidemocratic and perhaps even totalitarian.[6] This logic, Marcuse argues, vouchsafes the prevailing system of domination insofar as those who refer to the system of domination as such can be countered by the retort that this is only their opinion (or "view" or "perspective"). Likewise, patently misinformed or spurious assertions—recall a few from the introduction—are granted a certain legitimacy, if not acquiescence, by the warning notice that the speaker is merely offering an alternative opinion and must therefore be tolerated.

Of course, not every misinformed or spurious assertion is tolerated indiscriminately. David Icke's "view" that most world leaders are reptilian aliens does not receive much exposure on the platforms of public discourse, and such ideas are not usually taken seriously in private conversation either. So why does climate skepticism—no less false and no less unfounded—enjoy such permissibility as one "stance on the issue," to the point that many prominent political figures deny the existence of climate change and most deny its severity?[7] If a major politician endorsed Icke's theory, it would produce a laughingstock at best and a scandal at worst. Why, then, does no scandal follow when Senator Inhofe proclaims that climate change is a myth? Climate change is an empirical, scientific question, and as an empirical matter, there is no "debate" and there has not been for decades. That this continues to be regarded as an "issue" having "two sides" is something of a scandal in itself.

The first thing that must be said in the course of answering this question is that, unlike Icke-style conspiracy theories, climate denial (in one form or another) commands broad public support, at least in the United States. One aspect of its perceived legitimacy is its popularity. Here I point to an insight from Adorno, who begins his "Opinion Delusion Society" essay by noting how ridiculous and farcical anti-Semitic Nazi propaganda appears in retrospect. "Yet precisely this," he notes, "should make one suspicious of an inference habitually drawn from the widely held idea: namely, that in the majority the normal opinion necessarily prevails over the delusional one" (*Critical Models*, 105). That climate denial is a common belief does not alter its substance and render it deserving of deference any more than the widespread belief in the "Protocols of the Elders of Zion" should have been credentialed as one opinion among others in its own context. The abstract ideal of tolerance, to return to Marcuse's framework, dissolves the disquieting content of views like climate denial and anti-Semitism in the form of their presentation as opinions, buttressed by the (falsely) legitimating feature of their popularity. To do otherwise would be to abandon the standard of "impartiality" and the democratic values of political discourse, to pretend as though some individual or group is "in possession of the truth and capable of defining what is right and wrong, good and bad."

This is exactly what Marcuse recommends: to suspend the principle of tolerance and affirm the possession of truth, even if the result would be antidemocratic according to the present constitution of democracy. This, not in the name of a scrupulous respect for truth as such but as the necessary movement to attain the ideals signaled by the notion of tolerance:

> Withdrawal of tolerance from regressive movements *before* they can become active; intolerance even toward thought, opinion, and word, and finally, intolerance in the opposite direction, that is, toward the self-styled conservatives, to the political Right—these anti-democratic notions respond to the actual development of the democratic society which has destroyed the basis for universal tolerance. ("Repressive Tolerance," 110–11)

> As against the virulent denunciations that such a policy would do away with the sacred liberalistic principle of equality for "the other

side," I maintain that there are issues where either there is no "other side" in any more than a formalistic sense, or where "the other side" is demonstrably "regressive" and impedes possible improvement to the human condition. ("Repressive Tolerance," 120)

The predictable response to this claim—that what is "demonstrably regressive" or a "possible improvement" is a matter of political difference and can therefore only be made singular by totalitarian coercion—answers the critique of tolerance with an appeal to tolerance.[8] At this point we must ask if the dangers harbored by climate change are greater or lesser than those harbored by the withdrawal of tolerance from climate denial.[9] To be sure, there are many cases where the line between legitimate political disagreement and "demonstrably regressive" opinion is unclear or difficult. But unless we are prepared to grant legitimacy to climate denial and other such views indefinitely, and to accept the suffering, violence, and terror on the horizon if climate change is not addressed immediately and drastically, we must be prepared to "do away with the sacred liberalistic principle of equality for 'the other side'" in this case.[10]

What Marcuse effects here is a reversal of the standard narrative concerning the relationship between tolerance and totalitarian domination. To declare that one has the "right answer" to a political question, and that this answer applies to everyone else whether they like it or not, is to forsake the intrinsic value of pluralist democracy and to substitute indisputable "facts" for politics; it is the kernel of the totalitarian impulse. We heard variations on this theme from Ricœur, Lefort, Connolly, Fraser, Arendt, Rancière, Mouffe, and Laclau. For Marcuse (and Adorno), the relationship is exactly the opposite. The greatest danger lies in an excess of tolerance rather than a deficit, in a formal leveling of opinions removed from the question of their content. This is not without some motivation. The ostensibly undemocratic tendencies of the early Frankfurt School must be understood with reference to the fact that the Third Reich rose to power on a wave of democratic support, something largely ignored by the democratic turn. Marcuse writes, "If democratic tolerance would have been withdrawn when the future leaders started their campaign, mankind would have had a chance of avoiding Auschwitz and a World War" ("Repressive Tolerance," 109).

The critical inquiry into misinformed and spurious popular opinions cannot rest at this level, however, or it would risk settling into a superior complacency. It is not enough to point out that patently false or regressive beliefs have such currency and to recommend a withdrawal of tolerance; we must ask *why* these beliefs, and particular beliefs like climate denial, have such widespread acceptance and such perceived legitimacy. Adorno notes that "groundless and absurd [*unsinnige*] ideas of every stripe are by no means the exception and are by no means on the wane" (*Critical Models*, 116), but he is not content to simply record this as a matter of fact, as if the terminus of critique were to reveal the incompetence or incapacity of those who have not yet discovered critique. His use of the term "delusion" [*Wahn*] evokes its Freudian inheritance: a delusion is a patently false belief that is maintained because it fulfills or satisfies a need. For Adorno, the need that demands a delusion is not at its root a matter of individual psychological development but lies in "the real dynamic of society, a dynamic that produces such opinions, false consciousness [*falsches Bewusstsein*], necessarily" (*Critical Models*, 106). "Opinion Delusion Society"—rendered without punctuation to suggest the continuity of the three terms—is an attempt to understand popular irrationality as a reflection of irrationality at the level of social totality.

By "social totality" and other terms like "whole" or "real dynamic," Adorno does not refer to an ahistorical or immutable essence that might be deduced from first principles. He thinks that, as it is presently organized, society is riven by a contradiction, a fundamental antagonism, at the level of its material reproduction. He often frames it as an opposition between use value and exchange value, a conception that most clearly shows through in the lectures:

> Use values are produced not to satisfy human needs but for profit. . . . The only reason why goods are produced is so that the producers, by which I mean those who control the means of production, should be able as a class to profit from them as much as possible. . . . [G]iven this reality, the needs of human beings, the satisfaction of human beings, is never more than a sideshow and in great measure no more than ideology. If it is said that everything exists only for human beings, it sounds hollow because in reality production is for profit and people are planned in as consumers from the outset. In short, it sounds hollow because of this built-in conflict. (*History and Freedom*, 50–51)

> By calling this society irrational I mean that if the purpose of society as a whole is taken to be the preservation and the unfettering of the people of which it is composed, then the way in which this society continues to be arranged runs counter to its own purpose, its *raison d'être*, its *ratio*. . . . While the means used by society are rational, this rationality of the means is really . . . only a means-end rationality . . . one which obtains between the set ends and the means used to achieve them without having any relation to the real end or purpose of society, which is the preservation of the species as a whole in a way conferring fulfillment and happiness. (*Introduction to Sociology*, 133)[11]

The end of material production is the satisfaction of the needs of human beings, but under the profit principle, production is transfigured into an end in itself and needs are regarded solely as a means to that end.[12] This antagonism, which also creates, sustains, or activates various relations of domination and structural inequalities, produces a condition of reification, where the process of material reproduction—which is nothing other than a set of social relations—comes to appear as an alien force existing outside of human beings and their mediate and immediate needs.[13] Consequently, the subjects of this society, and even those with relative material privilege, are caught up in a system they can neither understand nor control, which perpetuates itself for its own sake and not for theirs. They are therefore not the subjects of this society at all, but its objects.[14]

This antagonism, along with all its dimensions and ramifications, informs Adorno's conception of "wrong life"; if this life "cannot be rightly lived," it is because of a contingent historical situation and not because of some failure of society "as such." "Opinion Delusion Society" situates the prevailing currency of "groundless and absurd ideas" in the context of this antagonistic social totality. Because the maintenance of the prevailing order comes into conflict with its nominal purpose, it must divert any discontent away from its fundamental structure in order to function. Any tension that might expose the contradiction at the heart of the system must be redirected or compensated for, even to the point of sustaining belief in outright falsities. This does not necessarily mean that ten men are sitting in a room conspiring to secure their power; it is more akin to an adaptive behavioral technique that operates on both individual and systemic levels. The logic of opinion performs this role, insofar as a terminal diagnosis of the status quo, however compelling, can be neutralized by dismissing it as only an opinion, and insofar as an apology for the status quo, however incoherent or facile, can be legitimated by excusing it as only an opinion. In Adorno's words, it "proffers explanations through which contradictory reality can without great exertion be rendered free of contradiction" (*Critical Models*, 111). Once this compulsion to explanation is entrenched, there is no great leap from "normal opinion" to pathological opinion. Furthermore, there is no guarantee that pathology will be confined to splinter groups, and in certain conditions delusion may become the rule rather than the exception. "Under the tenacious irrationality of the whole, the very irrationality of people is normal" (*Critical Models*, 116).

As we have seen, Adorno's typical model for understanding pathological opinion is anti-Semitism, especially in its Fascist expression. It is not adequate, he argues, to demonstrate that the dogmas of Nazism are false; to comprehend and confront the root of the problem, we must ask what social demands this collective derangement satisfied for its adherents, and whether or not the conditions that produced these demands have been addressed. He writes:

> That fascism lives on . . . is due to the fact that the objective conditions of society that engendered fascism continue to exist. Fascism essentially cannot be derived from subjective dispositions. The economic order, and to a great extent also the economic organization modeled upon it, now as then renders the majority of people dependent upon conditions beyond their control and thus maintains them in a state of political immaturity. To see through the nexus of deception, they would need to make precisely that painful intellectual effort that the organization of everyday life, and not least of all a culture industry inflated to the point of totality, prevents. (*Critical Models*, 98–99)

This does not absolve any particular individual of responsibility, but it does point to the importance of understanding pathological opinion as a social phenomenon. Rather than cultural backwardness or lack of information, the persistence of prejudicial or specious beliefs reflects the necessity of justifying the status quo or compensating for its torments, even at the cost of patent irrationality. In *History and Freedom*, Adorno addresses the "arch-deception" [*ur*-pseudos, *Urtäuschung*] of nationalism that culminates in "race delusion" [*Rassenwahn*]:

> The [*pseudos*] is that a form of association that is essentially dynamic, economic and historical misunderstands itself as a natural formation, or misconstrues itself ideologically as natural. . . . It is not sufficient, or rather it is too easy, to talk about the delusions of racism and to denounce them. What counts here is the ability to explain it and to recognize its place in the dynamics of history. . . . It is a delusion [*Wahn*] in the strict sense of the word. (*History and Freedom*, 106; cf. *An Introduction to Dialectics*, 123)

By the "strict sense" of delusion, as I have already intimated, he has in mind the Freudian definition.[15] As opposed to an illusion, which could be true or false, a delusion is demonstrably false but is still maintained because it satisfies the demands of successful adaptation and necessary repression. Adorno often speaks of "socially necessary appearance" or "socially necessary false consciousness." Because he transposes the psychoanalytic account of "delusion" from the individual level to the domain of social reproduction, we could without too much damage speak of a "socially necessary delusion."[16] It bears repeating that, in this theory, delusion is not a permanent feature of society *in abstracto*—it is only "necessary" for a society sustained by contingent, historically specific contradictions. A rational whole would not require the very irrationality of people.

CLIMATE SKEPTICISM AND THE FALSE DEMOS

Although Adorno was concerned about the ecological repercussions of the present system, he could not have foreseen the phenomenon of climate change or its persistent denial. Yet this catastrophic development furnishes the best possible model for the theory of socially necessary delusion. If we ask why climate denial is so widespread and inveterate in spite of overwhelming scientific evidence, we must first acknowledge the massive and organized campaign of misinformation spearheaded by giant corporations, their public relations firms, and think tanks. As chronicled by Michaels, in *Doubt Is Their Product*, and Oreskes and Conway, in *Merchants of Doubt*, the dissemination of climate skepticism is a well-funded and self-aware propaganda project—in this case, it really is ten men sitting in a room. But this answer does not strike at the root. Why are these business interests so intent on propagating lies about climate change, and why are so many so willing to believe the lies? Ostensibly, it is not because of a hostility to truth itself or a misanthropic indifference to the survival of the planet or even (for most) a narrow self-interest.[17] It is because, as a growing number of scholars argue, an adequate response to the crisis of anthropogenic climate change would require a fundamental reconstruction of the economic and political order.[18] A system based on the profit motive and the principle of unlimited growth cannot reconcile itself with the hard limit of ecological sustainability. From the perspective of the sustainable satisfaction of human needs (or "use value"), climate denial is completely irrational. But from the perspective of the realization of ever-increasing profit ("exchange value"), it is perfectly rational. Social reproduction thus comes into tension with its own objective; rationality becomes irrational and vice versa.[19] That the present course of society may soon render the planet uninhabitable is obviously an indictment of this course, and so the contradiction must be neutralized, smoothed over, denied, if the prevailing order is to be maintained.[20] This is poignantly revealed in those moments when climate skepticism goes beyond the stage of sheer denial. As Klein points out, the skeptics sometimes make an "economic" argument: climate change might be happening, but doing anything about it would hinder the economy, and so we should not take it seriously. In spite of itself, this argument contains some truth—"the Right is right," as she puts it—inasmuch as it reveals an antagonism between the economic system on one hand and the preservation of life on the other.[21] It is almost as if "the economy"—nothing except a set of social relations ostensibly designed for the maintenance of our needs—has a will of its own, independent of and now in direct conflict with ours.

From the point of view of the reproduction of society in its current form, *climate change cannot be true*. The people living in this society therefore cannot accept it. The iconography of speech, plurality, and dissensus, in which the democratic categorical imperative locates an ontology of the autonomous and indeterminate "political," is thus always already *mediated* by the contradictory demands of material reproduction in an antagonistic society. The demos, whatever its manifestation, must adapt itself to this alienated, heteronomous necessity. Those of us who acknowledge the reality of anthropogenic climate change still do not (and cannot) *live* as if we believe it. Even self-consciously sustainable "lifestyles" come up against the limits of a social system that requires constant consumption and the constant production of waste, and even public figures who pay lip service to the problem do not act differently in any substantial way. In this sense, those who explicitly deny the reality or severity of anthropogenic climate change are more faithfully reflecting the way all of us, insofar as we use plastic or drive cars, carry on the maintenance of this society.[22] I do not mean to suggest a moral equivalence between the climate activist and the climate skeptic, let alone an epistemological one; I only mean to reiterate the point that climate denial is not an *error* but a *delusion* necessary for the reproduction of the social totality in its current form. "If there really is no correct life in the false life," Adorno writes, "then actually there can be no correct consciousness in it either" (*Critical Models*, 120). It would be a mistake to read this remark as defeatist or deterministic or, again, as leveling all degrees of awareness to a common denominator of inadequacy. Rather, the passage suggests that the phenomenon of political delusion cannot be understood or challenged on an individual, apolitical level, and that it will persist as long as the fundamental antagonisms of society do. The critique of idealism in the Marxist tradition was never meant to establish that ideas are inconsequential or strictly determined by material conditions. It was meant to establish that alienation cannot be overcome simply by arriving at a correct consciousness, that alienation exists in reality and not just in ideas.

This brings me to the concept of false demos. Marcuse and Adorno argue that in a fundamentally antagonistic society, popular opinion is not an expression of a spontaneous or freely determined "will of the people" one that must be respected because it is their will, but a reflection of the alienated state in which people find themselves and to which they are compelled to conform. Adorno: "Because the world is not our world, because it is heteronomous, it can express itself only distortedly in stubborn and inflexible opinions" (*Critical Models*, 110). And Marcuse: "Universal toleration becomes questionable when its rationale no longer prevails, when tolerance is administered to manipulated and indoctrinated individuals who parrot, as their own, the opinion of their masters, for whom heteronomy has become autonomy" ("Repressive

Tolerance," 90). The object of critique is therefore not the antidemocratic forces that would obstruct the voice of the people but the false content of this voice and the antagonistic conditions that necessitate this content. An increase of democratization without a transformation of the alienated social totality will only produce more democratic delusions and pathologies, which vary in substance and severity according to historical specificities. To assume the a priori critical capacity of the figure of "the people"—in either a majoritarian or minoritarian sense, either epistemologically or morally—is to render invisible the wrong form of social reproduction that demands acquiescence from each of us (in various ways and with varying degrees of success). Adorno: "The progressive democratization of political institutions will do nothing to mitigate the loss of a sense of freedom, the growing indifference or the enfeeblement of the desire for freedom because the socio-economic reality of even the freest political institutions stands in the way of such a sense of freedom" (*History and Freedom*, 7). Marcuse even suggests that democratic control has already been realized, but with an alienated demos: "The people . . . indeed participate in the rule of the society. The people can indeed express their will, which is no longer their will but has been made their will by the ruling class and its instrumentalities" (*Paris Lectures*, 28–29).[23] There is no better indication of this than the present state of climate change and its systematic denial. Climate skepticism is in fact "the voice of the people," however heteronomously produced, and this fact will not be altered by amplifying this voice, extending its exposure, or granting it more power.

In such conditions, a critical political theory must ask how the demos came to have such a false tenor before it asks how to attain "true" democratic politics. It must criticize a false demos rather than a "false democracy."[24] This does not mean that no popular movement is worth supporting. On the contrary, it affirms the crucial importance of those movements that challenge the conditions that necessitate delusions like climate skepticism. It suggests, in other words, that movements must be evaluated according to their content, their adequacy to the terminal state of things, and not by the extent to which they meet the formal criteria of democracy.

Of course, climate denial is a relatively straightforward model and a relatively recent development. The mystifications of the *Front national* or "men's rights activism" would require different (and longer) treatments. The theoretical perspective that develops concepts like false demos and socially necessary delusion is not meant to excuse us from the difficult task of attending to the complexities of each specific phenomenon. It is meant, first of all, to situate these phenomena in relation to the objective structural conditions that sustain them (and that they sustain). It also allows us to analyze these tendencies at a level that goes beyond the necessary but not sufficient stage of moral indignation. Most importantly for the present project, however, it enables us to acknowledge and critique popular delusion, ignorance, and pathology in a way that is foreclosed by the categorical imperative of democracy (as well as the broader democratic turn in critical political theory).

As we explored throughout the first three chapters, the democratic categorical imperative depends upon two key assertions about the nature of "the political." First, it is "autonomous" with regard to "the economic," an end in itself that is neither a means to material production nor reducible to it. Second, it is "indeterminate," that is, not decidable by an appeal to truth. These two ontological presuppositions establish the critical force of democratic iconography (speech, dissensus, plurality, *doxa*, etc.), and forms of critique that depart from them are guilty of introducing a heteronomy that distorts the nature of the political and thus lapses into an antidemocratic disposition. The theorist becomes the guardian—Platonic reference intended—of political truth, and if people do not see this truth, it is because they are ensnared by some delusion or pathology that is "economic" in origin. If critical theory is to be democratic, to be adequate to the nature of the political, it must abandon this ambition to speak for the people and let the people speak for themselves; its task is to facilitate, elaborate, and theorize the proliferation of the multifarious and unpredictable voices of the demos.

As we have seen, however, the formalism of the democratic categorical imperative is never really a formalism. When confronted with right-wing populist movements (or in Arendt's case, the revolt of the poor), it no longer regards contestation and plurality as ends in themselves. It divests itself of the tools with which it could disqualify these movements but disqualifies them anyway, usually with no more than a passing reference and sometimes even with outright incredulity. Climate change is by any conceivable metric one of the most momentous political issues of our present conjuncture, but the prevailing "debate" over its existence or implications is completely unintelligible according to the ontological postulates of the democratic imperative. Decoupling it from the material reproduction of society ("the economic") obscures the motivations for its persistent denial, while regarding it as a matter of "opinion" betrays a callous disregard for the devastation and suffering looming on the horizon if it is not addressed.

One possible response is that climate change is simply not a *political* issue; it is an empirical or scientific issue that has been falsely politicized because of the antidemocratic forces at work in the prevailing system. Given the prevalence and the consequences of climate skepticism and other such views, we would then seem to be living at a time in which politics is not yet "the political" and in which the former systematically inhibits the establishment of the latter. In this case, a critical intervention based on the ontological features of "the political" becomes an ideal theory removed from, and bearing little or no relation to, the realities that urgently confront us at the present conjuncture. But the categorical imperative cannot even say this, because to separate "properly political questions" from empirical confusions is already to evacuate the specificity of democratic logic. If the people—en masse, whether majority or minority—affirm some form of climate skepticism, is this not "democratic"? Is it not a "demand," an "articulation," or a "distribution of the sensible"? By refusing to grant it the status of the political, or by explaining it by virtue of a propaganda campaign, we are denying the autonomy that the democratic turn was meant to give back to the people who had been so dispossessed by "vanguardist" critical theory. As I mentioned in chapter 1, the categorical imperative wants it both ways: to abdicate its prerogative to prescribe the "right" form of politics, diagnosing those who do not conform as deluded, *and* to avoid a critical analysis of phenomena that might force it to reconsider this abdication, instead deeming these phenomena "not truly political." If we take the democratic categorical imperative seriously, then climate denial must be granted the legitimacy of a political contestation. If we refuse to take climate denial seriously, then we must rethink the categorical imperative and give an account of the political—and an account of critique—which leaves behind the twin theses of autonomy and indeterminacy and, along with them, the foundational status accorded to the democratic iconography of speech, debate, plurality, public space, and *doxa*.

Another way of stating this difference is that, while the democratic categorical imperative begins with a formal and ahistorical political ontology, the concept of socially necessary delusion builds a critical theory out of the circumstances that confront us most pressingly at the present moment. In other words, the latter is not a principle brought to bear on particular events but an attempt to comprehend actually existing society in theory.[25] The democratic turn is forced to be extremely selective, focusing only on Left-progressive movements and either ignoring or summarily dismissing Right populism, because a sustained reflection on the latter would trouble the application of its categories. As I began to detail in the first chapter, climate denial is only the tip of the iceberg. An engagement with books like Jacoby's *The Age of American Unreason* or Hedges's *Empire of Illusion* is enough to make one long for the "dictatorship of the Enlightenment" that Laclau protested against, erroneously projecting a theoretical ambition onto the actual state of affairs. "What for Hegel was self-evident cannot possibly be claimed by the regnant philosophies today," Adorno writes. "No longer are they their own time comprehended in thought" (*Critical Models*, 16). Comprehending the "age of unreason" is what the categorical imperative of democracy has failed to do—more, what it cannot do given its theoretical structure. Likewise, this is what an account of false demos makes possible: a confrontation with the prevalence of delusional or pathological "opinions," one that goes beyond denigration, an approach that does not ignore them as unimportant, mischaracterize them as simple mistakes, or (as we will explore more fully in the next chapter) reify them as essential characteristics of the backward masses.

In one of the epigraphs above, Marcuse notes that the slogan "Power to the people" has fallen out of fashion, replaced by the question "Who are the people?" He said that in 1974. Today, though not in so many words, critical political theory has given itself over to the mantra of "Power to the people" again, leaving to one side the decisive question of who the people happen to be. If I suggest returning to this question, to an account of the actually existing demos and its entanglement with the contradictory demands of an antagonistic system of social reproduction, it is not only for the sake of theoretical consistency. We must replace the question of "How do we give the people a voice?" with the question "Why do the people speak so wrongly?"—not because of an intellectual commitment to the purity of truth but because a phenomenon like climate denial is too momentous, too grave, to avoid confronting in the name of democracy. The consequence of this is that the figure of democracy no longer functions as the fulcrum for critique. It is not that there is not enough democracy; it is that, under present conditions, the demos is bound up in an alienated social totality that produces delusions and pathologies which, if maintained, will lead to its own destruction. We would therefore not wait for a "democracy to come" but for a demos to come.

BACK TO IDEOLOGY?

The account of false demos and socially necessary delusion that I have sketched here points to the resuscitation of the contested and much maligned concept of "ideology."[26] As we have seen, Adorno and Marcuse use the word regularly, along with the expression "false consciousness."[27] The debate over the term is mired in inconsistent usage, with Althusser's account—which does not coincide with that of the early Frankfurt School—casting a long shadow. My description of climate denial as socially necessary delusion does not furnish a full-fledged theory of ideology; it only indicates some points of orientation.[28] Recently, critical theorists such as Maeve Cooke, Rahel Jaeggi, and Karen Ng have signaled a possible rehabilitation of ideology critique, and I regard this chapter as a contribution to that project.[29] Because this approach has become so controversial, however, I will anticipate and respond to some common objections, one here briefly and one in more detail in the concluding chapter.

A consistent objection is that ideology critique relies on an untenable or outmoded conception of truth as "correspondence" or "representation," a metaphysical claim about what is *Real* over and against some deceptive appearance—a "thought/reality opposition," in Laclau and Mouffe's formulation. This is the argument put forth by philosophers such as Richard Rorty, who insists against ideology critique that "there is no point in appealing to 'the way things really are.'"[30] A more sophisticated form of this criticism suggests that the criterion for what constitutes knowledge is itself produced by discourse and that consequently there is no extradiscursive standard of truth by which to measure the epistemic qualities of a given discourse. "Ideology," Foucault says,

> always stands in virtual opposition to something else which is supposed to count as truth. Now I believe that the problem does not consist in drawing the line between that in a discourse which falls under the category of scientificity or truth, and that which comes under some other category, but in seeing historically how effects of truth are produced within discourses which in themselves are neither true nor false.

He also objects that "ideology stands in a secondary position relative to something which functions as its infrastructure, as its material, economic determinant, etc."[31] It relies, in other words, on a shopworn "base-superstructure" model that reduces sociocultural illusions to an economic reality concealed beneath and determining them, again effecting a division between the real and the illusory. However different in context and formulation, the objections of Rorty and Foucault perform the same basic critical gesture: they suggest that it is no longer theoretically or politically viable to appeal to some fundamental reality hidden behind a deceptive appearance.

We may respond to this intervention by considering it in relation to another contemporary theoretical movement, the "epistemology of ignorance" as conceived by Charles Mills.[32] In *The Racial Contract,* Mills argues that the contemporary world order has been shaped by a system of white supremacy and by a sometimes tacit and sometimes explicit agreement among whites to establish racist myths that legitimate the domination and exploitation of nonwhites. The organization and maintenance of this "contract," he claims, "requires a certain schedule of structured blindnesses and opacities."[33] The mechanisms of white supremacy must be systematically obscured such that relations of domination come to appear as natural, a "cognitive and moral economy"[34] that obfuscates the conditions for the possibility of the present state of things. The result is that it is structurally deincentivized, though not by that token impossible, for whites to come to an adequate consciousness of the realities of white supremacy. In addition to its directly material consequences, then, the racial contract also produces "cognitive dysfunctions":

> [T]he Racial Contract prescribes for its signatories an inverted epistemology, an epistemology of ignorance, a particular pattern of localized and global cognitive dysfunctions (which are psychologically and socially functional), producing the ironic outcome that whites will in general be unable to understand the world they themselves have made.... To a significant extent... white signatories will live in an invented delusional world, a racial fantasyland.[35]

This delusional world is also reflected in the domain of philosophy, Mills argues, insofar as predominant approaches in political theory still rely on variations of "the social contract," a deracialized and therefore idealized model that inhibits social justice rather than facilitating it. This is explicable in part because of the overwhelmingly white makeup of the academy (especially philosophy), though he also notes that racism "needs to be understood as aiming at the minds of nonwhites as well as whites, inculcating subjugation."[36] Thus, while nonwhites are certainly more likely than whites to perceive the operation of the racial contract, there is not a mechanistic one-to-one determination in either direction between racial subject position and adequate consciousness.

The parallels between Mills's account and the discussion of mass delusion in Adorno and Marcuse are striking, particularly his characterization of "cognitive dysfunction" as a necessary feature of the reproduction of a bad status quo. "In the ideal polity one seeks to know oneself and to know the world," Mills writes. But in the real polity of the racial contract, "such knowledge may be dangerous."[37] This intimate connection between falsity and necessity—the "epistemically unreliable but socially functional,"[38] in Alcoff's words—forms the basis for ideology critique as the early Frankfurt School understands it. In fact, Mills describes his project as "really in the spirit of a racially informed *Ideologiekritik*," noting that "it lays claims to truth, objectivity, realism, the description of the world as it actually is."[39] In order for there to be an epistemology of ignorance, there must be something of which to be ignorant.

The familiar criticisms of ideology critique must then be applied to the epistemology of ignorance. If we dismiss the distinction between representation and reality as epistemologically untenable, we must also dismiss Mills's account of the "racial contract" insofar as it posits a distance between the prevailing consciousness of whites and the real conditions of white supremacy. In this case, the notion of a "racist myth" becomes unintelligible, either because everything is a myth or because nothing is. If we take the Foucauldian tack, the consequences for Mills's account are equally devastating. He presents the epistemology of ignorance as an ideological mechanism for legitimating and maintaining a system of material expropriation, by that token separating a knowledge of things as they are from the mystifying forces that distort this knowledge. In either case, the notion of a "racial fantasyland" assumes the existence of a space outside the fantasyland, a space of reality and truth against which delusion is measured. If we have rejected ideology critique for the stated reasons, we should conclude that the "racial contract" is not a false discourse that legitimates contingent relations of domination but another discourse not epistemologically better or worse than that which names white supremacy as a system. We happen to prefer one discourse to another, but we cannot say that the organization of the world is *really* characterized by a system of white supremacist domination.

We should be clear about the exact implications of this position. It would not necessarily apply to a metaethical debate about the foundations of antiracist political commitments but to discussions about what racism *is*, the form it has taken historically, and what its contemporary contours and parameters are. There are obviously vast debates about this in critical race theory, but any serious philosophical intervention takes for granted that, insofar as racism refers to anything, it refers to the historical or contemporary relative privilege of white people and the historical or contemporary relative oppression of people of color. But this is precisely what is being "contested" in the political arena at present. Public opinion polls indicate that roughly half of Americans disagree with the statement that "white people benefit from advantages in society that black people do not have."[40] In the wake of the National Football League's "kneeling" controversy, a popular coach asserted that "there has been no oppression [of African Americans] in the last hundred years."[41] A significant current in right-wing populism disseminates the view that whites are the victims of a massive and violent antiwhite conspiracy.[42] So while the Rorty-Foucault–style critic might try to disentangle the epistemological position required by ideology critique from the ethical commitments grounding an antiracist politics, it is not clear what an antiracist politics would entail once it was decoupled from "something that is supposed to count as truth." When confronted with the claim that the most serious form of oppression today is the oppression of white men by "political correctness," will the ideology skeptics' response be something like "actually, things are not as you say—really, things are quite different"? If so, then they have already granted the epistemological perspective that ideology critique requires. If they go further and understand these patent distortions as a facile attempt to preserve the socioeconomic privileges of a status quo under threat, then they are already doing ideology critique.

I juxtapose this common objection to ideology critique with the epistemology of ignorance to illustrate the kind of reductio ad absurdum that results if we apply the former consistently. Unless we are prepared to collapse the distinction between *real* racial domination and *false* racist or deracializing myths, we must reconsider the theoretical disposition that would renounce any separation of true and false consciousness; unless we refuse to acknowledge any relationship between the material exploitation of nonwhites and the discourses that legitimate and perpetuate racial ignorance, we must relinquish the idea that any account of this relationship amounts to "reductionism." Once we have done this, it becomes difficult to attack ideology critique using the same philosophical arsenal.

In the context of this chapter, I have indeed relied on a "thought/reality opposition" and on an account of truth as concealed behind certain discourses, motivated by the necessities of a socioeconomic order, that would distort it. Climate change is real and extraordinarily dangerous, and its denial has been a systematic political project—undertaken because the status quo demands it—successful enough that decisive numbers of people are now climate skeptics. I have argued that this situation calls for a theory of socially necessary delusion, or ideology. If it is objected that this account is faulty because it relies on an account of truth as opposed to delusion, we must be prepared to accept all of the consequences of this objection: that there is "no point" in appealing to the truth of climate science over and against the delusion of climate skepticism and that "the problem does not consist in drawing a line" between the epistemology of ignorance and something that would stand outside of it.[43]

A more substantial response to the criticism of ideology critique at the epistemological level would require another project and take us too far afield from this one. For the purposes of our investigation into the critical function of the figure of democracy, another objection is more salient: the problem of elitism. There is a danger that the turn to "false demos" and "socially necessary delusion" will inadvertently coincide with the pernicious forms of elitism that have prevailed for most of the history of political philosophy. In spite of itself, ideology critique may end up reasserting the prerogative of the philosopher kings. The categorical imperative of democracy, one could argue, functions as a safeguard against this troubling possibility. I will take up and respond to this objection in the final chapter.

5

WHAT IS ELITISM?

> It is a highly unstable theory about the world which has to assume that vast numbers of ordinary people, mentally equipped in much the same way as you or I, can simply be thoroughly and systematically duped into misrecognizing entirely where their real interests lie. Even less acceptable is the position that, whereas they, the masses, are the dupes of history, we—the privileged—are somehow without a trace of illusion and can see right through into the truth, the essence, of a situation.
> —Stuart Hall, "The Toad in the Garden"

The first few chapters of this project argued that the categorical imperative of democracy, which regards democratic iconography as an end in itself, is only able to maintain its critical credibility if it disqualifies certain elements of the demos in direct violation of its central theoretical commitments. As an alternative to this unsustainable ambivalence, the previous chapter argued that the present conjuncture is better diagnosed and confronted as a problem of false demos, that is, an understanding of the prevailing pathologies of "the people" as inextricable from, which is not to say reducible to or strictly determined by, antagonistic objective conditions. Therefore, the categorical imperative should be displaced by an account of socially necessary delusion, or ideology, which would elaborate the relationship between false and pathological political beliefs and the contradictory social relations that create, sustain, or activate them.

In order to be coherent, then, this theory requires some reference to a belief that would not be delusional. It cannot hypostatize social pathology as necessary in isolation from specific social relations; if the necessity of delusion were universal, the theoretical maneuver would lose its critical force. "Once [the concept of ideology] has ceased to differ from any true consciousness," Adorno writes, "it is no longer fit to criticize a false one" (*Negative Dialectics*, 198).[1] This is not a theory of political "ideologies" in the colloquial sense that applies indiscriminately; rather, it requires demarcating boundary lines between true and false political beliefs (which is not to say that the separation will be an absolute one without gradient). As Adorno puts it elsewhere (at his most confident): "It is a simple matter of distinguishing between truth and ideology . . . between a consciousness that is appropriate to the current state of society and one that conceals it" (*History and Freedom*, 140). Simple or not, this conception of ideology critique harkens back to an ominous-sounding, all-but-discredited project: that of "political education." This would not be an education in the practice or habitus of politics, which theorists of the democratic categorical imperative might affirm, but an education in the right content of politics, which, according to the understanding we have developed here, would be fundamentally antidemocratic.

An account of socially necessary delusion, in other words, obliges us to admit of a division, in a political register, between the deluded and those who perceive the mechanism of delusion. This is a consequence that some critics of ideology critique cannot accept. In addition to the epistemological concerns mentioned at the end of the last chapter, an account of socially necessary delusion also presents an ethical problem. Laclau frequently points to the checkered history of this ambition, warning that the impulse to diagnose "false consciousness" has "led to the establishment of an 'enlightened' despotism of intellectuals and bureaucrats who spoke in the name of the masses, explained to them their true interests, and imposed upon them increasing totalitarian forms of control" (*New Reflections on the Revolution of Our Time*, 91–92). His later evaluation of this "dinosaur notion" (*The Rhetorical Foundations of Society*, 144) is even more severe: "There is no longer any room for that childish talk about 'false consciousness,' which presupposes an enlightened elite whose possession of the truth makes it possible to determine what the 'true interests' of a class are" (*The Rhe-*

torical Foundations of Society, 166). Rancière also objects to this division on moral grounds, refusing to accept "the presupposition of the radical separation between a world doomed to ignorance and the very few who know about the way either toward a new society or toward an impending disaster" (*Recognition or Disagreement*, 154). Like Laclau, he justifies this aversion with an appeal to history: "The promise of emancipation linked with the endless critique of the illusions produced by the system of domination," he writes, "died in 1989" (*Recognition or Disagreement*, 153). As we have already seen in chapter 3, both Rancière and Laclau frequently associate the concept of ideology critique with the figure of the Platonic philosopher king, the former going far enough to say that Plato's intellectually stratified republic "made every future theory of ideology an academic joke" (*Recognition or Disagreement*, 135).[2] At the core of these morally infused criticisms, then, is the serious allegation that ideology critique, with its implicit notions of political education and the unenlightened, is inescapably *elitist*.

This criticism, I will argue in this chapter, relies on an equivocation between the markedly elitist notion of political incompetence developed by Plato (which is maintained throughout the subsequent tradition) and the radical departure represented by the project of ideology critique. The latter, I claim, retains only a superficial, metaphorical resemblance to the former. In fact, an account of socially necessary delusion is able to articulate the most compelling critique of Platonic elitism *and* avoid the inconsistencies of the democratic categorical imperative, while the indiscriminate repudiation of this account backfires by vindicating the anti-intellectualist tendencies of the contemporary Right. Finally, in its concurrent rejection of ideology critique and unsubstantiated exclusion of right-wing populism, the categorical imperative of democracy actually coincides with the very elitism that it indicts.

In what follows I will use the terms "ideology," "socially necessarily delusion," "false consciousness," and "false demos" interchangeably. This is in part to avoid repetition but also because the charge of elitism is indifferent to whatever terminological refinements might be developed. However we qualify the concept, the notion that there are widespread and firmly entrenched political beliefs that are *false*—and, by extension, that there are those who recognize and diagnose this falsity—is enough to activate the criticism. It does not matter *how* the divide between political truth and the unenlightened, or the education that would bridge that divide, is posited; the elitism lies in the fact that both the divide and the education *are* posited. It bears repeating, however, that "false consciousness" is not something that one either has or does not have in the way a light switch is either on or off; in this understanding, it is a broadly diffuse constellation of tendencies manifesting to various degrees and mobilized in various ways, depending on the contingencies of prevailing conditions.

THE INCOMPETENCE PRINCIPLE

Elitism has enjoyed a long and colorful life in political theory. In fact, the contention that the vast majority of people are not sufficiently intellectually or morally developed to make political decisions has been one of the omnipresent features of Western philosophy since Plato. As J. S. McClelland notes, "it could almost be said that political theorizing was *invented* to show that democracy . . . necessarily turns into rule by the mob."[3] Philippe Nemo also remarks on the antidemocratic origins of the tradition: "Plato's political thought is essentially *a long argument against the very principle of democracy*."[4]

At the heart of Plato's argument against democracy is the claim that some people are fit to rule while most, owing to their natural condition, are not. Politics requires an understanding of "the good," and an understanding of the good requires philosophical reflection, and philosophical reflection requires that one be capable of doing philosophy, which, Socrates says in a key passage in the *Republic*, the majority are not.[5] Most people, he goes on to explain, are guided by their irrational desires and by pleasure, rather than by reason or truth, and so are susceptible to manipulation by *demagogues* (the word "demagogue" meaning "leader of the people"). If these people control a city, then this city is doomed to descend into disorder and/or tyranny.[6] So the demos should not be given political power because, by its very nature, it is incapable of wielding it responsibly and in accordance with justice. It is this argument that leads Plato to imagine the infamous "philosopher kings" (or "guardians"), a class of wise and benevolent rulers who would administer a city according to philosophical insight.[7] He insists that just as one can be an expert in carpentry or cobbling, so one should be able to be an expert in political affairs. Democracy, which gives everyone access to political power regardless of political understanding, is like allowing anyone to be a carpenter or a cobbler despite a lack of training in these trades—but with far graver consequences.[8] Leave politics to those who are *competent* in politics, just as we leave carpentry to those who are competent in carpentry. The key difference between political expertise and carpentry—and this is the locus of Plato's elitism—is that anyone *could* be trained as a carpenter, while politics requires a philosophical understanding of the good, which by necessity is foreclosed to "the many."

This argument for elitism, which we might call *the incompetence principle*, is repeated—albeit with some notable variations—in Aristotle, Cato, Livy, Thomas, Hobbes, and Montesquieu, to name only a few.[9] With the advent of Edmund Burke and other antidemocratic reactionaries of the French Revolution, the concept of "the good" drops out, replaced by a notion of political experience. For this kind of elitist, it is not that the masses are incapable of insight into the true order of things (there is no such thing) but that they have not been maturated in practices of ruling and government; they are therefore uncultivated in the foundation of reliable politics, that is, customs and traditions hallowed by usage and consecrated by time.[10] Anti-Platonic in its theoretical justification, this argument remains Platonic in its conclusion: the demos is politically incompetent. Even John Stuart Mill argued for a socially stratified "plural voting" system out of fear that the laboring classes, whose mental and moral condition he regarded as degraded, would fail to respect the liberal values and institutions necessary for civic life.[11] Although Mill (unlike Plato and Burke) looked forward to a utopia of universal education, his estimation of contemporary incompetence was nevertheless demarcated along class (and racial) lines and so still conformed to the basic elitist impulse. In the history of Western political philosophy, the incompetence principle runs deeply enough that Platonists, conservatives, and progressive liberals are united in their fear of the ignorant and unreliable demos, however disparate the ultimate stakes of their respective projects.

From the late nineteenth to the early twentieth centuries, there was an explosion of literature on the rise of "mass society" and the threat this posed to political stability, tradition, morality, and culture. The population boom, the increasing democratization of political institutions, and the solidification of organized labor were ominous developments for those convinced of the ignorance, irrationality, and lack of cultivation of "the common man." The incompetence principle found its most fervent and explicit expressions during this period,[12] and it was also during this time that fear of popular power attained a veneer of scientific legitimacy as "crowd psychology" or "the sociology of mass behavior."[13] Important variations on the incompetence theme were then developed by Walter Lippmann (whose argument is essentially logistical) and by Joseph Schumpeter (whose account of "elitist democracy" prompted a lively midcentury debate).[14] As I attempted to show in chapter 2, Arendt's work belongs to this tradition as well.

After being a ubiquitous part of Western political philosophy for millennia, the incompetence principle went dormant in the last decades of the twentieth century. Under the scrutinizing eyes of what I have called the democratic turn, this way of thinking was dismissed as elitist. Recent political events, however, have revitalized the old argument from incompetence and sparked a renewed debate about the limits of democracy. Since the mid-2000s, especially in the United States, there has appeared a series of books in a genre that we might call "the incompetent demos exposé," an alarming catalog of the irrationality, ignorance, and misinformed opinion characteristic of the average American citizen. Sometimes this genre takes the form of cultural criticism (Susan Jacoby's *The Age of American Unreason*, Chris Hedges's *Empire of Illusion*) and sometimes of ethnographic report (Arlie Russell Hochschild's *Strangers in Their Own Land*, David Niewert's *Alt-America*); most important for our purposes, however, is the subsection of this genre that juxtaposes democratic theory with empirically informed pessimism about the capacity of people to live up to this theory. What is "exposed" in this case is that, contrary to our best ideal theoretical impulses, human psychology is just not equipped for the kind of rational and reflective disposition required for democracy to work in the way that its advocates think it should. Examples include Arthur Lupia's *Uninformed*, Bryan Caplan's *The Myth of the Rational Voter*, Ilya Somin's *Democracy and Political Ignorance*, and Achen and Bartels's *Democracy for Realists*. These texts differ in the way they situate their findings in relation to democracy, but in each case the conclusion is that democratic theory needs to be rethought or reconsidered in light of the revelation that "the people" have limited competence when it comes to politics.

This new tendency is complemented by a series of recent popular periodical articles that suggest, contrary to some of our preconceived notions, that people do not form beliefs (including political beliefs) on a rational basis. With titles like "The Science of Why We Don't Believe Science," "Why Facts Don't Change Our Minds," and "Why Facts Don't Matter to Trump Supporters," these articles draw on contemporary psychological or sociological research to show that human beings are cognitively predisposed toward ignorance and irrationality.[15] Sometimes the argument is that belief systems are based on emotional connection or identification with groups rather than "facts" or "reason"; other times the explanation comes down to a neurological "confirmation bias" couched in evolutionary terms. In either case, the conclusion is that the stubborn persistence of irrational or ignorance beliefs (like climate skepticism) is explicable in terms of the frailties of human psychology. Articles of this kind increased in frequency during and after the political events of 2016.

The notion of incompetence developed by these works is nothing so theoretically elaborate as the metaphysics of Plato, and their accounts are much more stolid than the paranoid forebodings of Burke. For the exposés, the incompetence principle is based only on an assertion about "what people are like." Looking at the raw data, the story goes, it turns out that "the people" are not rational, that they have a predisposition toward ignorance, and that they will probably never meet the high standards demanded by any theory that presupposes or recommends their competence. "The folk theory of democracy celebrates the wisdom of popular judgments by informed and engaged citizens," Achen and Bartels write. "The reality is quite different."[16] But the conclusion is not only academic; the common thread running throughout this genre—from Jacoby to Somin to the mainstream opinion pieces—is a warning about the dangers of popular power when this cognitively impaired "people" is angry, overzealous, and underinformed.

At the extremity of this tendency is Jason Brennan's *Against Democracy*. Because of the "ignorant, irrational, impaired, immoral, and corrupt electorate,"[17] he argues, we should replace democracy with "epistocracy," or rule by the knowledgeable.[18] This would work by restricting suffrage, instituting a political competency test as a prerequisite for the right to vote. If you can demonstrate that you know enough about politics to make a responsible and informed decision, then and only then do you earn your place among the electorate. In line with Caplan, Lupia, and others, Brennan frames his argument by appealing to "what human beings are like." The book is littered with phrases like this: "It turns out that most people process political information in deeply biased and irrational ways."[19] When this sobering empirical albatross is fully understood, the idealistic norm of popular sovereignty becomes at best an unreflective dogma and at worst a path to political ruin. If this is the case, then political philosophy's longstanding incompetence principle appears to be vindicated.

THE PROBLEM WITH THE PEOPLE

Contrary to the suggestion of its critics, ideology critique is something fundamentally different than the elitism of the incompetence principle and its legacy from Plato to Burke to Brennan. The concept of socially necessary delusion does in fact posit a distance between prevailing false consciousness and something that would constitute an enlightened politics, but it does not attribute this distance to an inherent quality of the demos. In other words, it accepts the premise of the incompetence principle (the mere fact of mass political ignorance and irrationality) but denies its conclusion (that this fact results from an unmediated psychological feature). It places responsibility not on the eternally limited vision of the many (Plato), the unrestrained whims of the inexperienced masses (Burke), the intellectual and moral deficiencies of the lower classes (Mill), or the indeclinable frailties of the human psyche (the exposés), but on the antagonistic objective social conditions that demand and sustain political incompetence. For Plato and for Brennan, the problem is the people. For Adorno and Marcuse, it is the contradictory system to which the people must adapt. The former: "The trouble is with the conditions that condemn [people] to impotence and apathy and would yet be changeable by human action; it is not primarily with people and with the way conditions appear to people" (*Negative Dialectics*, 190).[20] The latter: "I call this society insane—not the people in it" (*The New Left and the 1960s*, 96).

What the incompetence principle effects, and what a theory of socially necessary delusion avoids, is the reduction of a political problem to a psychological invariant. By regarding irrationality and ignorance as a structural fixture of human behavior as such, the psychologization of incompetence eliminates the need for a political economy of delusion and its systematic social production. From this perspective, it is not that prevailing forms of social reproduction foster or necessitate delusional beliefs, but that we are "hardwired" to be deluded. Climate denial is so obstinate not because the status quo demands it (and has worked so hard to nurture it) but because facts just plain do not appeal to people. This inflation of the empirical fact of popular ignorance and irrationality into an assertion about "what human beings are like" is at work in both Plato's argument for philosopher kings and Brennan's turn toward "epistocracy." A trait characteristic of individuals who must adapt to certain historical and socioeconomic conditions is inflated into a characteristic of human adaptation in the abstract, thus construing these conditions as irrelevant or above criticism. Returning to Mills's framework for a moment, the psychologization model could also tell us that "people tend to be racist" and then infer from this that racism is "hardwired,"[21] obscuring the long history of the racial contract as a historical production. This is the limitation of the approach that only registers mass political incompetence as a simple fact to be reckoned with. It is indeed a fact to be reckoned with—and here already there is an advance over the categorical imperative of democracy—but if we are not content to resign ourselves to this fact and all of its consequences, then critically confronting it means asking after its conditions of possibility and the conditions of possibility of its transformation. The incompetence principle confirms an ahistorical, apolitical understanding of mass delusion and pathology, treating it as a failure of the individual psyche or as the necessary curse of particular classes or groups. It regards ignorance not as something to be overcome but as something to be recognized and accepted as inevitable. By avoiding this mistake, an account of socially necessary delusion circumvents the problem of elitism.

In an interesting way, the return of the incompetence principle repeats the basic error of democratic thinking, namely, that the presumption that political opinion is autonomously rather than heteronomously produced. The two mistakes mirror one another: democracy and antidemocracy are complementary formalisms. The former insists on the value of democratic iconography in spite of the prevailing character of the demos, while the latter, believing itself (with some justification) to be closer to empirical reality, reifies this prevailing character and uses it to justify a rejection of the value of democratic iconography. The first distortion prevents us from rectifying the wrongs perpetrated in the name of the second. By completely bypassing the moment of truth in the elitist impulse, the categorical imperative of democracy defeats the emancipatory purpose originally intended by its critique of this impulse. The concept of false demos recognizes popular ignorance and irrationality without reifying it, situating it instead in terms of the conditions that engender it and placing its critical emphasis there.

To make this more concrete, consider again the model of climate skepticism. The categorical imperative of democracy would require us to either deny its prevalence outright or to legitimate it as a democratic intervention. Alternatively, as we have seen, it could decide that this phenomenon is simply not political (more on this below). The incompetence principle, on the other hand, would regard the popular currency of climate skepticism as confirming its elitist thesis: if the people deny climate change, then the people are clearly incompetent by nature. Ideology critique goes beyond the categorical imperative by refusing to ignore or minimize the significance of climate skepticism, and then goes beyond the incompetence principle by asking after the *causes* and the *social function* of climate skepticism, explicitly resisting an explanation that would project this pathology into an ahistorical, psychologized, and therefore depoliticized realm. The categorical imperative says that the demos is good as such, while the incompetence principle says that the demos is bad as such. A theory of socially necessary delusion answers that the demos is bound up with objective social conditions, which for the nonce are bad but which might be made good, and that the critical value of democratic iconography will depend on the relationship between the demos and these conditions.

With this response, ideology critique admits the provisional truth of the incompetence principle without inferring from this truth an argument for elitism. It can therefore formulate a criticism of the incompetence principle that goes beyond sheer denial, something the democratic turn is unable to do—either because its doctrinal faith blinds it to the realities of the people or because it has (ostensibly) forfeited its license to discriminate between true and false consciousness. By surpassing the incompetence principle rather than simply refusing it, ideology critique can criticize elitism at the same time that it acknowledges the prevalence of false and pathological political beliefs. To quote Adorno again: "If philosophers since Heraclitus have carped at the many for remaining captive to mere opinion instead of knowing the true essence of things, then their elitist thinking [*Elite Denken*] only put the blame [*Schuld*] on the *underlying population* for what properly lies with the institution of society" (*Critical Models*, 109).[22] In this gesture, elite thinking is rejected as a response to the perceived distance between the demos and the truth, but this distance is not thereby annulled.

Compare this approach to Arendt's remarks, detailed in chapter 2, about the "politically immature public." For her, this immaturity stems from the condition of the *animal laborans*, the political backwardness inherent in those who see things "from the viewpoint of the stomach." Her democratic impulse should lead away from the notion of political maturity insofar as politics is supposed to be autonomous and a matter of *doxa* rather than truth; but the elitist impulse requires that the desired exclusion be cast in terms of the inherent capacities or incapacities of certain people. Distressed about the intrusion of falsity into the formerly pure political sphere, she does not situate this infiltration in terms of the objective social necessities compelling it; instead, she chalks up the contemporary politicization of empirical facts to the immaturity of the demos itself. The approach I am suggesting would avoid this ambivalence by relinquishing both the critical primacy of democratic iconography and antidemocratic skepticism, thereby functioning as a critique of both.

There is a scene in Kazuo Ishiguro's novel *The Remains of the Day* that illustrates the respective, complementary deficiencies of the incompetence principle and the democratic categorical imperative. On a noble estate in 1930s England, a group of aristocrats are debating the value of democracy. One of them insists that "the will of the people [is] the wisest arbiter."[23] The others scoff incredulously. As if to test the hypothesis, the host calls in his butler, Stevens. One of the aristocrats then asks Stevens a series of questions on contemporary political issues, but the bewildered servant is unable to say anything in response. The skeptic feels vindicated by this: "You see gentlemen . . . our man here is unable to assist us in these matters. And yet we still go along with the notion that this nation's decisions be left in the hands of our good man here and the few million others like him."[24] While the democrat in the room remains stubbornly unconvinced, the rest commend the interrogator for proving his point. Incidentally, this is the exact justification that Brennan provides for his "epistocracy," only with a somewhat larger sample size.

In this scenario, the first aristocrat represents the democratic turn, while the other represents the incompetence principle. The former is rendered ridiculous by the fact that Stevens is unable to answer, while the latter is rendered facile by his elitist interpretation of this fact. Between the democrat's a priori faith in the opinions of the "ordinary man in the street" and the elitist's positive judgment of incompetence, the circumstances of Stevens's life are rendered invisible. Neither aristocrat is able to perceive the objective conditions that mediate Stevens's inability to answer—the realities of domestic servitude, the blind obedience and deference inculcated in him, and the inferiority complex necessitated by the maintenance of a hierarchical social order. The democrat insists that, in spite of being a butler, this ordinary man has valid opinions; through this gesture he obscures any possible relationship between political opinion and the social necessities of a world divided between domestic servants and lords of the manor. For his part, the elitist takes the ordinary man's lack of competence as a justification for the continued existence of this world rather than as a *product* of it. We should, of course, be outraged at the skeptical gentleman's willingness to humiliate Stevens and to use him as a prop in an argument. At the same time, the moral of this story cannot be that the more generous aristocrat wins the argument after all, for it is still the case that Stevens *is* ignorant. The elitist infers from the butler's lack of education a state of permanent incompetence, while the democrat simply denies that he needs education. In both cases, they bypass a critique of the bad reality of which this ignorance is a reflection.

Ishiguro's scene also provides occasion to clear up a potential category mistake. Here, the ignorant one is a servant and the (ostensibly) knowledgeable ones are the privileged members of an elite class. We might conclude that, whatever its merits over and against the incompetence principle, the critique of ideology maps on exactly to the economically, racially, and sexually stratified categories of the old model, thereby trading elitism for something like "paternalism" while retaining all of the former's problematic aspects. But in the interpretation I am developing here, consciousness is not *determined* by objective social conditions but only *mediated* by them; likewise, the ignorance, irrationality, and pathology generated by these conditions is not strictly bound to any particular group. There is no *absolute* correlation between Stevens's position as a butler and his lack of political perspective, nor is there any guarantee that his aristocratic tormenters (or his one patronizing supporter) will be politically enlightened simply by virtue of being aristocrats.[25] To say that delusion is socially necessary is not to say that people in specific structural positions within the social totality are doomed to delusion. Rather, it means that a generally diffused delusion is necessary for the reproduction of certain social relations; its relative success or failure among differently situated members is contingent rather than necessary—this is why it functions effectively but imperfectly. Recognizing and confronting false consciousness are not the unique prerogative of any particular class (and certainly not of academics).

At the same time, we should acknowledge two crucial caveats. The first is that those with a vested interest in maintaining the status quo and its systems of domination are, of course, less inclined to become aware of or challenge the delusions that reinforce this status quo. The second, which stands in a paradoxical relation to the first, is that the informed and sophisticated perspective required to approach the question of ideology is not equally accessible to everyone. "Criticizing privilege becomes a privilege," Adorno writes. "The world's course is as dialectical as that" (ND, 41). So there are structural incentives working against Stevens's level of political consciousness, even though it is not *determined* by his position as a butler. Likewise, while the aristocrats may have ample opportunity to form an enlightened view, they are structurally deincentivized to question the entitlement system or the delusions that underpin it. But accessibility and incentives aside, an account of socially necessary delusion does not provide any strict mechanism for cutting through messy contingencies and assigning prerogatives based on position.

The opponents of ideology critique charge that, perhaps in spite of its intentions, the diagnosis of false consciousness inevitably reverts to the elitism of Plato. As we have seen, Rancière and Laclau liken the critic of socially necessary delusion to the philosopher king, and ideology to the shadows on the wall of the cave. The crux of Plato's argument, however, is that "the many" are unfit to govern because, according to their inherent nature, they are incapable of thinking philosophically; governing should therefore be left to that small minority who are able to see what the majority cannot. In Plato, and in the reverberations of this argument throughout the tradition, there is a *necessary* disparity between the enlightened and the unenlightened. The first major difference in ideology critique is that this disparity is understood as contingent. The necessity in "socially necessary delusion" means "necessary to the reproduction of an antagonistic system" and not "necessary as a fixture of human nature" or "necessary for social organization as such." Likewise, it moves even further away from Plato by insisting that the critical aim is not merely a shift in consciousness but a shift in the conditions that necessitate this consciousness. The goal is not the successful management of the herd by the guardians, as it remains even in Brennan, but the establishment of social conditions in which ignorance and irrationality will no longer be necessary. Insofar as a theory of social delusion maintains the division between "the knowing" and "the rest"—and it does so only in a qualified, limited way—its understanding of the nature, causes, and consequences of this division are completely transformed. This departure is covered over in the criticisms of Rancière and Laclau. Placing emphasis on their superficial metaphorical similarities distorts the decisive difference between ideology critique and Platonic elitism.

It should be pointed out that, in their respective critiques of ideology critique, Rancière and Laclau (and Rorty and Foucault) probably have in mind the model developed by Althusser. Rightly or wrongly, his remarks on the subject could be understood as positing a necessary correlation between locations in the mode of production and degrees of consciousness, a permanent incongruity between the "ideology" of those engaged in the process and the "science" of intellectuals outside of it.[26] In this case, a certain vestige of Platonism would remain. As we have seen, the account of socially necessary delusion that I have sketched here departs from this approach in important ways. But insofar as it vetoes all accounts of false consciousness for establishing an intellectual disparity in the political realm, the moral opposition to ideology critique is unable to discriminate between these two models. The critics throw the Althusserian baby out with the Althusserian bathwater. Rancière in particular allows no space between a commitment to *necessary* intellectual inequality and a commitment to the "equality of intelligences." One is either Plato or Jacotot. An account of socially necessary delusion shows us a way between these two alternatives.

WHO ARE THE ELITISTS? AND WHO ARE THE POPULISTS?

Dismissing all diagnoses of ideological delusion as elitist has some further implications that we should consider. If we refuse to grant *any* distinction between true and false consciousness in a political register on the grounds that it reintroduces a form of the incompetence principle, then patently spurious or pathological beliefs—such as climate skepticism or xenophobic nationalism—are accorded the status of legitimate political interventions. We may still disagree with these positions, but this disagreement would only consist in two opposing conceptions of the world and not in more or less clear perceptions of things as they actually are; accordingly, we would not criticize the opposing viewpoint on the grounds that it did not adequately reflect reality but only on the grounds that it is not *our* viewpoint. The difference between a climate skeptic and one who thinks through the consequences of climate change is therefore *not* a difference between adequate and inadequate pictures of reality. This is consistent with a position that rejects the notion of political education *tout court*. In this case, the measure of elitism is not a theory's understanding of the need for or content of political education but the mere positing of an intellectual disparity as such. When political actors believe something delusional, pointing this out is enough to make one an elitist, and suggesting that this wrong belief ought not be tolerated is enough to make one totalitarian. That this theoretical disposition is not actually sustainable is revealed by the ambivalence I have been tracking throughout this book. In order to preside over the marriage of democracy and emancipation, the democratic turn must forbid the right-wing demos from attending the ceremony.[27] But in discarding political education, we cede the ground on which we could establish a critique of right-wing politics that goes beyond random negation. Isaac Asimov famously denounced the "cult of ignorance"—that is, the overriding cultural sentiment that "my ignorance is just as good as your knowledge"[28]—in the United States. By dismissing an account of false consciousness because it counts some forms of consciousness as false, we give license to this cult of ignorance.

There is an even greater danger implicit in this position. When the critique of elitism—in itself a noble impulse—takes the form of denying the distance between a rational, informed perspective and a delusional one, the violence that produced the latter is also denied. The refusal to acknowledge an intellectual disparity on moral grounds covers over the *fact* of this disparity—and with it all of the painful realities that are its condition of possibility: unequal access to education, the time and resources necessary for reflection, and the opportunity to develop critical thought without incurring social isolation. As Asimov observes, "As soon as someone shouts 'elitist' it becomes clear that he or she is a closet elitist who is feeling guilty about having gone to school."[29] Such a criticism, in other words, represents a kind of internalized anti-intellectualism, presented as humility and legitimated by the categorical imperative of democracy. By relinquishing the right to speak authoritatively, one shrewdly avoids the unpleasant fact that the status quo systematically dispossesses most people of the right to speak authoritatively. In spite of its emancipatory intentions, then, the critique of elitism performs an apologetic function. The wounds of a society that all but forces its population into a state of ignorance and irrationality are magically healed by the Pyrrhic consolation that no one is entitled to name this state.

This is not a speculative, theoretical worry. It is true that since the solidification of the familiar Right/Left spectrum, the incompetence principle has been closely associated with the Right. It is commonplace to say that modern conservatism began with Burke,[30] and the "mass society" literature that I mentioned above (in particular both Ortega and Lippmann) had a profound influence on the postwar development of right-wing philosophy and politics, especially in the United States.[31] There is some historical justification, therefore, in the frequent assertion that the Left represents the democratic impulse and the critique of elitism while the Right represents an antidemocratic fear of the masses.[32] This understanding, however, overlooks an important sea change that has taken place in the last few decades. Slowly, from the 1960s to the 1980s, the complexion of right-wing political thought and practice shifted dramatically; it went from a Platonic-Burkean defense of order against the unruly masses to an avowed *appeal* to popular support against "elites" and "experts." No longer relying on notions of political expertise or the incompetence of common people, the "majoritarian turn" in (particularly American) conservatism saw the Right become "populist" and declare faith in "the silent majority."[33] Massive political successes—from Reagan to the 1994 "revolution" to Trump—followed soon after. This development has been answered in turn by the exposé genre described above, especially the Jacoby and Hochschild variety, which exposes a shockingly misinformed right-wing demos from a progressive perspective. Anti-elitism, once a source of anxiety for the Right, has become the torment of the other side. The fear of the masses has switched its political allegiance.

The shifting political function of the criticism of elitism, besides illustrating this project's larger point about the prevailing character of the demos, also reveals the dangers of equating ideology critique with Platonism. The indiscriminate rejection of ideology critique as elitist conveniently mirrors the anti-intellectualism that has become an important part of the Right's political identity. We can see this at work in a 1968 episode of *Firing Line*, where *National Review* founder William F. Buckley cross-examines Black Panther leader Eldridge Cleaver:

> Buckley: You don't seem to be willing to grant precisely that freedom—which you theoretically cherish—of people to decide their own political future. When Dick Gregory ran for mayor of New York [*sic*], two percent of the black community there voted for him. Ninety-eight percent voted for another candidate. Now wouldn't this suggest a rather overwhelming repudiation of the point of view of Dick Gregory by people he nevertheless understands himself to be—
>
> Cleaver: It seems to me that the people who did participate in that election are in vast need of political education.
>
> Buckley: In other words, people will be voting correctly when they vote as you tell them to, or as you "educate" them to.
>
> Cleaver: When they begin to vote in their own interests.
>
> [. . .]

Buckley: There is a Marcuse-ian edge to your thought—that people don't vote for their own best interests because they are constantly deceived, and that only revolutionary experience will cause them—

Cleaver: I don't think there's any doubt that people are deceived. They have the pigs of the mass media who manipulate information . . . essentially they distort reality, so that people have their heads filled with lying and vicious propaganda, and they're in no position to really function in a realistic manner.

Buckley: Why are you uniquely situated to have penetrated this national delusion?[34]

Notice how closely Buckley's position aligns with the criticisms put forth by Rancière and Laclau. I do not mean to suggest by this comparison that, if the Right articulates an idea, then that idea is automatically discredited. Rather, I mean to show that these criticisms could be applied by the Right, with total justification, to dissolve any emancipatory intervention of the Left insofar as that intervention depends on an account of "how things are" over and against "how things appear." A mistrust of "political correctness" and of the "experts" who issue warnings about climate change would be vindicated by this perspective. It would be excused from having to listen to that philosopher king, Charles Mills, insofar as he posits a division between reality (white supremacy) and the delusions that conceal that reality (white ignorance), by extension positing a division between those who perceive the truth and those who are deluded—an inherently "elitist" gesture. This would not be a case of the Right seizing and misappropriating an argument that properly belongs to radical democracy but, if we take Rancière and Laclau at their word, a legitimate application of the latter's own hypothesis. There is a serious risk that in rejecting all notions of ideology as elitist, we would inadvertently forfeit the legacy of Cleaver and resign ourselves to the legacy of Buckley.

I have argued throughout this book that, in order to make its categories function in a critical or emancipatory way, the categorical imperative of democracy needs to exclude certain political currents from consideration. Democratic iconography and radical politics can be made to coincide if political interventions with undesirable content can be nullified, without regard for theoretical consistency, as undemocratic or as outside the realm of the political altogether. Reading this ambivalence alongside the reflections developed in this chapter allows us to see that the charge of elitism more properly belongs to the categorical imperative of democracy than to an account of socially necessary delusion. Through its twin elitist-populist impulses, it simultaneously establishes an undemocratic "other" *and* renounces any intention of improving or enlightening this other. In dismissing both political education and large parts of the demos, the categorical imperative reduces its excluded object to a status *beneath* the political and thus beneath education, in the same way that Plato regarded the nonphilosophical "many" as incorrigible and therefore best managed by the guardians. As we have seen, Rancière, Mouffe, and Laclau (along with Fraser, Connolly, and Marchart) refuse to count examples of right-wing political movements as instantiations of their normative concepts, but they also explicitly and emphatically forsake the categories—political education and enlightenment on one hand, delusion and false consciousness on the other—through which these movements might be understood or confronted as anything other than pure exteriority. If we deny that political education is necessary, we are essentially consigning democracy's political other to a state of permanent undesirability and therefore reinstating an elitism of the most extreme form. When it comes to the xenophobes that Rancière pathologizes, those who do not play by "the rules of the game" according to Mouffe, or the undemocratic "people" in Laclau's framework, there is no room for recovery. They are not to be acknowledged as equals with valid political interventions, but neither are they to be shown the error of their ways. Ostensibly, then, they are only to be looked down upon or to serve as a warning notice for other, true democrats. If instead we grant that, in these truly undemocratic, antipolitical cases, education is permissible, then we have reintroduced the enlightened/unenlightened division that prompted this discussion in the first place, only with a somewhat modified content.

The categorical imperative of democracy participates in the aversion to the masses so common in political philosophy, but under the pretense of a protest against this aversion. It thereby bypasses the moment of truth in the incompetence principle and simultaneously forsakes its only claim to a cogent criticism of this principle. It does not feel a pressing need to engage with the positions of the xenophobe, the men's rights activist, or the climate skeptic, that is, to engage them as serious phenomena that demand theoretical and critical analysis. It is content to invoke these currents as cautionary examples, disqualify them without justification, and then proceed with its valorization of democratic iconography as if the right-wing demos did not exist. Democracy, we are told, means abandoning the idea that there is one correct "worldview," but at the same time, aspects of a particular worldview are taken for granted—as if we all acknowledge the basic reality of anthropogenic climate change, as if we all understand the history of colonialism and racial oppression, as if no one really believes that homosexuality is an affront to God. The theorists of democracy operate on the presupposition that all members of the political community are reflective, educated, and Left-leaning—that is, that all members of the community are like themselves. The partisans of difference return us to identity under another name. While their accounts might be applicable to cases of difference, disagreement, and contestation among well-educated progressives, they leave us in the dark when confronted with ignorance, anti-intellectualism, and delusion—and it is this darkness that desperately needs illumination today.

CONCLUDING REMARKS: THE POLITICS OF FORM AND THE POLITICS OF CONTENT

We might describe the critical intervention of the democratic categorical imperative as a rejection of the theoretical disposition represented by Rousseau, specifically his distinction between the "general will" and the collection of individual wills. If the political is autonomous and a matter of *doxa* rather than truth, then the conceit of a *correct* politics that is accessible by rational reflection, but which may not coincide with the prevailing character of the public or its various contingent eruptions, becomes anathema. But however much the categorical imperative of democracy would like to reject the idea of the general will, it is constantly reintroducing it. A narrow circumscription of proper political content runs alongside its emphatic refusal of the prerogative to determine this content. To tweak Foucault's line about Hegel, we may say that at the end of the categorical imperative's anti-Rousseauian path, there stands Rousseau, "motionless, waiting for us."[35]

This tension, which I have called the elitist-populist ambivalence, reveals the poverty of democracy as a critical category insofar as democratic iconography is always *formal* and never pledged to any particular content. The democratic turn cannot answer the question posed by Schmitt, which I used as the epigraph to this work: if our object is a particular kind of politics, of what value is the general democratic form?[36] We have seen throughout this book many attempts to bypass this problem, to suture the figure of democracy and the concerns of critical theory without leaving a remainder. I have argued that this attempt cannot be successful, and that the critical currency of democracy relies on a legerdemain whereby right-wing populism is excluded without adequate justification. The danger in this does not lie in some damage done to the blacklisted movements; on the contrary, the categorical imperative of democracy deprives us of the tools necessary to understand and confront the false and pathological political tendencies that, today, constitute nothing short of an existential threat. This is why I claim that an account of "false democracy," which suggests that things would be better if only they were more democratic, should be displaced by an account of "false demos," which asks after the social conditions of prevailing popular delusions without lapsing into a Platonic elitism.

If we regard the politics of the *Front national*, men's rights activism, or climate skepticism as unacceptable and undesirable (as we should), it is not on the basis of the extent to which these tendencies are democratic in form (they are) but on the basis of their political content. This content is *wrong*, not in the sense that between us and them there are different and incompatible Weltanschauungen locked in a hegemonic, agonistic struggle, but in the sense that they reflect ignorance, irrationality, and delusion, a false demos. Rejecting the categories of a politics of content as outmoded, elitist, or totalitarian requires a certain forgetting—a forgetting of the size and scope of these political movements and of the explicitly stated justifications behind them. There are socioeconomic factors mediating this lapse of memory, not least the relative insularity of academic work and academic life. But to understand is not to forgive: in the era of climate skepticism, a dereliction of critical intellectuals' duty of formulating theoretical insight into their historical conjuncture is not only an intellectual failure but also a moral and political one.

At the beginning of the last century, G. K. Chesterton defended his traditionalist conservative politics by appealing to a "democracy of the dead."[37] Without exactly intending it, the democratic turn appeals to a democracy of those who do not yet (and may never) exist. The decisive question then becomes: Who can appeal to a democracy of the living? If a critical theory of society interested in emancipation cannot do this without embroiling itself in the contradictions narrated by this book, then it must look for the terms of its analysis beyond the limits of democracy.

NOTES

PREFACE

1. For a discussion of the "turn to ethics," along with references, see Antonio Y. Vázquez-Arroyo, *Political Responsibility* (New York: Columbia University Press, 2016), passim.
2. Sheldon S. Wolin, *Fugitive Democracy and Other Essays* (Princeton, NJ: Princeton University Press, 2016), 236.

INTRODUCTION

1. For catalogs of different approaches, see Held, *Models of Democracy*, as well as Terchek and Conte, *Theories of Democracy*.
2. See Brown, "We're All Democrats Now." Recently some dissident voices in critical theory have challenged the deification of democracy (see Rockhill, *Counter-History of the Present*, 51–102, and Dean, *Democracy and Other Neoliberal Fantasies*, 77–94). Though my argument follows a different trajectory, I regard my intervention as consonant with theirs. In the analytic tradition, Brennan's *Against Democracy* has directly argued against democracy and in favor of "epistocracy." I discuss Brennan's argument in chapter 5 and differentiate it from my own conclusions.
3. With the possible exception of Diamond, all of the contemporary democratic theorists cited in the first chapter fit this basic pattern, as do the radical democrats discussed in chapter 3. See also Wolin's *Democracy Incorporated*, Rahman's *Democracy against Domination*, Mair's *Ruling the Void*, MacLean's *Democracy in Chains*, Urbinati's *Democracy Disfigured*, and Milligan's *The*

Next Democracy? At the extremity of this tendency is Derrida's evocation of "democracy to come." "The 'to-come' not only points to the promise," he writes, "but suggests that democracy will never exist, in the sense of a present existence: not because it will be deferred but because it will always remain aporetic in its structure" (*Rogues*, 86).

4. Dahl, *Dilemmas of Pluralist Democracy*, 5.

5. One conspicuous omission is the model of democracy developed by Habermas. This is mainly because I cannot add anything to the critiques of the dangers and limits of Habermas's formalism that have already been developed, for example, by Thompson's *The Domestication of Critical Theory*, 51–59; Abromeit's "Right-Wing Populism and the Limits of Normative Critical Theory"; and Chari's *A Political Economy of the Senses*, 73–77.

1. THE CATEGORICAL IMPERATIVE OF DEMOCRACY

1. May, *Contemporary Political Movements and the Thought of Jacques Rancière*, 1. See also Robin, *The Reactionary Mind*, 3–4.

2. West, *Democracy Matters*, 23.

3. Ibid., 2.

4. Diamond, *In Search of Democracy*, 25.

5. See ibid., 33–44.

6. Harris, 11. Cf. Howard, *The Specter of Democracy*; Abensour, *Democracy against the State*; and Lukács, *The Process of Democratization*.

7. The cover image depicts a number of small fists rising up to combat one large, looming fist aimed downward.

8. Harris, 13.

9. Wolff, 133–34.

10. Francisco Panizza, introduction to *Populism and the Mirror of Democracy*, 30–31.

11. Ochoa Espejo, "Power to Whom? The People between Procedure and Populism," 61. See also Arato, "Political Theology and Populism," Abts and Rummens, "Populism versus Democracy," and Müller, *What Is Populism?*

12. Mudde and Kaltwasser, "Exclusionary vs. Inclusionary Populism: Comparing Contemporary Europe and Latin America."

13. Panizza, 30–31.

14. Quoted in Jonsson, *A Brief History of the Masses*, 57.

15. While still maintaining democracy as a critical foundation, Brown has forcefully criticized the Left's turn to "the autonomy of the political," arguing that it amounts to a tacit acceptance of global capitalism (see "Sovereignty and the Return of the Repressed," esp. 260–64).

16. Ricœur, *Histoire et vérité*, 261. This essay inaugurated the distinction between *le politique* (usually translated as "the political") and *la politique* (usually translated as "politics"). I quote here the original French in my own translation, as in the translated English version, "la politique" is misleadingly rendered as "polity."

17. Lefort, *Democracy and Political Theory*, 19.

18. Ibid., 12. Cf. Barber: "Where there is truth or certain knowledge there need be no politics. . . . But democratic politics begins where certainty ends" ("Foundationalism and Democracy," 349). This is also the defense of democracy developed by Dahl, *Democracy and Its Critics*, 66–78.

19. See Ricœur, 279–82, and Lefort, 19–20.

20. These two theses are not mutually inclusive. The primary figures under discussion here take them to be reciprocally implicating, but contemporary philosophers from other domains of democratic theory have advanced arguments that maintain "political cognitivism" while insisting on the specificity of the political and on the value of democracy. See Estlund, *Democratic Authority*, and Copp, "Could Political Truth Be a Hazard for Democracy?"

21. I quote here a formulation from the *Grounding for the Metaphysics of Morals*, 45.

22. See, for example, the discussion of marriage and sexuality in *Lectures on Ethics*, 155–62.

23. Connolly, *Pluralism*, 4.

24. Ibid., 65.

25. See Connolly, "An Interview with William Connolly," 314, and *Pluralism*, 145–47.

26. Connolly, "An Interview," 330. Cf. *Pluralism*, 5, 8.

27. Fraser, *Scales of Justice*, 21.

28. Ibid., 26.

29. Ibid., 27.

30. Ibid., 59.

31. See Shear, "Ryan Brings the Tea Party to the Ticket." See also Skoçpol and Williamson, *The Tea Party and the Remaking of Republican Conservatism*.

32. Fraser, 63.

33. Ibid., 65.

34. Fraser analyzes shifts in "the feminist imagination" with reference to her theory of "frame setting" (see ibid., 100–115). Especially interesting for our discussion are her remarks on "evangelicalism" (110–12), where she refers to "the obvious trick" pulled on working-class women by the Right, that is, persuading them to believe the "patently false" idea that feminism is elitist.

35. See Stack, "How the 'War on Christmas' Controversy Was Created."

36. Fraser, 68.

37. Marchart, *Post-Foundational Political Thought*, 2.

38. See ibid., 13–18.

39. Ibid., 159–62. Honig's work (especially *Political Theory and the Displacement of Politics*) draws extensively on the autonomy and indeterminacy theses.

40. Marchart, *Post-Foundational Political Thought*, 157.

41. Ibid., 159.

42. Ibid., 157–58, 161.

43. See Wollheim, "A Paradox in the Theory of Democracy," esp. 78–79. Cf. Gutmann, *Liberal Equality*, 176–77. This observation is also made by Schumpeter in *Capitalism, Socialism, and Democracy*, 240–42. In Wollheim's paradox, we can see the nucleus of the debate (which preoccupies the analytic tradition) between "intrinsic" and "instrumental" models of democratic justification (see Arneson, "Democracy Is Not Intrinsically Just"; Landemore, *Democratic Reason*, 42–50; and Christiano, *The Rule of the Many*, 16–17). Recently, there have been some attempts to overcome the instrumental/intrinsic divide, such as Chambers, "Balancing Epistemic Quality and Equal Participation in a System Approach to Deliberative Democracy." For a critique of this tendency, see Yack, "Democracy and the Love of Truth."

44. It should also be clear that I am not discussing "the boundary problem" (described by Dahl, *Democracy and Its Critics*, 119–31, 193–209). This is not a matter of deciding where the demos begins and ends in a geographical sense or in the sense of selective enfranchisement; rather, the elitist-populist ambivalence selectively decides which instances of democratic politics *within the same boundaries* to valorize and which to decry.

45. West, 2.

46. See Neuman, "Scientists, General Public Have Divergent Views on Science," as well as Klein, *This Changes Everything*, 34–35.

47. See "Sen. Jim Inhofe on the Fight over Climate Change."

48. See Pew Research Center, "Public's Views on Human Evolution."

49. See Rockmore, "How Texas Teaches History"; Hinckley, "Texas: We Don't Need Academics to Fact-Check Our Textbooks"; Hartmann, "Why Oklahoma Lawmakers Voted to Ban AP U.S. History"; A. Wong, "History Class and the Fictions about Race in America"; and Woolf, "US 'Little Rebels' Protest against Changes to History Curriculum."

50. See "RNC 2012: Mitt Romney Speech to GOP Convention (Full Text)."

51. See "Fifth Republican Primary Debate."

52. See Wang, "'Post-Truth' Named 2016 Word of the Year by Oxford Dictionaries."

53. See Sinderbrand, "How Kellyanne Conway Ushered in the Era of 'Alternative Facts.'"

54. Tocqueville, *Democracy in America*, 16.

55. Cf. Pichardo, "New Social Movements," on the selectiveness of the critical literature on this subject.

56. Fishkin, *When the People Speak*, 14. See also Offe and Preuss, "Democratic Institutions and Moral Resources."

57. Cohen, "Moral Pluralism and Political Consensus," 282.

58. There is an ongoing debate within the deliberative tradition about the status of truth in the democratic procedure, that is, whether appeals to truth can or should be made during deliberation, if democracy can be justified because it leads to epistemologically superior political results, and if there is such a thing as an epistemologically superior political result. For helpful accounts of the theoretical landscape, see Landemore, "Beyond the Fact of Disagreement?"; Elkins and Norris, *Truth and Democracy*, and Geenens and Tinnevelt, *Does Truth Matter?*

59. That the demos may not want democracy in any strong sense is no mere academic paradox, as is illustrated by Hibbing and Theiss-Morse's *Stealth Democracy*. They argue, based on empirical data, that most people actually have no interest in participating in politics at all.

60. Schmitt, *The Crisis of Parliamentary Democracy*, 28–29.

61. Ibid., 28.

62. Habermas: "Discourse theory has the success of deliberative politics depend not on a collectively acting citizenry but on the institutionalization of the corresponding procedures and conditions of communication" ("Three Normative Models of Democracy," 27).

2. ARENDT'S ISLAND OF FREEDOM

1. See *The Human Condition*, 8–9, 177–80, 191–92, 246–47; and *Between Past and Future*, 168–69.

2. In *Hannah Arendt: A Reinterpretation of Her Political Thought*, Canovan notes that, in several unpublished manuscripts, Arendt claims that "action" began *before* the polis in Homeric heroism and warfare, and that it was even the opposite of speech (136–38).

3. In *Hannah Arendt and Karl Marx*, Weisman argues that "the implications of conceiving of humans as *animal laborans* sets the tone for all of Arendt's explicit writings on Marx" (9; cf. Pitkin, *Attack of the Blob*, 131–34). Interestingly enough, Marx agrees with Arendt on the relationship between necessity and freedom: "The realm of freedom really begins only where labour determined by necessity and external expediency ends; it lies by its very nature beyond the sphere of material production proper.... The true realm of

freedom, the development of human powers as an end in itself, begins beyond it, though it can only flourish with this realm of necessity as its basis" (see *Capital, Volume III*, 958–59).

4. See Hannah Arendt and Karl Jaspers, *Correspondence*, 160.

5. As for the accuracy of Arendt's reading of Marx, Weisman is correct to note that "Arendt never opens her thinking to the possibility that the now mostly discredited orthodoxy of the Second International that conflates the works of Marx and Engels is mistaken" (*Hannah Arendt and Karl Marx*, 2; cf. Pitkin, *Attack of the Blob*, 133). As we have seen, however, this misreading of Marx nevertheless reveals interesting dimensions of her own thought.

6. Canovan (*Hannah Arendt*) understands Arendt's ontology as a reaction to the rise of totalitarianism, claiming that "responses to the most dramatic events of her time lie at the very centre of Arendt's thought" (7). Totalitarian ideology, as the final chapter of *Origins* argues, is the marriage of two contradictory principles: that everything is determined, and that anything is possible. This is why Arendt privileges "action" but also insists upon the *limits* of the public sphere; she wants to maintain spontaneity and freedom while preserving a space upon which politics cannot encroach. In "Hannah Arendt: Democracy and the Political," Wolin also reads the categorical schemata of *The Human Condition* as an outgrowth of Arendt's analysis of totalitarianism, but draws the connection quite differently. Whereas Canovan mines Arendt's critique of totalitarian ideology for its democratic fruits (plural spaces, action, speech), Wolin traces the *antidemocratic* strain of this same critique (what the earlier Canovan called the "elitist" element). Wolin argues that the public/private dichotomy is fundamentally antidemocratic, and that "the rise of the social" is so troubling for Arendt precisely because it is democratizing.

7. In *Arendt and America*, King details a friendly exchange of letters and ideas between Arendt and the famous theorist of "mass society," David Riesman (109–24), and argues that the figure of "the masses" informs Arendt's idea of "the social" (123).

8. Gines, *Hannah Arendt and the Negro Question*, 56–57.

9. See Breen, "Violence and Power."

10. See Dietz, "Feminist Receptions of Hannah Arendt."

11. This is the reading articulated by Clarke, "Social Justice and Political Freedom"; and by Klein, "Fit to Enter the World."

12. Isaac writes that "[Arendt's] 'aristocracy' is an aristocracy of civic-mindedness, not a hereditary elite based on access to wealth" ("Oases in the Desert," 158). Bokiniec writes that "Arendt's elites are not from aristocratic leisure class, it is aristocracy of human spirit, of engagement, of action, elite that can be joined by anyone who is willing to participate in the public sphere" ("Is 'Polis' the Answer?" 79).

13. See Christodoulidis and Schaap, "Arendt's Constitutional Question"; Ince, "Bringing the Economy Back In"; Emden, "Carl Schmitt, Hannah Arendt, and the Limits of Liberalism"; Canovan, "The Contradictions of Hannah Arendt's Political Thought"; Gines, *Hannah Arendt and the Negro Question*; and Breen, "Violence and Power." Benhabib gives a concise account of this general problem with Arendt's "public space" (*The Reluctant Modernism of Hannah Arendt*, 74–85).

14. In addition to those already cited, see McClure, "The 'Social Question,' Again."

15. Bernstein, while acknowledging that "the rise of the social" for Arendt is basically the rise of the poor, writes: "To claim . . . that *every person* must be given the opportunity to participate in politics, transforms the question of society. For it means that we must honestly face the issue of how we can achieve or strive to realize a society where every person has the opportunity to engage in politics. This becomes (in Arendt's account) a primary *political* question" ("Rethinking the Social and the Political," 120). This reading is also articulated by Knauer ("Rethinking Arendt's 'Vita Activa,'" especially 192–93) and by Benhabib (*Reluctant Modernism*, 166).

16. Cf. Gündoğdu: "Arendt applauds Marx as a theorist who shows that poverty is not a necessary and natural outcome due to a law of scarcity but a political phenomenon that results from 'exploitation' or 'expropriation by force'" (*Rightlessness in an Age of Rights*, 68).

17. Several scholars have noted this curious element, including Gines (*Hannah Arendt and the Negro Question*, 52–55); Disch (*Hannah Arendt and the Limits of Philosophy*, 59, 62); and Bernasconi ("The Double Face of the Political and the Social," 19). Canovan (*Hannah Arendt*), while praising Arendt's "classical Republican" political values (212–27), acknowledges that her participatory vision is impossible for most given the economic status quo, noting that Arendt "had grave doubts" about "taking what had been the rights of a few and extending them to all humanity" (239–40); Canovan seems to buy the "technological development" argument (230–31).

18. Bernasconi, "The Double Face of the Political and the Social," 4.

19. See Nisbet, "Hannah Arendt and the American Revolution"; King, "Hannah Arendt and the Concept of Revolution in the 1960s"; Dossa, "Hannah Arendt on Billy Budd and Robespierre"; Feher, "Freedom and the 'Social Question'"; Barnouw, "Speech Regained"; and Disch, "How Could Hannah Arendt Glorify the American Revolution and Revile the French?"

20. Arendt herself notes that the "founding fathers" were "by no means for pure democracy" (*Hannah Arendt*, 333).

21. See also "Through centuries the extermination of native people went hand in hand with the colonization of the Americas, Australia and Africa" (*The Origins of Totalitarianism*, 440).

22. Bernasconi puts it well: "She gave the distinction between the social and the political a normative status which led her to applaud the American Revolution, among other things, for ignoring the social and economic cost paid by those who did not share in the prosperity they helped to produce for others" ("The Double Face of the Political and the Social," 15).

23. This antinomy shows up in interesting ways in the literature. In her discussion of *On Revolution* (*Reluctant Modernism*, 157–66), Benhabib characterizes Arendt's distinction between the political and the economic as a "hapless ontological divide" that obscures the fact that "there is no neutral and nonpolitical organization of the economic; all economy is political economy" (158). But she then immediately congratulates Arendt for an "insight into the interdependence of liberation and freedom, or rather the interdependence of socioeconomic conditions and of political freedom" (159). Holman also (inadvertently) articulates this tension: "The polis was thus not a rule of some over others, but an isonomy, which assumes not a natural equality of condition or capacity between all, but an equality between those who are understood as existing with one another in a specific relation as peers" (*Politics as Radical Creation*, 109). Of course, the ancient Athenians did not take their slaves to be their peers, no more than the American "founding fathers" granted isonomy to the poor or to women.

24. The isonomic theme of this disturbing essay acts as a point of departure for several critics intent on drawing out the limits and flaws of Arendt's political ontology. The most expansive attempt on this front is Gines. The central focus of her book is Arendt's recurring but not unambiguous antiblack racism, which she reads as a cipher for the constitutive limits of Arendt's work as a whole. In "Hannah Arendt and the Liberal Tradition," Muhlmann makes a similar point about that piece (133–36). Other accounts of Arendt's racism include Johnson's "Reading between the Lines," which argues that Arendt is even more racist than Gines gives her credit for; and Norton's "Heart of Darkness," which offers a thoroughgoing account of her troubled relation to Africa and African Americans in general.

25. As Gines notes, Arendt develops a cogent argument against "abstract humanism" (close to the kind of isonomy she defends in the Little Rock essay) whenever it is a question of Jewish identity or social status, but this argument does not seem to extend to other "social" categories like "African American" (*Hannah Arendt and the Negro Question*, 6–11). This points to "glaring disjunctions" and "incongruities" (10) in Arendt's ontology. Cf. Bernasconi, "The Double Face of the Political and the Social," 4.

26. A good example of this tack is Disch (*Limits of Philosophy*, 172–203), who uses this analysis as "a way to break with Arendt's humanism on her own terms" (171).

27. Arendt's most sustained attempt to relate her political ontology to the democratic tradition is the essay "Nation-State and Democracy," found in *Thinking without a Bannister*, 255–61.

28. See Wood, *Democracy against Capitalism*, 181–237.

29. Disch (*Limits of Philosophy*, 31–40); Benhabib (*Reluctant Modernism*, 104–7, 146); Canovan (*Hannah Arendt*, 205ff); Curthoys ("The Refractory Legacy of Algerian Decolonization," 111); Hirsch ("The Promise of the Unforgiven," 55); and Flathman (*Pluralism and Liberal Democracy*, 53–75).

30. In a book synthesizing Arendt and Marcuse, for instance, Holman argues that while Marcuse's work should act as a corrective to Arendt's exclusion of "social" issues from public debate, Marcuse's Marxism likewise needs an Arendtian corrective insofar as it (according to Holman) conceives of politics as "instrumentally aimed at the achievement of a certain extrinsic goal" rather than as "a performative good in itself" (*Politics as Radical Creation*, 4). See also Wenman, *Agonistic Democracy*; Kalyvas, *Democracy and the Politics of the Extraordinary*; Honig, *Political Theory and the Displacement of Politics*; Disch, *Hannah Arendt and the Limits of Philosophy*; Hirsch, "The Promise of the Unforgiven,"; Isaac, "Oases in the Desert"; Heather and Stolz, "Hannah Arendt and the Problem of Critical Theory"; Buckler, *Hannah Arendt and Political Theory*; and Markell, "The Rule of the People."

31. Cf. Canovan, "Contradictions," 19.

32. Bernstein, "Rethinking the Social and the Political," 121.

33. Cf. Sari, at the conclusion of her essay "Arendt, Truth, and Epistemic Responsibility": "Arendt's articulation of a political decision can be understood as a decision of a 'we' to keep the space of appearance open, which depends on meaningful and responsible human togetherness in the formation and exchange of opinions *informed by the acknowledgment of factual truths about the world* that give us our bearings" (170, emphasis mine).

34. D'Entrèves: "Against Plato and Hobbes, who denigrated the role of opinion in political matters, Arendt reasserts the value and importance of political discourse, of *deliberation* and *persuasion*, and thus of a politics that acknowledges difference and the plurality of opinions" ("Arendt's Theory of Judgment," 257–58).

35. See, respectively, Disch (*Limits of Philosophy*, 170–71); Canovan (*Hannah Arendt*, 201–2); Horowitz, *Hannah Arendt: Radical Conservative*; Muhlmann; Honig (*Displacement*, 76–125); Hirsch (65–73); and Benhabib (*Reluctant Modernism*).

3. DEMOCRACY AT ITS LIMITS

1. Breaugh et al., *Thinking Radical Democracy*, 4.
2. "It would be impossible to speak of a radically democratic return of the political in France without [Arendt's] intervention" (ibid., 21).
3. Wenman, for example, counts Badiou and Žižek along with Rancière and Laclau as "radical democrats" and opposes them to the "agonistic democrats" (among whom he counts Mouffe). See "Laclau or Mouffe?"
4. See *Disagreement*, 48–52; and *On the Shores of Politics*, 16, 51. Cf. Chambers: "[For Rancière] we cannot derive politics from any essential features of the human subject[. . . .] Rancière rejects all ontology" (*The Lessons of Rancière*, 17).
5. Rancière almost always uses *la politique* to refer to politics/the political (as opposed to *la police*). He almost never makes use of the distinction between *la politique* (usually translated as "politics") and *le politique* (usually translated as "the political"). Among the few exceptions in Rancière's case is *Recognition or Disagreement*, 125, where he writes that "the political" (*le politique*) "consists in the tension between the police order . . . and the enactment of the egalitarian principle." This supports Marchart's claim that, for Rancière, *le politique* represents the point of collision between *la politique* and *la police* (see "The Second Return of the Political"). Thus, while it is not a major part of his theory, Chambers is wrong to deny altogether that Rancière makes use of the *la/le* distinction. See *The Lessons of Rancière*, 50–57. At the same time, we should recognize that Rancière does not always use his key term consistently, as is pointed out by Rockhill in *Radical History and the Politics of Art*, 165–67.
6. See *On the Shores of Politics*, 45, 50, 89; *Disagreement*, 133; *Hatred of Democracy*, 16, 23, 38, 52–53, 58, 61.
7. "Politics is first of all a sphere of appearance" ("Democracy, Dissensus and the Aesthetics of Class Struggle," 296).
8. "The only kind of dialogue compatible with democracy is one where the parties hear one another but do not agree with one another, the kind of dialogue which takes place on the stage" (*On the Shores of Politics*, 102).
9. "By *subjectification* I mean the production through a series of actions of a body and a capacity for enunciation not previously identifiable within a given field of experience, whose identification is thus part of the reconfiguration of the field of experience" (*Disagreement*, 35). "Parties do not exist prior to the declaration of a wrong" (*Disagreement*, 39).
10. See his contribution to *Democracy in What State?* collection: "Democracies against Democracy"; cf. *On the Shores of Politics*, 60–61.
11. Chambers: "Politics can do nothing else than this: renegotiate and reconfigure the police order" (*The Lessons of Rancière*, 65). This is why Rancière

sometimes criticizes the true/false democracy dichotomy, as in *On the Shores of Politics*, 39-40. Cf. Tanke: "For Rancière, the police is a distribution of the sensible that denies the ability of the part to supplement the *polis* with a claim of equality" (*Jacques Rancière*, 45). Tanke's interpretation renders the term "police" as a pejorative and suggests, contrary to Rancière, that it is possible to live in a permanent state of democracy.

12. For a critique of Rancière's formalism along different lines than mine, see Chari, *A Political Economy of the Senses*, 54–60.

13. Labelle offers an interpretation of this claim by Rancière: "The cleavage we find between a perfectly integrated society and its monstrous and unsayable otherness allows for the proliferation of neo-liberal and populist rhetoric which states that if the immigrant, the homeless or the unemployed remain unassimilated into society, it is simply by choice, in other words it is due to their refusal to be included" ("Two Refoundation Projects of Democracy in Contemporary French Philosophy," 94). But this presupposes that racist/xenophobic populist movements represent established homogeneity against multiplicity or plurality, bypassing the possibility that, according to their own speech, these movements represent "contestations" of the false homogeneity of liberal progressivism/multiculturalism.

14. Theorists who "apply" Rancière's ideas to concrete cases tend to do the same; for instance, see every example provided by May in *Contemporary Political Movements and the Thought of Jacques Rancière*. See also Lorey, "The 2011 Occupy Movements."

15. Though with a markedly different theoretical agenda, Marchart ("The Second Return of the Political") has also criticized Rancière for what he deems the "emancipatory apriorism" of his work: "The idea of politics being egalitarian *eo ipso*. Politics, for Rancière . . . is either egalitarian, *or it is not politics*" (135).

16. In the sixth thesis on politics, however, Rancière contrasts "two ways of counting the parts of the community"—a distribution of parts with no remainder (the police) and the count of those who have no part (politics).

17. Tanke: "The key question with respect to any distribution of the sensible is to know whether it is founded upon equality or inequality" (*Jacques Rancière*, 2). If Rancière says that equality is the disruption of *any* distribution, how can a distribution be *founded* on equality?

18. Cf. "Jacques Rancière": "A common thread throughout my work is . . . attention to the ways in which arguments circulate between reasons of order and the reasons of those claim to attack it" (240).

19. In "Rancière's Leftism, or, Politics and Its Discontents," Bosteels perceptively argues that Rancière inadvertently reproduces the "speculative Left-

ism" that he criticizes in others with his opposition between "police fictions" and "true politics."

20. The extent to which Rancière's notion of "the equality of intelligences" should be taken literally is the subject of scholarly debate. In *The Political Thought of Jacques Rancière*, May argues that, for Rancière, "the equality of anyone and everyone" is a necessary presupposition for progressive politics and does not reflect an actual universal capacity to learn any subject matter. Magnusson, however, insists against May that the term should be taken literally. See her "A Politics in Writing."

21. Rancière explicitly names this connection in "A Few Remarks on the Method of Jacques Rancière," 115.

22. Of course, the claim that there is a *necessary* disparity between the knowledge of intellectuals and the ignorance of "the masses" is substantially different from the claim that the categories of truth, illusion, knowledge, and ignorance are essential for an emancipatory politics. Rancière, however, collapses this distinction—I will return to this point at length in chapter 5.

23. Rancière explores these issues at more length in *Staging the People: The Proletarian and His Double* and *The Intellectual and His People: Staging the People Volume 2*. For more on his critique of "explication," see Tanke (*Jacques Rancière*, 7–12); Biesta, "A New Logic of Emancipation"; Davis, *Jacques Rancière* (15–25); and Mecchia, "Philosophy and Its Poor."

24. He also rejects the label "intellectual" insofar as it distinguishes certain political actors over and against others. See *Moments Politiques*, 65–68.

25. Immediately after this comment, however, he proceeds to give an account of Plato's "lie" of a necessary distribution of parts that justifies domination.

26. Rancière's rejection of the truth/illusion approach extends even to "postmodern" criticisms of this model, which he claims simply reproduce its basic logic (see *The Emancipated Spectator*, 25–49).

27. See Hesse, "Men's Rights Activists"; Fell, "Toxic Appeal"; and Landsbaum, "Men's Rights Activists Are Flocking to the Alt Right."

28. Cf. "Seven Ways to Spread Racist Ideas in France" (*Moments Politiques*, 55–58), an ironic Swiftian piece in which Rancière suggests that racist ideas are attributable more to intellectuals' assumption that racism is prevalent than to its actual prevalence among the demos.

29. Tanke: "One might read many of Rancière's core convictions . . . as emerging through a reversal of his former teacher's positions" (*Jacques Rancière*, 10).

30. Chambers attempts to dissociate Rancière from Arendt insofar as the latter rejects the "conception of politics as the production of a pure, protected political sphere" (*The Lessons of Rancière*, 39–49). While it is true that

Rancière escapes some of Arendt's elitist tendencies, I hope to have shown in this section that the distance between them is not so decisive as Chambers suggests.

31. Vasilev notes that Mouffe's characterization of necessary antagonism, which "upholds conflict as an end in itself," has a disquietingly ahistorical and abstract character. See "On Mouffe's Agonism."

32. Mouffe draws from Rancière favorably (*On the Political*, 29).

33. As we will see, Mouffe usually cites Arendt positively. In *Agonistics*, however, she criticizes Arendt for still believing in the possibility of "consensus," referring to Arendt's political model as "agonism without antagonism" (*Agonistics*, 9–10). For Mouffe, antagonism is never entirely eliminable. Cf. Breckman: "The presiding figure in Mouffe's later work is not Schmitt, but Hannah Arendt" (*Adventures of the Symbolic*, 213).

34. I will explain this term when I discuss *Hegemony and Socialist Strategy*, below.

35. "Political questions are not mere technical issues to be solved by experts. Properly political questions always involve decisions which require us to make a choice between conflicting alternatives" (*On the Political*, 10, cf. *On the Political*, 104).

36. In *Laclau and Mouffe*, Smith notes that "reactionary causes" often "appropriate key elements from the democratic tradition," but "in actuality, the religious right, neo-conservatives and new racists only pretend to champion liberal democratic rights and freedoms in order to defend traditional class, race, gender and sexual inequalities" (178). Again, positing a difference between "actuality" and certain "articulations" suddenly becomes permissible when we are discussing the Right. In this vein, Leggett comments on Mouffe's equivocal relation to empirical referents, observing that she oscillates between "realist" and "anti-realist" positions and arguing that radical democracy should be supplemented by a nondiscursive account of "society" ("Restoring Society to Post-Structuralist Politics," 310–14).

37. See "Marine Le Pen." Cf. Mouffe: "It is the idea of equality which provides the backbone of the left vision while the right . . . has always condoned diverse forms of inequality" (*The Democratic Paradox*, 123).

38. Cf. the way Mouffe describes "communitarian" critics of liberalism such as McIntyre and Sandel: "[They] believe that a critique of liberal individualism necessarily implies the rejection of pluralism. So, they end up by proposing to return to a politics of the common good based on shared moral values" ("Liberalism and Modern Democracy," 186–87).

39. Torfing: "The extension of the Democratic Revolution to still new areas of society provides sufficient condition for the creation of democratic antagonism, but it does not predetermine how these democratic antagonisms are to

be articulated. Democratic antagonisms do not necessarily lead to democratic struggles as they can be articulated with different kinds of discourse, even with anti-democratic right-wing discourses demanding 'less state and more market'" (*New Theories of Discourse*, 257). What in Mouffe's (or Laclau's) theory accounts for a distinction between democratic antagonisms and democratic struggles? Why are demands for less state and more market automatically antidemocratic?

40. See "France's Marine Le Pen."

41. By this I do not merely mean to point out, with Dean (*Democracy and Other Neoliberal Fantasies*), that "the right speaks the language of democracy" (73). I mean that Le Pen's intervention *is* democratic as Mouffe understands democracy.

42. In "The Illusion of Purity," Thaler notes the "performative contradiction" (787) involved in Mouffe's affirmation of "multipolarity" over and against cosmopolitan universalism: it still requires universalizing the moral principle of multipolarity understood in a specific and precise way. Cf. Jones: "How is it that Mouffe believes that a rational consensus is impossible, yet argues that the same parties are able to pledge allegiance to the ethico-political principles of liberal democracy, namely liberty and equality?" ("Chantal Mouffe's Agonistic Project," 22). Jones addresses this tension by appealing to a Mouffian distinction between "rational consensus" and "conflictual consensus"—but this only relocates the problem and does not solve it. As we have said, what counts as a violation of "the rules of the game" will depend upon the content of one's politics.

43. In "Laclau or Mouffe?" Wenman cautions against conflating Mouffe and Laclau. He argues that after establishing a common framework in *Hegemony and Socialist Strategy*, the two authors proceed in markedly different directions. While I think the case is overstated, I hope I have avoided the charge of conflation by treating Mouffe's work in a separate section; I introduce *Hegemony and Socialist Strategy* at this juncture because, in my reading, Laclau's subsequent work is more reliant on the theoretical framework outlined there than is Mouffe's. When I write "Laclau and Mouffe . . . ," I refer only to what is specified in *Hegemony and Socialist Strategy*.

44. Laclau first uses the term "hegemonic articulation" in *Politics and Ideology in Marxist Theory*, 100–101. In that early work, he still posits the reality, if not the determinacy, of class struggle: "To deny the dialectic between 'the people' and classes would be, then, to deny the ideological class struggle" (195). This is exactly what the later Laclau does.

45. In this section I can only scratch the surface of the theoretical issues with the basic argumentative structure of *Hegemony and Socialist Strategy*. Several detailed dissections of the book (Hunter; Rustin; Aronowitz) were

NOTES

published shortly after its appearance. Also worth mentioning in this context is Laclau and Mouffe's colorful exchange (PM) with Geras ("Post-Marxism?" and "Ex-Marxism without Substance"). For an account of the book's reception, see Sim, *Post-Marxism*, 34–47. In my estimation, the two strongest overall critiques of *Hegemony and Socialist Strategy* can be found in Wood (*The Retreat from Class*, 43–89) and Osborne, "Radicalism without Limit?"

46. Norris ("Against Antagonism" and "Ernesto Laclau and the Logic of 'the Political'") offers compelling critiques of Laclau's formalistic projection of the political into the ontological realm, arguing that it ultimately comes to contradict his commitments to democracy and to the Left. Kingsbury ("Populism as Post-Politics") argues along these lines as well, observing that the formalism involved in Laclau's understanding of "democracy" comes to resemble the "post-political" liberalism that he so opposes.

47. See for example, *New Reflections on the Revolution of Our Time*, 14–15.

48. See *Emancipation(s)*, 16–17; *New Reflections on the Revolution of Our Time*, 77–78, 91–92; and "Post-Marxism without Apologies," 129.

49. See also *Emancipation(s)*, 33, 57; and "Post-Marxism without Apologies," 129.

50. Sim highlights this passage and observes that Laclau and Mouffe seem to be breaking their own rules and reverting back to "essentialism" here (29–30). Smith offers a commentary on this passage (19–25) but begins with the claim that "capitalism, by its very nature, systematically denies large sections of the population access to the resources necessary for self-determination" (19)—forgetting, first, that for radical democratic theory "capitalism" has no "very nature," and second, that the opposite articulation of the relationship between capitalism and subordination ("capitalism helps to overcome relations of subordination by giving everyone equal opportunity for advancement") could be just as "democratic."

51. Without intending to criticize radical democracy, Lowndes demonstrates this point by giving an account of George Wallace's ultraright populism while staying faithful to Laclau's vocabulary. See "From Founding Violence to Political Hegemony."

52. Laclau criticizes Žižek for structuring his discourse "around entities—'class, class struggle, capitalism'—which are largely fetishes dispossessed of any precise meaning" (*Contingency, Hegemony, and Universality*, 201). One wonders if he would likewise criticize a feminist theorist for appealing to the "fetishes" of gender, patriarchy, or women's struggle. Cf. the discussion of the "sex/gender system" in *Hegemony and Socialist Strategy*, 103–4.

53. While trying to save Laclau and Mouffe from this dilemma, Smith effectively demonstrates the *petito principii* involved: "[Laclau and Mouffe] impose strict conditions on the value of difference for radical democracy. Difference

should be celebrated as a positive good, but only insofar as difference does not promote domination and inequality[. . . .]For radical democratic pluralism, only those fragments of the social movement that uphold democratic principles should be valued as progressive differences" (34). The problem we have been narrating—namely, that what constitutes "domination" will depend upon what "hegemonic articulation" one prefers, and that therefore the former cannot be used as a criterion to adjudicate acceptable and unacceptable forms of the latter—is obscured by Smith when she introduces the new term "structural position" to the radical democratic vocabulary, distinguishing it from "subject position": "A 'subject position' refers to the ensemble of beliefs through which an individual interprets and responds to her structural positions within a social formation" (*Laclau and Mouffe*, 58). But to claim that there are *given* "structural positions" within an intelligible, pre-discursive "social formation" that are then *interpreted* is to have already abandoned radical democracy as Laclau and Mouffe understand it, to revert back to the "thought/reality opposition." She acknowledges later in the book that for Laclau and Mouffe, "political discourses and identities are wholly constituted through articulation" (ibid., 87), however inconsistent this is with the addition of the "structural position" category.

54. This is the conclusion of Torfing's chapter (*New Theories of Discourse*, 191–209) on the relation between the discourse theory of Laclau and Mouffe and racist nationalism.

55. See "Debate on Immigration, Refugees in Polish Parliament."

56. "Destroying the hierarchies on which sexual or racial discrimination is based will, at some point, always require the construction of other exclusions for collective identities to be able to emerge" (*New Reflections on the Revolution of Our Time*, 33).

57. Critchley: "If all societies are *tacitly hegemonic*, then the distinguishing feature of democratic society is that it is *explicitly hegemonic*. Democracy is thus the name for that political form of society that makes explicit the contingency of its foundations" ("Is There a Normative Deficit in the Theory of Hegemony?" 115). Breckman: "The constitution of 'objectivity' seems to be a condition of all social movements, thereby rendering all of them instances of false consciousness [in Laclau's terms.] . . . [H]ow many social movements could survive in the full light of Laclau and Mouffe's knowledge?" (*Adventures of the Symbolic*, 206).

58. In "Hegemony, Political Subjectivity, and Radical Democracy," Howarth comments on the problem of normativity in Laclau's theory (269–71). He argues that the normative force of Laclau's analysis lies in the distinction between democratic and antidemocratic "articulations." But in the midst of making this argument, he notes that "an anti-foundational [i.e., democratic] per-

spective does not determine a certain set of political and ethical positions, though it does rule some positions out—those based on essentialist presuppositions for example." If an antifoundational articulation can be "anti-democratic," it has not been made clear how.

59. Keenan: "What both Arendt and Laclau and Mouffe highlight is the importance to democratic politics of recognizing and in some way affirming . . . collective uncertainty as the basic condition of democratic freedom" (*Democracy in Question*, 19).

4. FROM "FALSE DEMOCRACY" TO FALSE DEMOS

1. In response to the increasing visibility of right-wing populism, some scholars have called for a return to "first generation" Frankfurt School critical theory, arguing that the development represented by Habermas inhibits our understanding of this phenomenon and therefore possible responses to it. See Abromeit, "Critical Theory and the Persistence of Right-Wing Populism," and "Right-Wing Populism and the Limits of Normative Critical Theory," as well as O'Kane, "A Hostile World." I regard this chapter as consonant with these efforts; while they focus more on *The Authoritarian Personality*, I foreground "Opinion Delusion Society" and Marcuse's "Repressive Tolerance" to expand and enrich the analysis. In his insightful "The Authoritarian Personality Revisited," Gordon notes that this psychological text is fraught with methodological problems that Adorno himself criticized.

2. Adorno elaborates the "model" approach in several places, most helpfully in *An Introduction to Dialectics*, 169–70.

3. The one source I have found that explores the contradiction between democratic values and the pressing urgencies of climate action is Kitcher's "Plato's Revenge," where he writes that "sustaining democracy seems incompatible with saving our planet." The limitation of Kitcher's approach is that he does not situate climate denial in terms of its social necessity; this is what an account informed by the critical theory of Adorno and Marcuse makes possible. The inadequacy of the democratic form for confronting the climate crisis is also mentioned in Malm, *The Progress of This Storm*, 152; and Mann and Wainwright, *Climate Leviathan*, 182.

4. Cf. the second type of epistemology of ignorance discussed by Alcoff, which she attributes to Harding. See "Epistemologies of Ignorance: Three Types," 43–47.

5. See Popper, *The Open Society and Its Enemies*, 546.

6. Dunlap and McCright: "By creating the appearance of controversy within the *public realm*, [climate] denialists are able to appeal to values such as freedom of speech, fairness to both sides, and respecting minority viewpoints to add legitimacy to their claims." See "Challenging Climate Change," 309.

7. In the United States, prominent right-wing politicians often claim, in spite of all evidence, that there is "no consensus" among scientists (see Oreskes and Conway, *Merchants of Doubt*, 213). But while one major party outright denies climate change (see E. Wong, "Trump Has Called Climate Change a Chinese Hoax"), the other acknowledges it nominally while continuing to act as if nothing had changed (see Prasad et al., "Obama's Dirty Secret").

8. Lichtman: "Marcuse's position becomes identical with the old Scholastic dogma that error has no right. . . . Marcuse . . . opens himself to the charge of despotism or totalitarianism which was so widely and passionately brought against him. For he is clearly required to nominate some elite to break the hold of one-dimensional consciousness and lead the multitude from false-consciousness to emancipation" ("Repressive Tolerance," 201–2). Long dismissed on these grounds, Fopp has recently defended the essay as an exercise in social epistemology. See "Herbert Marcuse's 'Repressive Tolerance' and His Critics."

9. "I have been fully aware of the danger involved in my position; I believe that it is infinitely smaller than the danger we risk if we continue to tolerate the forces which drag this country ever deeper into war, waste, and violence" (*Marxism, Revolution, and Utopia*, 221).

10. "We would have to conclude that liberation would mean subversion against the will and against the prevailing interests of the great majority of the people" (*An Essay on Liberation*, 17). Cf. the discussion of democracy in *An Essay on Liberation*, 65–71.

11. Adorno articulates this critique in several places (*Negative Dialectics*, 320, *Lectures on Negative Dialectics*, 8–9); there is an especially lucid discussion of the use/exchange contradiction, reification, and the concept of "society" in *Introduction to Sociology*, 27–34.

12. Hammer: "It is the commodity form which, in the final instance, explains, in both Lukács, Benjamin, and Adorno, the deformations of contemporary social reproduction" (*Adorno and the Political*, 29). The same can be said for Marcuse (see esp. *Reason and Revolution*, 280–322, and *Counterrevolution and Revolt*, 15–20).

13. For Adorno, the critical capacity of the category of need does not lie in a distinction between "social and natural, primary and secondary, correct and false" needs but in "the question of the *suffering* of the vast majority of all humans on earth. If we produced that which *all* humans now most urgently need, then we would be relieved of inflated social-psychological concerns

about the legitimacy of their needs." See "Theses on Need," 104. Cf. *Minima Moralia*, 155–57.

14. In *Freedom in the Anthropocene*, Stoner and Melathopoulos connect the disconcerting political situation of the anthropocene—that human beings have created climate change but seem completely unable to stop it—to the theory of reification in Lukács, Adorno, and Postone. In *Imperiled Life*, Sethness-Castro applies Adorno's "new categorical imperative" to the present climate crisis (111–35). My argument below complements these analyses by situating climate *skepticism* in terms of Adorno's account of social delusion.

15. Livingstone translates "pseudos," *täuschung*, and *Wahn* indiscriminately as "delusion." For the sake of precision, I have translated the terms before the indented quote myself, from *Zur Lehre von der Geschichte und von der Freiheit*, 154–55. I have also altered the translation in the indented quote where necessary.

16. The phrase "socially necessary illusion" in the translation of *Lectures on Negative Dialectics* (100) is actually *gesellschaftlich notwendiger Schein* (147)—better rendered as "socially necessary appearance" or "semblance" to avoid confusion with Freud's "illusion." The same goes for the translation of "necessary illusion" in *An Introduction to Dialectics* (3). The word *Schein* is also used in *Negative Dialectics* (196) but translated there as "delusion" (197), which is equally misleading in a context where we are also invoking the Freudian terminology.

17. As Schweickart points out, relatively few of the corporations funding and propagating climate denial are directly linked to the fossil fuel industry (16). He also sums up the logic of socially necessary delusion in two sentences: "They know, but they don't know. They can't afford to know" (17). See "Capitalism vs. the Climate."

18. See Klein, *This Changes Everything*; Dunlap and McCright, "Challenging Climate Change"; Li, "The 21st Century"; Parr, *The Wrath of Capital*; Foster et al., *The Ecological Rift*; Malm, *Fossil Capital*; Hornborg, "Cornucopia or Zero-Sum Game?"; and Wright and Nyberg, *Climate Change, Capitalism, and Corporations*.

19. See also the discussion of the relationship between rationality and irrationality in *The Stars Down to Earth*, esp. 152–66. For a discussion of this antagonism as it relates to climate change, see Short, "Natural History, Sovereign Power, and Global Warming," 257–62. Cf. Jamieson: "We are bringing about a climate change that we do not want but do not know how to stop. Human action is the driver, but it seems that things, not people, are in control. . . . Instead of humanity rationally governing the world and itself, we are at the mercy of monsters that we have created" (*Reason in a Dark Time*, 1). Despite this, Jamieson leaves the economic system (as opposed to the actions

of particular corporations) entirely to one side in his analysis. The political economy of climate denial (and inaction) is also left out of Gardiner's *A Perfect Moral Storm*, which construes climate failure as an "ethical tragedy" stemming from "moral corruption" (see esp. 301–38).

20. From a staunchly empirical social-psychological point of view, Feygina et al. track a negative correlation, in individual subjects, between feelings of protectiveness over the status quo and acknowledgment of the severity of anthropogenic climate change, concluding that "*system justification motivation is a significant obstacle to attaining pro-environmental change*" (328, my italics). See "System Justification, the Denial of Global Warming, and the Possibility of 'System Sanctioned Change.'"

21. See Klein, *This Changes Everything*, 31–63.

22. In "Ideological Obstacles to Effective Climate Policy," Gunderson et al. insightfully point out that even prevailing "responses" to the climate crisis ("green growth" models and other forms of "sustainable capitalism") have an ideological character insofar as they function to obscure the "systemic socio-ecological contradictions" at the root of the problem. There is only a difference in degree between outright climate skepticism and optimism about the possibility of "market-based solutions"—they are both "strategies for denial" (134). At the end of the article, Gunderson et al. turn to Marcuse's account of "new technology" as an alternative to the ideological responses. Cf. the "stages of denial" as described by Mann and Toles, *The Madhouse Effect*, 53–67.

23. Cf. the famous opening sentence of *One-Dimensional Man*. Notice that Marcuse identifies a "democratic unfreedom" rather than an antidemocratic stifling of freedom.

24. Despite their abiding suspicion of the demos, Adorno and Marcuse still occasionally make use of the "false democracy" argument, that is, that present conditions prevent the establishment of a "true democracy" (e.g., *History and Freedom*, 76; *An Essay on Liberation*, 13, and Adorno's essay "Democratic Leadership and Mass Manipulation"). This leads some Adorno commentators to characterize his project as essentially democratic (Mariotti, *Adorno and Democracy*; and Douglas, "Democratic Darkness and Adorno's Redemptive Criticism"). At the same time, scholars who explore the status of democracy in Adorno consistently express a tension, in Heins's formulation, "between the ideal of moral and aesthetic standards being handed down authoritatively and the alternative ideal of norms devised in common by a community of actors and perceivers" ("Saying Things That Hurt," 79). Though she insists on reading Adorno as a democratic thinker, Mariotti expresses this tension also: "Adorno wants to fulfill the promise of democracy by fostering the kind of dispositional and intellectual, social and psychic, change on the part of individuals that would allow 'the people' to truly wield power and rule, for the *demos* to have

kratos" (6). This is the equivocation I have been tracking throughout this project: if democracy is only desirable when the demos has a certain "dispositional and intellectual, social and psychic" makeup, then democracy is not an end in itself. While I would not describe Adorno's (or Marcuse's) project as *anti*democratic, it seems to me that the figure of democracy does not and cannot do the foundational critical work.

25. Of course, Adorno and Marcuse are dialectical thinkers and as such do not conceive of theory as a simple transcription or interpretation of empirical data. One could sum up the intellectual project of the Frankfurt School as a protest against positivist social science. At the same time, they insist that theory maintain a close relationship with its object, and that the former must be guided by the latter without abandoning its distance from it. Adorno even argues that there is a necessary positivist *moment* in dialectical thinking (*An Introduction to Dialectics*, 116–18; cf. *Counterrevolution and Revolt*, 34).

26. In my estimation, Larraín (*The Concept of Ideology* and *Marxism and Ideology*) offers the best panoramic synthesis of the concept of ideology. For an account of ideology critique's fall from grace, see Žižek's introduction to *Mapping Ideology*.

27. Adorno discusses ideology and false consciousness in numerous places, most directly (though not necessarily most productively) in "Beitrag zur Ideologienlehre" (translated as "Ideology" in *Aspects of Sociology*). For accounts of Adorno's use of ideology, see Jarvis, *Adorno*, 65–67; and Cook, "Adorno, Ideology, and Ideology Critique." Marcuse uses the terminology in a similar way; for an account of Marcuse's use of ideology, see Kellner, *Herbert Marcuse and the Crisis of Marxism*, 254–55.

28. Geuss (*The Idea of a Critical Theory*, 12–22) and Morris (*Knowledge and Ideology*, 5–15) distinguish between "epistemic," "functional," and "genetic" forms of ideology critique. Adorno and Marcuse's explanation of "socially necessary delusion" contains elements of all three forms: such delusions are ideological because they are false, because they function to sustain a bad status quo, and because they owe their prevalence (if not necessarily their origin) to the necessity of sustaining this status quo.

29. See, respectively, "Resurrecting the Rationality of Ideology Critique," "Rethinking Ideology," and "Ideology Critique from Hegel and Marx to Critical Theory." All three focus on Adorno's account, specifically his formulation (from the "Ideology" essay) that ideology is "consciousness which is objectively necessary and yet at the same time false . . . the intertwining of truth and falsehood" (189).

30. Rorty, "Feminism, Ideology, and Deconstruction: A Pragmatist View," 229.

31. Foucault, *Power/Knowledge*, 118. This line of critique is explored in detail in Barrett, *The Politics of Truth*, 123–56 (though, interestingly, Barrett concludes by endorsing the Frankfurt School model).

32. While it is acknowledged that Mills coined this phrase, it has since developed an expansive theoretical life—see, for example, Sullivan and Tuana's *Race and Epistemologies of Ignorance*, as well as Proctor and Schiebinger's *Agnotology*. In her contribution to the former, Alcoff argues that the theory of the epistemology of ignorance could be productively complemented with an early Frankfurt School perspective (though she focuses on Horkheimer). In her essay on ideology critique, Ng briefly connects Mills and Adorno ("Ideology Critique from Hegel and Marx to Critical Theory," 400). In "Ideology, Racism, and Critical Social Theory," Shelby argues that an account of ideology is necessary for understanding racism, but he does not draw on the Frankfurt School model.

33. Mills, *The Racial Contract*, 19.

34. Ibid.

35. Ibid., 18.

36. Ibid., 89.

37. Ibid., 98.

38. Alcoff, "Epistemologies of Ignorance," 39.

39. Mills, *The Racial Contract*, 129. Cf. Mills's essays "Ideology" and "Ideal Theory as Ideology."

40. Cited in Hochschild, *Strangers in Their Own Land*, 255.

41. See Rosenthal, "Mike Ditka: 'No Oppression in Last 100 Years.'"

42. See Berger, "How 'The Turner Diaries' Changed White Nationalism."

43. Malm: "Just as global warming is only one additional, particularly urgent reason to break with the neoliberal political paradigm, so it is but another nail in the coffin of anti-realism" (*The Progress of This Storm*, 23).

5. WHAT IS ELITISM?

1. This should distinguish the early Frankfurt School's account of ideology from the understanding developed by, for example, Haslanger, for whom ideology is "not a pejorative term. It is an essential part of any form of social life because it functions as the background that we assimilate and enact in order to navigate our social world." See *Resisting Reality*, 18.

2. Ricœur draws this analogy as well: "Marx and Lenin return to a theme which can be called Platonic, the problem of 'false consciousness'" (*Histoire et vérité*, 272). Dahl, too, draws a direct line from Plato to Lenin (*Democracy and Its Critics*, 53).

3. McClelland, *The Crowd and the Mob*, 1.

4. Nemo, *A History of Political Ideas from Antiquity to the Middle Ages*, 74. Cf. Ober: "Classical Greek political thought arose from an extended . . . battle for discursive authority between two powerful and multifaceted communities: the internally diverse Athenian citizenry and the internally competitive Athenian educated elite" (*Political Dissent in Democratic Athens*, 12). Ober's extensive and nuanced account locates antidemocratic political thought in ancient Athens even prior to Plato in the work of Aristophanes, Thucydides, and the anonymous "Old Oligarch."

5. "Can the majority in any way tolerate or accept the reality of the beautiful itself? . . . Then the majority cannot be philosophic" (*Republic* 493e–494).

6. Plato articulates this argument in many passages, especially *Republic* 431c, 561d, and 563d–564b, as well as *Protagoras* 319be.

7. See *Republic* 473d.

8. See *Republic* 434ab, as well as the passage from *Protagoras*, cited above.

9. Roberts's *Athens on Trial* provides an indispensable history of antidemocratic thinking in the Western tradition. From her account, we see that the perceived negative *consequences* of democratic power shift dramatically—democracy sometimes leads to decadence, sometimes to instability, sometimes to sin—but in each case it leads there because of the fundamental incompetence of the common people, interpreted as either a natural feature or as the curse of situation (and often, inconsistently, as both).

10. Burke's *Reflections on the Revolution in France* combines an explicit defense of the incompetence principle with an unmistakable anti-intellectualism.

11. He develops this system in *Considerations on Representative Government* (chapter 8), and in *Thoughts of Parliamentary Reform* (esp. 11–12), where he writes, "No lover of improvement can desire that the predominant power should be turned over to persons in the mental and moral condition of the English working classes" (14).

12. Key examples include Le Bon's *The Crowd*, Trotter's *Instincts of the Herd in Peace and War*, Ortega's *The Revolt of the Masses*, Martin's *The Behavior of Crowds*, and Riesman, Glazer, and Denney, *The Lonely Crowd*. Also worth mentioning in this context are Lippmann's progenitors in the sociological tradition such as Pareto, Taine, Mosca, and Michels.

13. See Jonsson, *A Brief History of the Masses*, 78ff.

14. See Bachrach, *Political Elites in a Democracy*. I am thinking of Lippmann's *The Phantom Public*, and Schumpeter's *Capitalism, Socialism, and Democracy* (esp. 237–83).

15. See Kolbert, "Why Facts Don't Change Our Minds," Ignatius, "Why Facts Don't Matter to Trump Supporters," Mooney, "The Science of Why We

Don't Believe Science," Ehrenfreund, "I Asked Psychologists to Analyze Trump Supporters," and Graham, "Why Fact-Checking Doesn't Faze Trump Fans."

16. Achen and Bartels, *Democracy for Realists*, 299.

17. Brennan, *Against Democracy*, 158.

18. He adopts the term "epistocracy" from Estlund. As we have seen, Rancière uses the more etymologically precise term "epistemocracy."

19. Brennan, *Against Democracy*, 24.

20. Ashton misleadingly translates *die Menschen* (189) as "Man."

21. This has in fact been done. See Waugh, "Racism Is 'Hard-Wired' into the Human Brain."

22. Cf. Adorno's discussion of elitism in *Introduction to Sociology*, 129–35.

23. In Ismail Merchant's film version, this character says, "You cannot go wrong if you listen to the opinions of your ordinary man in the street. They're perfectly entitled to give opinions on politics."

24. Ishiguro, *The Remains of the Day*, 194–99.

25. Ishiguro juxtaposes this scene with another in which an older Stevens is confronted by the devastation of the Second World War—and, implicitly, by the fact that his former employer was an advocate of appeasement and an occasional Nazi sympathizer. The lesson is clear: the enlightened perspective of the aristocrats did not prevent them from casting their lot with political disaster. At the same time, we should hesitate before inferring from this that Stevens is the truly enlightened one; at the time, he dutifully supported his master and staunchly defended his political choices. In other words, if the course of British politics in the interwar years *were* in Stevens's hands, we have little reason to believe that the result would have been different.

26. As for the accuracy of this interpretation of Althusser, the most that can be said here is that, despite the popularity of the essay on "Ideological State Apparatuses," his theory of ideology remained incomplete. It is most thoroughly elaborated in the recently published manuscript, *On the Reproduction of Capitalism* (esp. 171–209).

27. The hypocrisy involved in this has not gone unnoticed by the Right. See Bauer, "The Left and 'Discriminating Tolerance'"; and O'Sullivan, foreword to Legutko, *The Demon in Democracy*.

28. Asimov, "A Cult of Ignorance," 19.

29. Ibid.

30. See, for example, Robin, 4

31. See Nash, *The Conservative Intellectual Movement in America since 1945*, 33–38; Critchlow, *The Conservative Ascendancy*, 11; Kirk, *The Conservative Mind*, 197; Lora, *Conservative Minds in America*, 202; and Allitt, *The Conservatives*, 153.

32. See, for example, the opening paragraph of Robin; Allitt, *The Conservatives*, 3; Critchlow, *The Conservative Ascendancy*, 9; or the passage from May quoted in chapter 1.

33. See Nash, *The Conservative Intellectual Movement in America since 1945*, 230–57 and 308–17; Critchlow, *The Conservative Ascendancy*, 114–31; Story and Laurie, *The Rise of Conservatism in America*, 13–14; Hoeveler, *Watch on the Right*, 7–8; and Boyer, "The Evangelical Resurgence in 1970s American Protestantism."

34. See "Firing Line with William F. Buckley Jr." This exchange happens from around 00:17:30 to around 00:20:00. Later on (00:31:45), Buckley compares Cleaver to American Nazi Party leader George Lincoln Rockwell.

35. Foucault, *The Archaeology of Knowledge*, 235.

36. This passage can be found in Schmitt, *The Crisis of Parliamentary Democracy*, 24.

37. Chesterton, *Orthodoxy*, 84–86.

BIBLIOGRAPHY

WORKS BY THEODOR W. ADORNO

"Beitrag zur Ideologienlehre." In *Gesammelte Schriften 8.1: Soziologische Schriften I*. Edited by Rolf Tiedemann. Frankfurt am Main: Suhrkamp, 1986.
"Ideology." In Frankfurt Institute for Social Research, *Aspects of Sociology*, translated by John Viertel, 182–203. Boston: Beacon Press, 1973.
Critical Models: Interventions and Catchwords. Translated by Henry W. Pickford. New York: Columbia University Press, 2005.
Eingriffe: Neun kritische Modelle. Frankfurt am Main: Suhrkamp Verlag, 1963.
"Democratic Leadership and Mass Manipulation." In *Studies in Leadership*, edited by Alvin Gouldner, 417–21. New York: Russell and Russell, 1965.
History and Freedom: Lectures 1964–1965. Edited by Rolf Tiedemann. Translated by Rodney Livingstone. Cambridge: Polity, 2006.
Zur Lehre von Der Geschichte und von Der Freiheit. Edited by Rolf Tiedemann. Frankfurt am Main: Suhrkamp Verlag, 2001.
An Introduction to Dialectics. Edited by Christoph Ziermann. Translated by Nicholas Walker. Cambridge: Polity, 2017.
Einführung in die Dialektik. Edited by Christoph Ziermann. Berlin: Suhrkamp Verlag, 2015.
Introduction to Sociology. Edited by Christoph Gödde. Translated by Edmund Jephcott. Stanford, CA: Stanford University Press, 2000.
Lectures on Negative Dialectics: Fragments of a Lecture Course 1965/1966. Edited by Rolf Tiedemann. Translated by Rodney Livingstone. Cambridge: Polity, 2008.
Vorlesung über Negative Dialektik. Edited by Rolf Tiedemann. Frankfurt am Main: Suhrkamp Verlag, 2003.
Minima Moralia: Reflections from Damaged Life. Translated by E. F. N. Jephcott. London: Verso, 2006.
Negative Dialectics. Translated by E. B. Ashton. New York: Bloomsbury Academic, 1981.
Negative Dialektik. Frankfurt am Main: Suhrkamp Verlag, 1966.
Prisms. Translated by Shierry Weber Nicholsen and Samuel Weber. Cambridge, MA: MIT Press, 1983.
The Stars Down to Earth. Edited by Stephen Crook. London: Routledge, 2001.
"Theses on Need." Translated by Martin Schuster and Iain Macdonald. *Adorno Studies* 1, no. 1 (2017): 101–4.

WORKS BY HANNAH ARENDT

Arendt, Hannah, and Karl Jaspers. *Correspondence: 1926–1969*. Edited by Lotte Kohler and Hans Saner. Translated by Robert and Rita Kimber. Boston: Houghton Mifflin Harcourt, 1992.
Between Past and Future. New York: Penguin Classics, 2006.
Crises of the Republic. New York: Mariner Books, 1972.
Essays in Understanding. Edited by Jerome Kohn. New York: Schocken, 1994.
Hannah Arendt: The Recovery of the Public World. Edited by Melvyn A. Hill. New York: St. Martin's Press, 1979.
The Human Condition. Chicago: University of Chicago Press, 1998.
On Revolution. New York: Penguin Classics, 2006.
The Origins of Totalitarianism. New York: Harcourt Brace Jovanovich, 1973.
The Promise of Politics. Edited by Jerome Kohn. New York: Schocken, 2007.
"Public Rights and Private Interests." In *Small Comforts for Hard Times: Humanists on Public Policy*, edited by Michael Mooney and Florian Stuber, 103–8. New York: Columbia University Press, 1977.
Responsibility and Judgment. Edited by Jerome Kohn. New York: Schocken, 2005.
Thinking without a Bannister. Edited by Jerome Kohn. New York: Schocken, 2018.

WORKS BY ERNESTO LACLAU

Butler, Judith, Ernesto Laclau, and Slavoj Žižek. *Contingency, Hegemony, and Universality*. London: Verso, 2000.
Emancipation(s). London: Verso, 2007.
New Reflections on the Revolution of Our Time. London: Verso, 1990.
Politics and Ideology in Marxist Theory: Capitalism, Fascism, Populism. London: Verso, 1977.
On Populist Reason. New York: Verso, 2005.
"Populism: What's in a Name?" In *Populism and the Mirror of Democracy*, edited by Francisco Panizza, 32–49. London: Verso, 2005.
The Rhetorical Foundations of Society. London: Verso, 2014.
"The Signifiers of Democracy." In *Democracy and Possessive Individualism: The Intellectual Legacy of C. B. Macpherson*, edited by Joseph H. Carens, 221–33. Albany, NY: SUNY Press, 1993.

WORKS BY LACLAU AND MOUFFE

Hegemony and Socialist Strategy. New York: Verso, 2014.
"Post-Marxism without Apologies." In *New Reflections on the Revolution of Our Time*, by Ernesto Laclau, 97–132. London: Verso, 1990.

WORKS BY HERBERT MARCUSE

Counterrevolution and Revolt. Boston: Beacon Press, 1972.
An Essay on Liberation. Boston: Beacon Press, 1971.
Marxism, Revolution, and Utopia : Collected Papers of Herbert Marcuse,

Volume Six. Edited by Douglas Kellner and Clayton Pierce. London: Routledge, 2014.
Negations: Essays in Critical Theory. Translated by Jeremy J. Shapiro. Boston: Beacon Press, 1968.
The New Left and the 1960s: Collected Papers of Herbert Marcuse, Volume Three. Edited by Douglas Kellner. Oxford: Routledge, 2005.
One-Dimensional Man. 2nd edition. Boston: Beacon Press, 1991.
Paris Lectures at Vincennes University, 1974: Global Capitalism and Radical Opposition. Edited by Peter-Erwin Jansen and Charles Reitz. Limited edition publication presented at the International Herbert Marcuse Society Conference, 2015.
Reason and Revolution. Oxford: Oxford University Press, 1941.
"Repressive Tolerance." In *A Critique of Pure Tolerance,* edited by Robert Paul Wolff, Barrington Moore Jr., and Herbert Marcuse, 81–123. Boston: Beacon Press, 1969.

WORKS BY CHANTAL MOUFFE

Agonistics: Thinking the World Politically. London: Verso, 2013.
The Democratic Paradox. New York: Verso, 2009.
"The 'End of Politics' and the Challenge of Right-Wing Populism." In *Populism and the Mirror of Democracy,* edited by Francisco Panizza, 50–71. London: Verso, 2005.
"For an Agonistic Public Sphere." In *Radical Democracy: Politics between Abundance and Lack,* edited by Lars Tønder and Lasse Thomassen, 123–32. Manchester: Manchester University Press, 2014.
"Liberalism and Modern Democracy." In *Democracy and Possessive Individualism: The Intellectual Legacy of C. B. Macpherson,* edited by Joseph H. Carens, 175–91. Albany, NY: SUNY Press, 1993.
On the Political. London: Routledge, 2005.
"Radical Democracy or Liberal Democracy?" In *Radical Democracy: Identity, Citizenship, and the State* edited by David Trend, 19–26. London: Routledge, 2013.
The Return of the Political. New York: Verso, 2006.

WORKS BY JACQUES RANCIÈRE

Althusser's Lesson. Translated by Emiliano Battista. London: Bloomsbury, 2011.
"Democracies against Democracy." In *Democracy in What State?* by Giorgio Agamben, Alain Badiou, Daniel Bensaïd, Wendy Brown, Jean-Luc Nancy, Jacques Rancière, Kristin Ross, and Slajoj Žižek, 76–81 Translated by William McCuaig. New York: Columbia University Press, 2012.
"Democracy, Dissensus and the Aesthetics of Class Struggle: An Exchange with Jacques Rancière," interview by Rafeeq Hasan, Max Blechman, and Anita Chari, *Historical Materialism* 13, no. 4 (2005): 285–301.
Disagreement: Politics and Philosophy. Translated by Julie Rose. Minneapolis: University of Minnesota Press, 2004.
Le Mésentente. Paris: Galilée, 1995.
Honneth, Axel, and Jacques Rancière. *Recognition or Disagreement: A Critical Encounter on the Politics of Freedom, Equality, and Identity.* Edited by Katia Genel and Jean-Philippe Deranty. New York: Columbia University Press, 2016.
The Emancipated Spectator. Translated by Gregory Elliott. London: Verso, 2011.
"A Few Remarks on the Method of Jacques Rancière." *Parallax* 15, no. 3 (2009): 114–23.
Hatred of Democracy. Translated by Steve Corcoran. London: Verso, 2014.
The Ignorant Schoolmaster: Five Lessons in Intellectual Emancipation. Translated by Kristin Ross. Stanford, CA: Stanford University Press, 1991.

The Intellectual and His People: Staging the People Volume 2. Translated by David Fernbach. London: Verso, 2012.
"Jacques Rancière: Against an Ebbing Tide." In *Reading Rancière: Critical Dissensus*, edited by Paul Bowman and Richard Stamp, 238–51. London: Bloomsbury Academic, 2011.
Moments Politiques. Translated by Mary Foster. New York: Seven Stories Press, 2014.
On the Shores of Politics. Translated by Liz Heron. London: Verso, 2007.
The Philosopher and His Poor. Edited by Andrew Parker. Translated by Corinne Oster, John Drury, and Andrew Parker. Durham, NC: Duke University Press, 2004.
The Politics of Aesthetics. Translated by Gabriel Rockhill. New York: Bloomsbury: 2013.
"The Populism That Is Not to Be Found." In *What Is a People?* by Alain Badiou, Judith Butler, Georges Didi-Huberman, Sadri Khiari, Jacques Rancière, Pierre Bourdieu, Bruno Bosteels, and Kevin Olson. Translated by Jody Gladding, 101–5. New York: Columbia University Press, 2016.
Staging the People: The Proletarian and His Double. Translated by David Fernbach. London: Verso, 2011.
"Ten Theses on Politics." In *Dissensus: On Politics and Aesthetics*, translated by Steven Corcoran, 35–52. London: Bloomsbury, 2010.

WORKS BY OTHERS

Abensour, Miguel. *Democracy Against the State: Marx and the Machiavellian Movement*. Translated by Max Blechman and Martin Breaugh. Cambridge: Cambridge University Press, 2011.
Abromeit, John. "Critical Theory and the Persistence of Right-Wing Populism." *Logos* 15, nos. 2–3 (2016).
———. "Right-Wing Populism and the Limits of Normative Critical Theory." *Logos* 16, nos. 1–2 (2017).
Abts, Koen, and Stefan Rummens. "Populism versus Democracy." *Political Studies* 55 (2007): 405–24.
Achen, Christopher H., and Larry M. Bartels. *Democracy for Realists: Why Elections Do Not Produce Responsive Government*. Princeton, NJ: Princeton University Press, 2016.
Alcoff, Linda Martín. "Epistemologies of Ignorance: Three Types." In *Race and Epistemologies of Ignorance*, edited by Shannon Sullivan and Nancy Tuana, 39–57. Albany, NY: SUNY Press, 2007.
Allitt, Patrick. *The Conservatives*. New Haven, CT: Yale University Press, 2009.
Althusser, Louis. *On the Reproduction of Capitalism: Ideology and Ideological State Apparatuses*. Translated by G. M. Goshgarian. New York: Verso, 2014.
Arato, Andrew. "Political Theology and Populism." In *The Promise and Perils of Populism*, edited by Carlos de la Torre, 31–58. Lexington: University of Kentucky Press, 2015.
Arneson, Richard J. "Democracy Is Not Intrinsically Just." In *Justice and Democracy*, edited by Keith Dowding, Robert E. Goodin, and Carole Pateman, 40–58. Cambridge: Cambridge University Press, 2004.
Aronowitz, Stanley. "Theory and Socialist Strategy." *Social Text* 16 (1986): 1–16.
Asimov, Isaac. "A Cult of Ignorance." *Newsweek*, January 21, 1980.
Bachrach, Peter, ed. *Political Elites in a Democracy*. New York: Atherton Press, 1971.
Barber, Benjamin. "Foundationalism and Democracy." In *Democracy and Difference*, edited by Seyla Benhabib, 348–59. Princeton, NJ: Princeton University Press, 1996.
Barnouw, Dagmar. "Speech Regained: Hannah Arendt and the American Revolution." *Clio* 15, no. 2 (1986): 137–52.
Barrett, Michèle. *The Politics of Truth: From Marx to Foucault*. Stanford, CA: Stanford University Press, 1991.

BIBLIOGRAPHY

Bauer, Fred. "The Left and 'Discriminating Tolerance.'" *National Review*, June 22, 2015. http://www.nationalreview.com/article/420094/left-and-discriminating-tolerance-fred-bauer.
Benhabib, Seyla, ed. *Democracy and Difference*. Princeton, NJ: Princeton University Press, 1996.
———. "Models of Public Space: Hannah Arendt, the Liberal Tradition, and Jürgen Habermas." In *Habermas and the Public Sphere*, edited by Craig Calhoun, 73–98. Boston: MIT Press, 1993.
———. *The Reluctant Modernism of Hannah Arendt*. Lanham, MD: Rowman & Littlefield, 2003.
Berger, J. M. "How 'The Turner Diaries' Changed White Nationalism." *The Atlantic*, September 16, 2016. https://www.theatlantic.com/politics/archive/2016/09/how-the-turner-diaries-changed-white-nationalism/500039.
Bernasconi, Robert. "The Double Face of the Political and the Social: Hannah Arendt and America's Racial Divisions." *Research in Phenomenology* 26, no. 1 (1996): 3–24.
Bernstein, Richard J. "Rethinking the Social and the Political." *Graduate Faculty Philosophy Journal* 11, no. 1 (1986): 111–30.
Biesta, Gert. "A New Logic of Emancipation: The Methodology of Jacques Rancière." *Educational Theory* 60, no. 1 (2010): 39–59.
Bobbio, Norberto. *Liberalism and Democracy*. Translated by Martin Ryle and Kate Soper. London: Verso, 1990.
Bokiniec, Monika. "Is 'Polis' the Answer? Hannah Arendt on Democracy." *Santalka: Filosofija* 17, no. 1 (2009): 76–82.
Bosteels, Bruno. "Rancière's Leftism, or, Politics and Its Discontents." In *Jacques Rancière: History, Politics, Aesthetics*, edited by Gabriel Rockhill and Philip Watts, 158–75. Durham, NC: Duke University Press, 2009.
Bowman, Paul, and Richard Stamp, eds. *Reading Rancière: Critical Dissensus*. London: Bloomsbury Academic, 2011.
Boyer, Paul. "The Evangelical Resurgence in 1970s American Protestantism." In *Rightward Bound*, edited by Bruce J. Schulman and Julian E. Zelizer, 29–70. Cambridge, MA: Harvard University Press, 2008.
Breaugh, Martin, Christopher Holman, Rachel Magnusson, Paul Mazzocchi, and Devin Penner, eds. *Thinking Radical Democracy: The Return to Politics in Post-War France*. Toronto: University of Toronto Press, 2015.
Breckman, Warren. *Adventures of the Symbolic: Post-Marxism and Radical Democracy*. New York: Columbia University Press, 2015.
Breen, Keith. "Violence and Power." *Philosophy and Social Criticism* 33, no. 3 (2007): 343–72.
Brennan, Jason. *Against Democracy*. Princeton, NJ: Princeton University Press, 2016.
Brown, Wendy. "Sovereignty and the Return of the Repressed." In *Democracy and Difference*, edited by Seyla Benhabib, 250–72. Princeton, NJ: Princeton University Press, 1996.
———. *Undoing the Demos: Neoliberalism's Stealth Revolution*. New York: Zone Books, 2015.
———. "'We're All Democrats Now. . . .'" In *Democracy in What State?* by Giorgio Agamben, Alain Badiou, Daniel Bensaïd, Wendy Brown, Jean-Luc Nancy, Jacques Rancière, Kristin Ross, and Slavoj Žižek, 44–57. New York: Columbia University Press, 2012.
Buckler, Steve. *Hannah Arendt and Political Theory: Challenging the Tradition*. Edinburgh: Edinburgh University Press, 2012.
Burke, Edmund. *Reflections on the Revolution in France*. Edited by L. G. Mitchell. New York: Oxford University Press, 2009.
Canovan, Margaret. "The Contradictions of Hannah Arendt's Political Thought." *Political Theory* 6, no. 1 (1978): 5–26.
———. *Hannah Arendt: A Reinterpretation of Her Political Thought*. Cambridge: Cambridge University Press, 1992.
Caplan, Bryan. *The Myth of the Rational Voter: Why Democracies Choose Bad Policies*. Princeton, NJ: Princeton University Press, 2008.

Carens, Joseph H., ed. *Democracy and Possessive Individualism: The Intellectual Legacy of C. B. Macpherson.* Albany, NY: SUNY Press, 1993.

Chambers, Samuel A. *The Lessons of Rancière.* Oxford: Oxford University Press, 2014.

Chambers, Simone. "Balancing Epistemic Quality and Equal Participation in a System Approach to Deliberative Democracy." *Social Epistemology* 31, no. 3 (2017): 266–76.

Chari, Anita. *A Political Economy of the Senses.* New York: Columbia University Press, 2015.

Chesterton, G. K. *Orthodoxy.* New York: John Lane Company, 1908.

Christiano, Thomas. *The Rule of the Many.* Boulder, CO: Westview Press, 1996.

Clarke, James P. "Social Justice and Political Freedom: Revisiting Hannah Arendt's Conception of Need." *Philosophy & Social Criticism* 19, nos. 3–4 (1993): 333–47.

Cohen, Joshua. "Moral Pluralism and Political Consensus." In *The Idea of Democracy*, edited by David Copp, Jean Hampton, and John E. Roemer, 270–91. Cambridge: Cambridge University Press, 1993.

Connolly, William E. "An Interview with William Connolly, December 2006." In *The New Pluralism: William Connolly and the Contemporary Global Condition*, edited by David Campbell and Morton Schoolman, 305–36. Durham, NC: Duke University Press, 2008.

———. *Pluralism.* Durham, NC: Duke University Press, 2005.

Cook, Deborah. "Adorno, Ideology, and Ideology Critique." *Philosophy and Social Criticism* 27, no. 1 (2001): 1–20.

Cooke, Maeve. "Resurrecting the Rationality of Ideology Critique: Reflections on Laclau on Ideology." *Constellations* 13, no. 1 (2006): 4–20.

Copp, David. "Could Political Truth Be a Hazard for Democracy?" In Copp, Hampton, and Roemer, 101–17.

———, Jean Hampton, and John E. Roemer, eds. *The Idea of Democracy.* Cambridge: Cambridge University Press, 1993.

Christodoulidis, Emilios, and Andrew Schaap. "Arendt's Constitutional Question." In *Hannah Arendt and the Law*, edited by Marco Goldoni and Christopher McCorkindale, 101–16. Oxford: Hart Publishing, 2013.

Critchley, Simon. "Is There a Normative Deficit in the Theory of Hegemony?" In *Laclau: A Critical Reader*, edited by Simon Critchley and Oliver Marchart, 113–22. New York: Routledge, 2004.

———, and Oliver Marchart, eds. *Laclau: A Critical Reader.* New York: Routledge, 2004.

Critchlow, Donald T. *The Conservative Ascendancy.* Cambridge, MA: Harvard University Press, 2009.

Curthoys, Ned. "The Refractory Legacy of Algerian Decolonization: Revisiting Arendt on Violence." In *Hannah Arendt and the Uses of History*, edited by Richard H. King and Dan Stone, 109–29. New York: Berghahn Books, 2008.

Dahl, Robert A. *Democracy and Its Critics.* New Haven, CT: Yale University Press, 1989.

———. *Dilemmas of Pluralist Democracy.* New Haven, CT: Yale University Press, 1982.

Davis, Oliver. *Jacques Rancière.* Cambridge: Polity, 2010.

Dean, Jodi. *Democracy and Other Neoliberal Fantasies.* Durham, NC: Duke University Press, 2009.

———. "Politics without Politics." In *Reading Rancière: Critical Dissensus*, edited by Paul Bowman and Richard Stamp, 73–94. London: Bloomsbury Academic, 2011.

"Debate on Immigration, Refugees in Polish Parliament. Jaroslaw Kaczynski Speech (English SUB) 2015." September 19, 2015. https://www.youtube.com/watch?v=6NlRstWinSU.

D'Entrèves, Maurizio Passerin. "Arendt's Theory of Judgment." In *The Cambridge Companion to Hannah Arendt*, edited by Dana Villa, 245–60. Cambridge: Cambridge University Press, 2000.

Derrida, Jacques. *Rogues: Two Essays on Reason.* Translated by Pascale-Anne Brault and Michael Naas. Stanford, CA: Stanford University Press, 2005.

Diamond, Larry. *In Search of Democracy.* New York: Routledge, 2015.

Dietz, Mary G. "Feminist Receptions of Hannah Arendt." In *Feminist Interpretations of Hannah Arendt*, edited by Bonnie Honig, 17–50. University Park: Penn State Press, 1995.

Disch, Lisa Jane. *Hannah Arendt and the Limits of Philosophy.* Ithaca, NY: Cornell University Press, 1996.

———. "How Could Hannah Arendt Glorify the American Revolution and Revile the French? Placing *On Revolution* in the Historiography of the French and American Revolutions." *European Journal of Political Theory* 10, no. 3 (2011): 350–71.

Dossa, S. "Hannah Arendt on Billy Budd and Robespierre: The Public Realm and the Private Self." *Philosophy and Social Criticism* 9, nos. 3–4 (1982): 305–18.

Douglas, Andrew J. "Democratic Darkness and Adorno's Redemptive Criticism." *Philosophy and Social Criticism* 36, no. 7 (2010): 819–36.

Dunlap, Riley E., and Aaron M. McCright. "Challenging Climate Change: The Denial Countermovement." In *Climate Change and Society*, edited by Riley E. Dunlap and Robert J. Brulle, 300–332. Oxford: Oxford University Press, 2015.

Dyrberg, Torben Bech. "Radical and Plural Democracy: In Defence of Right/Left and Public Reason." In *Radical Democracy: Politics between Abundance and Lack*, edited by Lars Tønder and Lasse Thomassen, 167–84. Manchester: Manchester University Press, 2014.

Ehrenfreund, Max. "I Asked Psychologists to Analyze Trump Supporters. This Is What I Learned." *Washington Post*, October 15, 2015. https://www.washingtonpost.com/news/wonk/wp/2015/10/15/i-asked-psychologists-to-analyze-trump-supporters-this-is-what-i-learned.

Elkins, Jeremy, and Andrew Norris, eds. *Truth and Democracy*. Philadelphia: University of Pennsylvania Press, 2012.

Emden, Christian J. "Carl Schmitt, Hannah Arendt, and the Limits of Liberalism." *Telos* 142 (2008): 110–34.

Estlund, David M. *Democratic Authority*. Princeton, NJ: Princeton University Press, 2008.

Feher, Ferenc. "Freedom and the 'Social Question' (Hannah Arendt's Theory of the French Revolution)." *Philosophy and Social Criticism* 12, no. 1 (1987): 1–30.

Fell, James S. "The Toxic Appeal of the Men's Rights Movement." *Time*, May 29, 2014. http://time.com/134152/the-toxic-appeal-of-the-mens-rights-movement/.

Feygina, Irina, John T. Jost, and Rachel E. Goldsmith. "System Justification, the Denial of Global Warming, and the Possibility of 'System Sanctioned Change.'" *Personality and Social Psychology Bulletin* 36, no. 3 (2010): 326–38.

"Fifth Republican Primary Debate—Undercard—December 15 2015 on CNN." 2016. https://www.youtube.com/watch?v=GsgS0sTGbtY.

"Firing Line with William F. Buckley Jr.: The Black Panthers." *Firing Line*, November 13, 1968. https://www.youtube.com/watch?v=5NPwk_Dbin8.

Fishkin, James S. *When the People Speak*. Oxford: Oxford University Press, 2011.

Flathman, Richard E. *Pluralism and Liberal Democracy*. Baltimore: Johns Hopkins University Press, 2005.

Fopp, Rodney. "Herbert Marcuse's 'Repressive Tolerance' and His Critics." *Borderlands* 6, no. 1 (2007).

Foster, John Bellamy, Richard York, and Brett Clark. *The Ecological Rift: Capitalism's War on the Earth*. New York: Monthly Review Press, 2011.

Foucault, Michel. *The Archaeology of Knowledge*. Translated by A. M. Sheridan Smith. New York: Vintage Books, 1972.

———. *Power/Knowledge: Selected Interviews and Other Writings, 1972–1977*. Edited and translated by Colin Gordon. New York: Random House, 1988.

"France's Marine Le Pen: Donald Trump Win Shows Power Slipping from 'Elites' (Full Interview)—CNBC." CNBC, 2016. https://www.youtube.com/watch?v=cX4bSCnxIfE.

Fraser, Nancy. *Scales of Justice*. New York: Columbia University Press, 2010.

Gardiner, Stephen M. *A Perfect Moral Storm: The Ethical Tragedy of Climate Change*. Oxford: Oxford University Press, 2011.

Geenens, Raf, and Ronald Tinnevelt, eds. *Does Truth Matter? Democracy and Public Space*. New York: Springer, 2009.

Geras, Norman. "Ex-Marxism Without Substance: Being A Real Reply to Laclau and Mouffe." *New Left Review* 1, no. 169 (1988): 34–61.

———. "Post-Marxism?" *New Left Review* 1, no. 163 (1987): 40–82.

Geuss, Raymond. *The Idea of a Critical Theory: Habermas and the Frankfurt School*. Cambridge: Cambridge University Press, 1981.

Gines, Kathryn T. *Hannah Arendt and the Negro Question.* Bloomington: Indiana University Press, 2014.

Gordon, Peter E. "The Authoritarian Personality Revisited: Reading Adorno in the Age of Trump." In *Authoritarianism: Three Inquiries in Critical Theory*, edited by Wendy Brown, Peter E. Gordon, and Max Pensky, 45–84. Chicago: University of Chicago Press, 2018.

Graham, David A. "Why Fact-Checking Doesn't Faze Trump Fans." *The Atlantic*, July 5, 2017. www.theatlantic.com/politics/archive/2017/07/the-strange-effect-fact-checking-has-on-trump-supporters/532701.

Gunderson, Ryan, Diana Stuart, and Brian Peterson. "Ideological Obstacles to Effective Climate Policy: The Greening of Markets, Technology, and Growth." *Capital & Class* 42, no. 1 (2018): 133–60.

Gündoğdu, Ayten. *Rightlessness in an Age of Rights: Hannah Arendt and the Contemporary Struggles of Migrants.* Oxford: Oxford University Press, 2015.

Gutmann, Amy. *Liberal Equality.* Cambridge: Cambridge University Press, 1980.

Habermas, Jürgen. "Three Normative Models of Democracy." In *Democracy and Difference*, edited by Seyla Benhabib, 20–30. Princeton, NJ: Princeton University Press, 1996.

Hall, Stuart. "The Toad in the Garden: Thatcherism among the Theorists." In *Marxism and the Interpretation of Culture*, edited by Cary Nelson and Lawrence Grossberg, 35–57. Champaign: University of Illinois Press, 1988.

Hammer, Espen. *Adorno and the Political.* New York: Routledge, 2005.

Harris, Jerry. *Global Capitalism and the Crisis of Democracy.* Atlanta: Clarity Press, 2016.

Hartmann, Margaret. "Why Oklahoma Lawmakers Voted to Ban AP U.S. History." *New York Magazine*, February 18, 2015. http://nymag.com/daily/intelligencer/2015/02/why-oklahoma-lawmakers-want-to-ban-ap-us-history.html.

Haslanger, Sally. *Resisting Reality: Social Construction and Social Critique.* Oxford: Oxford University Press, 2012.

Heather, Gerard P., and Matthew Stolz. "Hannah Arendt and the Problem of Critical Theory." *Journal of Politics* 41, no. 1 (1979): 2–22.

Hedges, Chris. *Empire of Illusion.* New York: Nation Books, 2010.

Heins, Volker. "Saying Things That Hurt: Adorno as Educator." *Thesis Eleven* 110, no. 1 (2012): 68–82.

Held, David. *Models of Democracy.* 3rd ed. Stanford, CA: Stanford University Press, 2006.

Hesse, Monica. "Men's Rights Activists, Gathering to Discuss All the Ways Society Has Done Them Wrong." *Washington Post*, June 30, 2014. https://www.washingtonpost.com/lifestyle/style/mens-rights-activists-gathering-to-discuss-all-the-ways-society-has-done-them-wrong/2014/06/30/a9310d96-005f-11e4-8fd0-3a663dfa68ac_story.html.

Hibbing, John R., and Elizabeth Theiss-Morse. *Stealth Democracy.* Cambridge: Cambridge University Press, 2002.

Hinckley, Story. "Texas: We Don't Need Academics to Fact-Check Our Textbooks." *Christian Science Monitor*, November 19, 2015. http://www.csmonitor.com/USA/Education/2015/1119/Texas-We-don-t-need-academics-to-fact-check-our-textbooks-video.

Hirsch, Alexander Keller. "The Promise of the Unforgiven: Violence, Power and Paradox in Arendt." *Philosophy and Social Criticism* 39, no. 1 (2013): 45–61.

Hochschild, Arlie Russell. *Strangers in Their Own Land: Anger and Mourning on the American Right.* New York: The New Press, 2018.

Hoeveler, J. David, Jr. *Watch on the Right.* Madison: University of Wisconsin Press, 1991.

Holman, Christopher. *Politics as Radical Creation: Herbert Marcuse and Hannah Arendt on Political Performativity.* Toronto: University of Toronto Press, 2013.

Honig, Bonnie, ed. *Feminist Interpretations of Hannah Arendt.* University Park: Penn State Press, 1995.

———. *Political Theory and the Displacement of Politics.* Ithaca, NY: Cornell University Press, 1993.

Hornborg, Alf. "Cornucopia or Zero-Sum Game? The Epistemology of Sustainability." *Journal of World-Systems Research* 9, no. 2 (2003): 205–16.

BIBLIOGRAPHY

Horowitz, Irving Louis. *Hannah Arendt: Radical Conservative*. New Brunswick, NJ: Transaction Publishers, 2012.

Howard, Dick. *The Specter of Democracy*. New York: Columbia University Press, 2006.

Howarth, David. "Hegemony, Political Subjectivity, and Radical Democracy." In *Laclau: A Critical Reader*, edited by Simon Critchley and Oliver Marchart, 256–76. New York: Routledge, 2004.

Hunter, Allen. "Post-Marxism and the New Social Movements." *Theory and Society* 17, no. 6 (1988): 885–900.

Ignatius, David. "Why Facts Don't Matter to Trump's Supporters." *Washington Post*, August 4, 2016. https://www.washingtonpost.com/opinions/why-facts-dont-matter-to-trumps-supporters/2016/08/04/924ece4a-5a78-11e6-831d-0324760ca856_story.html.

Ince, Onur Ulas. "Bringing the Economy Back In: Hannah Arendt, Karl Marx, and the Politics of Capitalism." *Journal of Politics* 78, no. 2 (2016): 411–26.

Isaac, Jeffrey C. "Oases in the Desert: Hannah Arendt on Democratic Politics." *American Political Science Review* 88, no. 1 (1994): 156–68.

Ishiguro, Kazuo. *The Remains of the Day*. New York: Knopf, 1989. Film version: *The Remains of the Day*, 1992. Directed by Ismail Merchant.

Jacoby, Susan. *The Age of American Unreason*. New York: Vintage, 2009.

Jaeggi, Rahel. "Rethinking Ideology." Translated by Eva Engels. In *New Waves in Political Philosophy*, edited by Boudewijn de Bruin and Christopher F. Zurn, 63–86. Basingstoke, UK: Palgrave Macmillan, 2009.

Jamieson, Dale. *Reason in a Dark Time: Why the Struggle against Climate Change Failed— and What It Means for Our Future*. Oxford: Oxford University Press, 2014.

Jarvis, Simon. *Adorno: A Critical Introduction*. Cambridge: Polity, 1998.

Johnson, Clarence Sholé. "Reading between the Lines: Kathryn Gines on Hannah Arendt and Antiblack Racism." *Southern Journal of Philosophy* 47 (2009): 77–83.

Jones, Matthew. "Chantal Mouffe's Agonistic Project: Passions and Participation." *Parallax* 20, no. 2 (2014): 14–30.

Jonsson, Stefan. *A Brief History of the Masses*. New York: Columbia University Press, 2008.

Kalyvas, Andreas. *Democracy and the Politics of the Extraordinary*. Cambridge: Cambridge University Press, 2009.

Kant, Immanuel. *Grounding for the Metaphysics of Morals*. Translated by James Ellington. New York: Hackett Publishing, 1993.

———. *Lectures on Ethics*. Edited by Peter Heath, J. B. Schneewind, and Peter Heath. Cambridge: Cambridge University Press, 1997.

Keenan, Alan. *Democracy in Question: Democratic Openness in a Time of Political Closure*. Stanford, CA: Stanford University Press, 2003.

Kellner, Douglas. *Herbert Marcuse and the Crisis of Marxism*. Berkeley: University of California Press, 1984.

King, Richard H. *Arendt and America*. Chicago: University of Chicago Press, 2015.

———. "Hannah Arendt and the Concept of Revolution in the 1960s." *New Formations* 71 (2011): 30–45.

Kingsbury, Donald. "Populism as Post-Politics: Ernesto Laclau, Hegemony, and the Limits of Democracy." *Radical Philosophy Review* 19, no. 3 (2016): 569–91.

Kirk, Russell. *The Conservative Mind*. 7th ed. Washington, DC: Regnery Publishing, 1986.

Kitcher, Philip. "Plato's Revenge: An Undemocratic Report from an Overheated Planet." *Logos* 12, no. 2 (2013).

Klein, Naomi. *This Changes Everything: Capitalism vs. the Climate*. New York: Simon & Schuster, 2015.

Klein, Steven. "'Fit to Enter the World': Hannah Arendt on Politics, Economics, and the Welfare State." *American Political Science Review* 108, no. 4 (2014): 856–69.

Knauer, James T. "Rethinking Arendt's 'Vita Activa': Toward a Theory of Democratic Praxis." *Praxis International* 5, no. 2 (1985): 185–94.

Kolbert, Elizabeth. "Why Facts Don't Change Our Minds." *New Yorker*, February 20, 2017. http://www.newyorker.com/magazine/2017/02/27/why-facts-dont-change-our-minds.

Labelle, Giles. "Two Refoundation Projects of Democracy in Contemporary French Philosophy: Cornelius Castoriadis and Jacques Ranciere." *Philosophy and Social Criticism* 27, no. 4 (2001): 75–103.
Landemore, Hélène. "Beyond the Fact of Disagreement? The Epistemic Turn in Deliberative Democracy." *Social Epistemology* 31, no. 3 (2017): 277–95.
———. *Democratic Reason*. Princeton, NJ: Princeton University Press, 2013.
Landsbaum, Claire. "Men's Rights Activists Are Flocking to the Alt-Right." *New York Magazine*, December 14, 2016. http://nymag.com/thecut/2016/12/mens-rights-activists-are-flocking-to-the-alt-right.html.
Larraín, Jorge. *The Concept of Ideology*. Athens: University of Georgia Press, 1979.
———. *Marxism and Ideology*. London: Macmillan, 1983.
Le Bon, Gustave. *The Crowd: A Study of the Popular Mind*. No translator given. Mineola, NY: Dover, 2012.
Lefort, Claude. *Democracy and Political Theory*. Translated by David Macey. Minneapolis: University of Minnesota Press, 1989.
Leggett, Will. "Restoring Society to Post-Structuralist Politics: Mouffe, Gramsci and Radical Democracy." *Philosophy and Social Criticism* 39, no. 3 (2013): 299–315.
Li, Minqi. "The 21st Century: Is There an Alternative (to Socialism)?" *Science & Society* 77, no. 1 (2013): 10–43.
Lichtman, Richard. "Repressive Tolerance." In *Marcuse: Critical Theory and the Promise of Utopia*, edited by Robert Pippin, Andrew Feenberg, and Charles P. Webel, 189–211. South Hadley, MA: Bergin & Garvey Publishers, 1988.
Lippmann, Walter. *The Phantom Public*. New Brunswick, NJ: Transaction Publishers, 1993.
Lora, Ronald. *Conservative Minds in America*. Chicago: Rand McNally, 1971.
Lorey, Isabell. "The 2011 Occupy Movements: Rancière and the Crisis of Democracy." *Theory, Culture & Society* 31, nos. 7–8 (2014): 43–65.
Lowndes, Joseph. "From Founding Violence to Political Hegemony: The Conservative Populism of George Wallace." In *Populism and the Mirror of Democracy*, edited by Francisco Panizza, 144–71. London: Verso, 2005.
Lukács, Georg. *The Process of Democratization*. Translated by Susanne Bernhardt and Norman Levine. Albany, NY: SUNY Press, 1991.
Lupia, Arthur. *Uninformed: Why People Seem to Know So Little about Politics and What We Can Do about It*. New York: Oxford University Press, 2015.
MacLean, Nancy. *Democracy in Chains*. New York: Penguin, 2017.
Magnusson, Rachel. "A Politics in Writing: Jacques Rancière and the Equality of Intelligences." In *Thinking Radical Democracy: The Return to Politics in Post-War France*, edited by Martin Breaugh, Christopher Holman, Rachel Magnusson, Paul Mazzocchi, and Devin Penner, 189–209. Toronto: University of Toronto Press, 2015.
Mair, Peter. *Ruling the Void: The Hollowing of Western Democracy*. London: Verso, 2013.
Malm, Andreas. *Fossil Capital*. New York: Verso, 2016.
———. *The Progress of This Storm*. New York: Verso, 2018.
Mann, Geoff, and Joel Wainwright. *Climate Leviathan*. New York: Verso, 2018.
Mann, Michael, and Tom Toles. *The Madhouse Effect*. New York: Columbia University Press, 2016.
Marchart, Oliver. *Post-Foundational Political Thought*. Edinburgh: Edinburgh University Press, 2007.
———. "The Second Return of the Political: Democracy and the Syllogism of Equality." In *Reading Rancière: Critical Dissensus*, edited by Paul Bowman and Richard Stamp, 129–47. London: Bloomsbury Academic, 2011.
"Marine Le Pen: Front National 'Not Racist'—BBC News." BBC News, 2016. https://www.youtube.com/watch?v=LkYi9x8tHW0.
Mariotti, Shannon L. *Adorno and Democracy: The American Years*. Lexington: University of Kentucky Press, 2016.
Markell, Patchen. "The Rule of the People: Arendt, Arche, and Democracy." *American Political Science Review* 100, no. 1 (2006): 1–14.

BIBLIOGRAPHY

Martin, Everett Dean. *The Behavior of Crowds: A Psychological Study.* n.p.: Leopold Classic Library, 2015.
Marx, Karl. *Capital: A Critique of Political Economy, Vol. III.* Translated by David Fernbach. New York: Penguin, 1993.
May, Todd. *Contemporary Political Movements and the Thought of Jacques Rancière: Equality in Action.* Edinburgh: Edinburgh University Press, 2010.
———. *The Political Thought of Jacques Rancière: Creating Equality.* Edinburgh: Edinburgh University Press, 2008.
McClelland, J. S. *The Crowd and the Mob.* Boston: Unwin Hyman, 1989.
McClure, Kirstie M. "The Social Question, Again." *Graduate Faculty Philosophy Journal* 28, no. 1 (2007): 85–113.
Mecchia, Giuseppina. "Philosophy and Its Poor: Rancière's Critique of Philosophy." In *Jacques Rancière: Key Concepts*, edited by Jean-Philippe Deranty, 38–54. New York: Routledge, 2014.
Menga, Ferdinando G. "The Seduction of Radical Democracy. Deconstructing Hannah Arendt's Political Discourse." *Constellations* 21, no. 3 (2014): 313–26.
Michaels, David. *Doubt Is Their Product.* Oxford: Oxford University Press, 2008.
Mill, John Stuart. *Considerations on Representative Government.* n.p.: Anodos Books: 2017.
———. *Thoughts on Parliamentary Reform.* CreateSpace Independent Publishing Platform, 2017.
Milligan, Tony. *The Next Democracy? The Possibility of Popular Control.* Lanham, MD: Rowman & Littlefield, 2016.
Mills, Charles. *Black Rights/White Wrongs.* New York: Oxford University Press, 2017.
———. "Criticizing Critical Theory." In *Critical Theory in Critical Times*, edited by Penelope Deutscher and Cristina Lafont, 233–50. New York: Columbia University Press, 2017.
———. "Ideology." In *The Routledge Handbook of Epistemic Injustice*, edited by Ian James Kidd, José Medina, and Gaile Pohlhaus Jr., 100–111. New York: Routledge, 2017.
———. *The Racial Contract.* Ithaca, NY: Cornell University Press, 1997.
Mooney, Chris. "The Science of Why We Don't Believe Science." *Mother Jones*, June 2011. http://www.motherjones.com/politics/2011/03/denial-science-chris-mooney.
Morris, Michael. *Knowledge and Ideology.* Cambridge: Cambridge University Press, 2016.
Mounk, Yascha. *The People vs Democracy.* Cambridge, MA: Harvard University Press, 2018.
Mudde, Cas, and Cristóbal Rovira Kaltwasser. "Exclusionary vs. Inclusionary Populism: Comparing Contemporary Europe and Latin America." *Government and Opposition* 48, no. 2 (2013): 147–74.
Muhlmann, Geraldine. "Hannah Arendt and the Liberal Tradition: Heritage and Differences." Translated by Ella Brians. *Graduate Faculty Philosophy Journal* 28, no. 2 (2007): 117–38.
Müller, Jan-Werner. *What Is Populism?* Philadelphia: University of Pennsylvania Press, 2016.
Nash, George H. *The Conservative Intellectual Movement in America since 1945.* 30th anniversary ed. Wilmington, DE: Intercollegiate Studies Institute, 2006.
Neiwert, David. *Alt-America: The Rise of the Radical Right in the Age of Trump.* New York: Verso, 2017.
Nemo, Philippe. *A History of Political Ideas from Antiquity to the Middle Ages.* Translated by Kenneth Casler. Pittsburgh, PA: Duquesne University Press, 2013.
Neuman, Scott. "Scientists, General Public Have Divergent Views on Science, Report Says." NPR, January 29, 2015. http://www.npr.org/sections/thetwo-way/2015/01/29/382464912/scientists-general-public-have-divergent-views-on-science-report-says.
Ng, Karen. "Ideology Critique from Hegel and Marx to Critical Theory." *Constellations* 22, no. 3 (2015): 393–404.
Nisbet, Robert. "Hannah Arendt and the American Revolution." *Social Research* 44 (1977): 63–79.
Norris, Andrew. "Against Antagonism: On Ernesto Laclau's Political Thought." *Constellations* 9, no. 4 (2002): 554–73.

———. "Ernesto Laclau and the Logic of 'the Political.'" *Philosophy and Social Criticism* 32, no. 1 (2006): 111–34.
Norton, Anne. "Heart of Darkness: African and African Americans in the Writings of Hannah Arendt." In *Feminist Interpretations of Hannah Arendt*, edited by Bonnie Honig, 247–62. University Park: Penn State Press, 1995.
Ober, Josiah. *Political Dissent in Democratic Athens: Intellectual Critics of Popular Rule*. Princeton, NJ: Princeton University Press, 1998.
Ochoa Espejo, Paulina. "Power to Whom? The People between Procedure and Populism." In *The Promise and Perils of Populism*, edited by Carlos de la Torre, 59–90. Lexington: University of Kentucky Press, 2015.
Offe, Claus, and Ulrich K. Preuss. "Democratic Institutions and Moral Resources." In *Political Theory Today*, edited by David Held, 143–71. Stanford, CA: Stanford University Press, 1991.
O'Kane, Chris. "'A Hostile World': Critical Theory in the Time of Trump." *Logos* 16, nos. 1–2 (2017).
Osborne, Peter. "Radicalism without Limit? Discourse, Democracy, and the Politics of Identity." In *Socialism and the Limits of Liberalism*, edited by Peter Osborne, 201–25. London: Verso, 1991.
Oreskes, Naomi, and Erik M. Conway. *Merchants of Doubt: How a Handful of Scientists Obscured the Truth on Issues from Tobacco Smoke to Global Warming*. New York: Bloomsbury, 2011.
Ortega y Gasset, José. *The Revolt of the Masses*. Translated by Anonymous. New York: W. W. Norton and Company, 1964.
O'Sullivan, John. Foreword to Ryszard Legutko, *The Demon in Democracy*. New York: Encounter Books, 2016.
Panizza, Francisco, ed. *Populism and the Mirror of Democracy*. London: Verso, 2005.
Parr, Adrian. *The Wrath of Capital: Neoliberalism and Climate Change Politics*. New York: Columbia University Press, 2014.
Pew Research Center. "Public's Views on Human Evolution." December 30, 2013. http://www.pewforum.org/2013/12/30/publics-views-on-human-evolution.
Pichardo, Nelson A. "New Social Movements: A Critical Review." *Annual Review of Sociology* 23, no. 1 (1997): 411–30.
Pitkin, Hanna Fenichel. *The Attack of the Blob: Hannah Arendt's Concept of the Social*. Chicago: University of Chicago Press, 1998.
Plato. *Complete Works*. Edited by John M. Cooper and D. S. Hutchinson. New York: Hackett Publishing, 1997.
Popper, Karl. *The Open Society and Its Enemies*. Rev. ed. Princeton, NJ: Princeton University Press, 1950.
Prasad, Sonali, Jason Burke, Michael Slezak, and Oliver Milman. "Obama's Dirty Secret: The Fossil Fuel Projects the US Littered around the World." *The Guardian*, December 1, 2016. http://www.theguardian.com/environment/2016/dec/01/obama-fossil-fuels-us-export-import-bank-energy-projects.
Proctor, Robert N., and Londa Schiebinger, eds. *Agnotology: The Making and Unmaking of Ignorance*. Stanford, CA: Stanford University Press, 2008.
Rahman, K. Sabeel. *Democracy against Domination*. Oxford: Oxford University Press, 2016.
Ricœur, Paul. *Histoire et vérité*. 3rd ed. Paris: Editions du Seuil, 1978.
Riesman, David, Nathan Glazer, and Reuel Denney. *The Lonely Crowd: A Study of the Changing American Character*. 2nd edition. New Haven, CT: Yale University Press, 2001.
"RNC 2012: Mitt Romney Speech to GOP Convention (Full Text)." *Washington Post*, August 30, 2012. https://www.washingtonpost.com/politics/rnc-2012-mitt-romney-speech-to-gop-convention-excerpts/2012/08/30/7d575ee6-f2ec-11e1-a612-3cfc842a6d89_story.html.
Roberts, Jennifer Tolbert. *Athens on Trial: The Antidemocratic Tradition in Western Thought*. Princeton, NJ: Princeton University Press, 2011.
Rockhill, Gabriel. *Counter-History of the Present*. Durham, NC: Duke University Press, 2017.
———. *Radical History and the Politics of Art*. New York: Columbia University Press, 2014.

BIBLIOGRAPHY

Rockmore, Ellen Bresler. "How Texas Teaches History." *New York Times*, October 21, 2015. https://www.nytimes.com/2015/10/22/opinion/how-texas-teaches-history.html.

Rorty, Richard. "Feminism, Ideology, and Deconstruction: A Pragmatist View." In *Mapping Ideology*, edited by Slavoj Žižek, 227–34. New York: Verso, 1994.

Rosenthal, Phil. "Mike Ditka: 'No Oppression in Last 100 Years.'" *Chicago Tribune*, September 10, 2017. https://www.chicagotribune.com/sports/breaking/ct-ditka-20171010-story.html.

Rubin, Corey. *The Reactionary Mind: Conservatism from Edmund Burke to Sarah Palin*. Oxford: Oxford University Press, 2011.

Rustin, Michael. "Absolute Voluntarism: Critique of a Post-Marxist Concept of Hegemony." *New German Critique* 43 (1989): 146–71.

Sari, Yasemin. "Arendt, Truth, and Epistemic Responsibility." *Arendt Studies* 2 (2018): 149–70.

Schmitt, Carl. *The Crisis of Parliamentary Democracy*. Translated by Ellen Kennedy. Cambridge, MA: MIT Press, 1988.

Schumpeter, Joseph. *Capitalism, Socialism, and Democracy*. 3rd ed. New York: HarperCollins, 2008.

Schweickart, David. "Capitalism vs the Climate: What Then Should We Do? What Then Should I Do?" *Radical Philosophy Review* 21, no. 1 (2017): 11–29.

"Sen. Jim Inhofe on the Fight over Climate Change." 2015. https://www.youtube.com/watch?v=ksHjhXY2CYU.

Sethness-Castro, Javier. *Imperiled Life: Revolution against Climate Catastrophe*. Oakland, CA: AK Press, 2012.

Shear, Michael D. "Ryan Brings the Tea Party to the Ticket." *New York Times*, August 12, 2012. https://thecaucus.blogs.nytimes.com/2012/08/12/ryan-brings-the-tea-party-to-the-ticket.

Shelby, Tommie. "Ideology, Racism, and Critical Social Theory." *The Philosophical Forum* 34, no. 2 (June 1, 2003): 153–88.

Short, Jonathan. "Natural History, Sovereign Power, and Global Warming." In *Critical Ecologies: the Frankfurt School and Contemporary Environmental Crises*, edited by Andrew Biro, 255–77. Toronto: University of Toronto Press, 2011.

Sim, Stuart. *Post-Marxism: An Intellectual History*. London: Routledge, 2013.

Sinderbrand, Rebecca. "How Kellyanne Conway Ushered in the Era of 'Alternative Facts.'" *Washington Post*, January 22, 2017. https://www.washingtonpost.com/news/the-fix/wp/2017/01/22/how-kellyanne-conway-ushered-in-the-era-of-alternative-facts.

Skocpol, Theda, and Vanessa Williamson. *The Tea Party and the Remaking of Republican Conservatism*. Updated ed. New York: Oxford University Press, 2016.

Smith, Anna Marie. *Laclau and Mouffe: The Radical Democratic Imaginary*. London: Routledge, 1998.

Somin, Ilya. *Democracy and Political Ignorance*. 2nd ed. Stanford, CA: Stanford University Press, 2016.

Stack, Liam. "How the 'War on Christmas' Controversy Was Created." *New York Times*, December 19, 2016. www.nytimes.com/2016/12/19/us/war-on-christmas-controversy.html.

Stoner, Alexander M., and Andony Melathopoulos. *Freedom in the Anthropocene: Twentieth-Century Helplessness in the Face of Climate Change*. New York: Palgrave Macmillan, 2015.

Story, Ronald, and Bruce Laurie, eds. *The Rise of Conservatism in America, 1945-2000*. New York: Bedford/St. Martin's, 2008.

Sullivan, Shannon, and Nancy Tuana, eds. *Race and Epistemologies of Ignorance*. Albany, NY: SUNY Press, 2007.

Tanke, Joseph J. *Jacques Rancière: An Introduction*. London: Continuum, 2011.

Terchek, Ronald J., and Thomas C. Conte, eds. *Theories of Democracy: A Reader*. Lanham, MD: Rowman & Littlefield, 2000.

Thaler, Mathias. "The Illusion of Purity: Chantal Mouffe's Realist Critique of Cosmopolitanism." *Philosophy and Social Criticism* 36, no. 7 (2010): 785–800.

Thomassen, Lasse. "In/Exclusions: Towards a Radical Democratic Approach to Exclusion." In *Radical Democracy: Politics between Abundance and Lack*, edited by Lars Tønder and Lasse Thomassen, 103–19. Manchester: Manchester University Press, 2014.

Thompson, Michael J. *The Domestication of Critical Theory*. London: Rowman & Littlefield, 2016.

Tocqueville, Alexis de. *Democracy in America*. Translated by Gerald E. Bevan. New York: Penguin, 2003.

Tønder, Lars, and Lasse Thomassen, eds. *Radical Democracy: Politics between Abundance and Lack*. Manchester: Manchester University Press, 2014.

Torfing, Jacob. *New Theories of Discourse: Laclau, Mouffe and Zizek*. Oxford: Wiley-Blackwell, 1999.

Trend, David, ed. *Radical Democracy: Identity, Citizenship, and the State*. London: Routledge, 2013.

Trotter, Wilfred. *Instincts of the Herd in Peace and War*. CreateSpace Independent Publishing Platform, 2016.

Urbinati, Nadia. *Democracy Disfigured*. Cambridge, MA: Harvard University Press, 2014.

Vasilev, George. "On Mouffe's Agonism: Why It Is Not a Refutation of Consensus." *Democratic Theory* 2, no. 1 (2015): 4–21.

Villa, Dana. "The 'Autonomy of the Political' Reconsidered." *Graduate Faculty Philosophy Journal* 28, no. 1 (2007): 29–45.

Wang, Amy B. "'Post-Truth' Named 2016 Word of the Year by Oxford Dictionaries." *Washington Post*, November 16, 2016. https://www.washingtonpost.com/news/the-fix/wp/2016/11/16/post-truth-named-2016-word-of-the-year-by-oxford-dictionaries.

Waugh, Rob. "Racism Is 'Hardwired' into the Human Brain—and People Can Be Prejudiced without Knowing It." *Daily Mail*, June 26, 2012. http://www.dailymail.co.uk/sciencetech/article-2164844/Racism-hardwired-human-brain--people-racists-knowing-it.html.

Weisman, Tama. *Hannah Arendt and Karl Marx: On Totalitarianism and the Tradition of Western Political Thought*. Lanham, MD: Lexington Books, 2015

Wenman, Mark. *Agonistic Democracy: Constituent Power in the Era of Globalisation*. Cambridge: Cambridge University Press, 2015.

———. "Laclau or Mouffe? Splitting the Difference." *Philosophy and Social Criticism* 29, no. 5 (2003): 581–606.

West, Cornel. *Democracy Matters*. New York: Penguin, 2005.

Wolff, Richard D. *Democracy at Work: A Cure for Capitalism*. Chicago: Haymarket Books, 2012.

Wolin, Sheldon S. *Democracy Incorporated*. Princeton, NJ: Princeton University Press, 2010.

———. "Hannah Arendt: Democracy and the Political." In *Hannah Arendt: Critical Essays*, edited by Lewis P. Hinchman and Sandra K. Hinchman, 289–306. Albany: SUNY Press, 1994.

Wollheim, Richard. "A Paradox in the Theory of Democracy." In *Philosophy, Politics, and Society, Second Series*, edited by Peter Laslett and W.G. Runciman, 71–87. Oxford: Basil Blackwell, 1972.

Wong, Alia. "History Class and the Fictions About Race in America." *The Atlantic*, October 21, 2015. https://www.theatlantic.com/education/archive/2015/10/the-history-class-dilemma/411601.

Wong, Edward. "Trump Has Called Climate Change a Chinese Hoax. Beijing Says It Is Anything But." *New York Times*, November 18, 2016. https://www.nytimes.com/2016/11/19/world/asia/china-trump-climate-change.html.

Wood, Ellen Meiksins. *Democracy Against Capitalism: Renewing Historical Materialism*. New York: Verso, 2016.

———. *The Retreat from Class*. London: Verso, 1999.

Woolf, Nicky. "US 'Little Rebels' Protest against Changes to History Curriculum." *The Guardian*, September 26, 2014. https://www.theguardian.com/world/2014/sep/26/-sp-colorado-ap-history-curriculum-protest-patriotism-schools-students.

Wright, Christopher, and Daniel Nyberg. *Climate Change, Capitalism, and Corporations: Processes of Creative Self-Destruction.* Cambridge: Cambridge University Press, 2015.

Yack, Bernard. "Democracy and the Love of Truth." In *Truth and Democracy*, edited by Jeremy Elkins and Andrew Norris, 166–80. Philadelphia: University of Pennsylvania Press, 2012.

Žižek, Slavoj, ed. *Mapping Ideology.* New York: Verso, 1994.

INDEX

2016 United States presidential election, 16, 113; Trump, Donald, 122

Achen, Christopher H., and Larry M. Bartels, 112, 113
Althusser, Louis, 58, 62, 101, 120, 152n26
anti-Semitism, 45, 89, 93–94
Asimov, Isaac, 121–122

Brennan, Jason, 113, 114, 117, 119
Brown, Wendy, xix, 3, 130n15
Buckley, William F., 123–124
Burke, Edmund, 111, 114, 122, 151n10

capitalism, 3, 49, 63, 75, 87, 91–92
categorical imperative of democracy, xviii, 7–8, 15, 19, 48–49, 82, 95–100
Chesterton, G. K., 128
Cleaver, Eldrige, 123–124
climate change, 3, 86, 90, 98–99, 105, 116, 121, 125, 145n3, 147n18
climate skepticism/climate denial, 16, 88, 94–96, 124, 146n6, 146n7, 147n17, 148n20, 148n22
Cohen, Joshua, 17
Connolly, William, 8–9
Cooke, Maeve, 101

Dahl, Robert, xix, 131n18, 132n44, 150n2
deliberative democracy, 17–18, 48, 133n58

Derrida, Jacques, 64, 70, 129n3
Diamond, Larry, 2–3

elitist-populist ambivalence, xviii, 5, 14, 34, 47, 82, 124, 127
enlightenment, 64, 74, 78, 100, 124
epistocracy. *See* Brennan, Jason
"equality of intelligences" (Ranciére), 56, 58–60, 140n20

false demos, xviii, 86, 96–97, 100, 115, 127
feminism/feminist politics, 11, 33, 57, 60, 76, 78, 80, 131n34, 143n52
Fishkin, James, 17
Foucault, Michel, 70, 101–102, 126
Fraser, Nancy, 10–11
Front national (French political party), 65–68, 76, 80, 97, 127

Gines, Kathryn, 33, 136n24, 136n25

Habermas, Jürgen, 130n5, 133n62, 145n1
Harris, Jerry, 3
Honig, Bonnie, 12, 132n39

ideology, 101–105, 107–109, 114–120, 149n26, 149n27, 149n28, 149n29, 150n1, 150n32, 152n26
immigration. *See* racism
Ishiguro, Kazuo, 117–118, 152n25

Kant, Immanuel, 7–8

Law and Justice Party (Poland), 80
Lefort, Claude, 6
Le Pen, Jean-Marie, and Marine Le Pen. *See* Front national (French political party)
LGBTQ activism/politics, 57
liberalism, 18, 64
Lippmann, Walter, 111

Marchart, Oliver, 12–13
Marx, Karl/Marxism, 3, 28–29, 37–38, 51, 58, 70, 133n3, 134n5, 135n16, 150n2
May, Todd, 1
Meiksins Wood, Ellen, 3
men's rights activism (MRA), 11, 57, 60, 76, 78, 125, 127, 140n27
Mill, John Stuart, 111
Mills, Charles, 102–104, 114, 124, 150n32
Mudde, Cas, and Critóbal Rovira Kaltwasser, 4

new social movements, 17, 133n55

Ochoa Espejo, Pauline, 4

Panizza, Francisco, 4
Plato, 110, 119, 124
pluralism, 4, 8–9, 17, 64, 67–68, 71
Popper, Karl, 87
populism (vs. democracy), 4–5
post-truth. *See* 2016 United States presidential election

racism, 16, 18–19, 45, 55–57, 60–61, 66–68, 86, 93–94, 102–104, 114, 124, 136n24, 140n28; "Reflections on Little Rock" (Arendt), 44
Ricoeur, Paul, 6, 131n16, 150n2
right-wing politics, 1, 2, 4, 9, 13, 15–16, 56–57, 60–61, 65–68, 76–80, 83, 104, 121–126. *See also* 2016 United State presidential election; *Front national* (French political party); men's rights activism (MRA); racism; Tea Party (United States)
Rorty, Richard, 64, 101–102
Rousseau, Jean-Jacques, 6, 17, 126

Schmitt, Carl, 17–18, 127
Schumpeter, Joseph, 111, 132n43
"the social" (Arendt), 27–32, 33, 36–37, 38, 40, 42, 46
socially necessary delusion, 93–94, 100, 108–109, 114–120

Tea Party (United States), 3, 10–11
Thiers, Adolphe, 5
Tocqueville, Alexis de, 16
Trump, Donald. *See* 2016 United States presidential election

vanguardism, 71, 74, 76, 78, 81, 99

West, Cornel, 2, 15
Wolff, Richard, 2, 3
Wollheim, Richard, 14, 132n43

xenophobia. *See* racism

ABOUT THE AUTHOR

Larry Alan Busk received his doctorate from the University of Oregon and currently teaches philosophy at California State University Stanislaus. His articles have appeared in many journals, including *Philosophy Today*, *Radical Philosophy Review*, and *Constellations*.

ABOUT THE BOOK

www.ingramcontent.com/pod-product-compliance
Lightning Source LLC
Chambersburg PA
CBHW022013300426
44117CB00005B/168